# THE STORY OF IRISH FILM

# THE STORY OF
# IRISH FILM

Arthur Flynn

CURRACH PRESS

First published in 2005 by
CURRACH PRESS
55A Spruce Avenue, Stillorgan Industrial Park, Blackrock, Co Dublin, Ireland

www.currach.ie

1 3 5 4 2

Cover by Anú Design
Origination by Currach Press
Index by Therese Carrick
Printed by Nørhaven Books A/S, Denmark

ISBN 1-85607-914-7

*Acknowledgements*
I would like to acknowledge the help of a large number of people and organisations without which this book would not have been written. I would like to begin with people who gave me interviews about their experiences or expertise of film-making in Ireland over a number of decades. They include Patrick Carey, Neil Jordan, Tomás MacAnna, Justin Collins, John Ford, John Huston, Louis Marcus, Harry Alan Powers, Roger Corman, Colm O'Laoghaire, Vincent Corcoran, Bob Quinn, Sheamus Smith, Annie O'Sullivan, George Morrison, Fred O'Donovan, Cyril Cusack, Joseph Strick, Kieran Hickey, Liam O'Leary, Ed Guiney, Seamus de Burca, Noel Pearson, Seamus Byrne, Michael O'Herlihy, O Z Whitehead, John Boorman, Jim Sheridan, Kevin Barker, Eamonn O'Higgins, Paul Fitzgerald, John Lynch, Tony Barry and Paddy Breathnach.

A number of organisations have also been extremely helpful: Kevin Moriarty, Ardmore Studios, Morgan O'Sullivan and Grainne Dunne, staff of the National Film Archives, Ferndale Films, Gael Linn, Raidió Telefís Éireann, Civic Museum, the National Library, The Arts Council, Michael Kelleher Bray Library, National Library, The Irish Film Institute, the editor and staff of *Film Ireland*, *The Irish Times*, *Sunday Tribune*, *Bray People* and *Irish Independent*. I would like to thank Tony Hanna for access to his film photograph collection. I would also like to thank Wicklow Film Commission and Wicklow County Council for their support and assistance.

# CONTENTS

*Dedicated to Barry*

# PREFACE

My love for cinema began as a child in Bray, Co Wicklow. I was a regular matinee-goer to the Royal and Roxy, and savoured the adventures of Hopalong Cassidy, Old Mother Reilly and Humphrey Bogart chasing The Maltese Falcon.

Some years later, with the opening of Ardmore Studios in the town, I could actually see films being shot. I remember watching Robert Mitchum and a youthful Richard Harris being directed in a scene on the banks of the Dargle, of seeing James Cagney barking orders on a hilltop in Glencree, of witnessing spectacular dog-fights over Calary Bog, and Laurence Harvey in a makeshift graveyard beside the gasometer. I saw how a scene was created from words on a page, how sets were constructed, and how the tricks of the trade, like back-production and painted backdrops had deceived me and millions of cinema-goers.

Over the following years I conducted interviews with stars and directors for numerous newspaper and magazine articles. I also wrote a book on Irish films for the Irish Environmental Library Series. This gave me a deeper insight into the motivation and philosophies of film makers.

In this book I have outlined the development of film-making in Ireland from the first screening at the Star of Erin Music Hall in Dame Street on 20 April 1896, through the jerky one-reelers at the turn of the century to the multi-dollar productions of today. I have also detailed the efforts of an emerging band of contemporary vibrant young Irish film-makers.

My task was to write the story of film-making in Ireland, which was chiefly the production of feature films by foreign directors. Up to the late 1970s the Irish contribution was confined almost entirely to shorts and documentaries. Native feature film-making only began on an acceptable level following the foundation of the Irish Film Board. Prior to this important one-off works did emerge from Irish directors. One of the earliest examples was *The Dawn* in 1936, acted by amateurs in Killarney and directed by Tom Cooper. Unfortunately there was no follow-up.

The notable point about the pre-Ardmore days was that the majority of films shot on location had an Irish setting, e.g. *Odd Man Out*, *The Quiet Man* and *Captain Boycott*. There were some exceptions such as Olivier's *Henry V* and Huston's *Moby Dick*. When Ardmore opened, the balance swung in the opposite direction with settings as varied as Germany, France, China and the United States. During the 1970s, Dublin was the location for a series of quickie Italian and German films.

I outline the turbulent forty-six year history of Ardmore Studios in which it changed ownership several times with a number of receivers to its present position. I describe the films produced there by leading directors ranging from Carol Reed, Martin Ritt, Henry Hathaway to John Huston, John Boorman and Stanley Kubrick. A little known fact is that a thriller entitled *Dementia 13*, made at the studio in 1963, was directed by Francis Ford Coppola – ten years before he directed *The Godfather*. Ardmore brought in the big names – Cagney, Mitchum, Olivier, Burton, Hepburn, Steiger, O'Toole and Connery. It was still only a service industry that supplied facilities for visiting production companies. It did little to foster an indigenous Irish film industry.

The early 1990s saw the first indications of an unprecedented upturn in the fortunes of film-making in Ireland by both indigenous directors and foreign companies availing of the tax breaks of Section 35 of the Finance Act and locations in the country. A number of factors contributed to this welcome development, beginning with the two Oscars for *My Left Foot*, the nomination of Richard Harris for *The Field* and Neil Jordan's Oscar for the screenplay of *The Crying Game*. Coinciding with these achievements, Michael D. Higgins, on his appointment as Minister for Arts, Culture and the Gaeltacht, took a keen interest in the film industry. He immediately re-established the Irish Film Board and set various training programmes in motion, dealing with all aspects of film. This resulted in a number of low budget films being produced such as Gerry Stembridge's *Guiltrip* to the multi-million dollar productions from *Michael Collins* and *Braveheart* to *King Arthur*.

The book includes a filmography of all feature films, made partly or entirely in Ireland, complete with date, director and stars.

# 1

# BIRTH OF THE CINEMA

No one man invented the 'motion picture'. It was the product of scientists, artists and businessmen working independently in many parts of the world.

The magic lantern, which appeared in the sixteenth century, was the precursor of the film. It consisted of a series of drawings which, when spun and viewed through slits, gave the illusion of motion. A form of this technique – little figures on the corners of copybook pages – has amused children for generations.

The next development was the replacement of the drawings with photographs. This process, called chronophotography, was developed by a number of scientists towards the end of the nineteenth century. Continuous research and advancing technology led the American, George Eastman, to perfect a system of printing images onto a continuous roll of celluloid film. Numerous variations on this format were made, including Thomas Edison's Kinetoscope, a type of peep show through which moving pictures could be viewed.

It seemed a natural progression to project the moving images onto a screen large enough for an audience to view. The efforts to do so turned into a worldwide race with many countries intent on being the first onto the field. The blueprints and experiments of the competitors were closely guarded secrets.

Finally, on 20 February 1896, at the Grand Café, Boulevard des Capucines in Paris, Louis and Auguste Lumière showed the first moving pictures to a paying public. This new form of entertainment was an instant success with the audience clamouring for more. Depicted in those first films were action sequences of people and transport and newsreel footage of processions and meetings.

The success of the Paris cinema led to the opening of many more around the world. Outside the major cities, films were screened wherever a showing could be arranged – in parish halls, fairgrounds, music halls, markets and anywhere people were liable to gather. Films were sometimes included in music-hall bills. In the initial years cinema passed into the hands of the travelling fairground showmen who transformed their puppet shows and lit-up theatres. This was particularly the case in Ireland. By 1908, permanent cinemas were being built on a wide scale.

In May 1897, the gradually developing cinema in France suffered a severe blow when a projectionist's carelessness resulted in a fire that claimed 140 lives. Following this, the authorities imposed more stringent controls on public performances. France was also to the forefront in producing the first dramatic film, *The Story of a Crime*, in 1901. America followed two years later with Edwin Porter's *The Great Train Robbery*.

The earliest producers in England had been in the main either enthusiastic photographers or inventors who created short films at very little cost and were astonished at the profits they could accrue on a successful production. Cecil Hepworth, one of the most prominent film pioneers in England, was responsible for many of the early short films in Ireland. In 1905 he was to make England's first dramatic film, *Rescued by Rover*.

In Ireland, films began to be produced from the end of the nineteenth century. They were in the main current affairs shorts that dealt with meetings, exhibitions, races and visits of prominent people. There was even a brief record of the Dublin Horse Show. Most of these films were combined to form an evening's entertainment. Dan Lowry exhibited them at the Star of Erin Music Hall in Dame Street, Dublin on 20 April 1896, when it was temporarily converted into a cinema. The following year the tinted films of Professor Joly of Paris were shown. Later that year, films were also shown at the Rotunda and Gaiety Theatres.

What must be the earliest Irish newsreel of any length was a documentary on the State visit of Queen Victoria to Dublin in 1900, starting with her arrival at Kingstown (now Dún Laoghaire) and following her progress through streets lined with flag-waving crowds. Incidental films of Irish scenery and topicalities were also shot around the turn of the century. These include *The Fire Brigade Going out on a Call*, *A View from the Train on the Blackrock Line*, *Demolition of a Building* and *The Gordon Bennett Motor Race in Kildare*.

On 2 January 1905, the Irish Animated Photo Company showed a pictorial record of the major events of the preceeding year in the Town Hall, Rathmines. The programme featured the ceremonies of the Consecration of Saint Patrick's

Cathedral, Armagh. There were close-ups of the prelates assisting at the event, and Cardinal Vanutell giving the papal blessing to the multitude. Local shots included congregations leaving churches in Rathgar and Rathmines in which individuals were clearly recognisable. The motion in them was jerky, the people goose-stepping much as they were to do in the later Mack Sennett comedies.

In America, production companies mushroomed and there was a vigorous battle to gain control of the booming film business. By 1909 there were at least nine separate companies. D. W. Griffith emerged as the architect of that country's supremacy in cinema. His pioneering forms and techniques were to remain largely unchanged for the next half-century. Initially, film production was based in New York, mainly because the leading actors worked on Broadway, but a number of factors, including better weather conditions and lower costs, soon drew the film-makers to Hollywood on the west coast.

1910 is an important date in the history of cinema, as it was the first occasion on which an American film company travelled outside the United States to film on location. The company was Kalem, founded in 1907 by Frank Marion, Samuel Long and George Klein.

In the spring of that year Marion called their top director, Sidney Olcott, to his office. Opening a large map of the world in front of him, he asked Olcott to choose whichever country he would like to visit with a full film-making unit. Olcott promptly pointed to the small island, where his mother was born, on the west coast of Europe. She was born in Dublin.

Olcott, who ranked second only to Griffith, was one of the most creative directors in America. He had begun his career as an actor and had directed his first screen version of *Ben Hur* in 1907. His brief was to search for new material and subsequently to produce films with suitable themes.

In August 1910, Olcott landed at Queenstown (now Cobh) and remained for a short period at the Victoria Hotel in Cork. Having toured Ireland, he went to Killarney where he stayed at the Glebe Hotel. He brought with him his leading lady, Gene Gauntier; Robert Vignola; and his cameraman, George Hollister. Gauntier later wrote *Blazing Trail*, describing her work with Olcott. The manuscript is on display in the Museum of Modern Art Film Library in New York. She and Olcott also collaborated on film projects and scenarios. They were two of the first people in the world to write specifically for the cinema.

Olcott's first film in Ireland was *The Lad from Old Ireland*, described as 'Kalem's Great Trans-Atlantic Drama'. Olcott also shot a number of shorts in Irish beauty spots such as Blarney Castle, Glengarriff and the Lakes of Killarney.

*Opposite*: Louis and August Lumière, who showed the first moving pictures to a paying public in Paris.

*Below left*: D. W. Griffith, dubbed by Charlie Chaplin as 'the teacher of us all'.

*Below right*: Sidney Olcott, from a promotional postcard, proclaiming him to be 'the original feature producer now making features in Ireland and Europe'.

On leaving Ireland the company moved to England, where they filmed *The Irish Honeymoon* and to Germany to make *The Little Spreewald Mädchen*.

*The Lad from Old Ireland* was such a huge success with Irish emigrants in America that Kalem decided to send a larger company the following year. In addition to Gauntier, Vignola and Hollister, Olcott also brought Jack P. McGowran from Australia, Alice Hollister (cinema's first vamp), Alice Maples, Jack Clarke, Pat O'Malley, Allan Farnham, Arthur Donaldson and Helen Lindroth.

When they returned in June 1911, Olcott felt that a country setting would better suit his purpose. While touring in a jaunting car, he discovered the village of Beaufort, about eight miles from Killarney and decided this was an ideal location. His efforts to explain his intentions caused much hilarity among the locals, as they knew nothing about motion pictures. Olcott enquired if they had ever seen a magic lantern show. Yes, they knew about lantern entertainments. 'Well,' said Olcott, 'films are like magic lantern slides, but they move.' They were still bewildered but were willing to assist Olcott and learn about this amazing new invention.

The company lodged in the hotel of Patrick O'Sullivan and his daughter, Annie. Olcott worked throughout the summer, filming interiors in a mock-up set on a platform which they constructed behind the hotel. They travelled throughout the county for exterior locations. On one occasion they travelled fifty miles to Dingle only to discover on arrival they had forgotten the camera.

Olcott's next film, *Rory O'Moore,* centred on the adventurers of the rebels of 1798 and principally of O'Moore, the romantic Emmet-like figure. The film made for boisterous, fast-moving entertainment. A print of the film is lodged in the British Film Institute Distribution Library. It is worth noting that this copy does not include the closing scene in which Rory departs by sailing boat for America. This sequence was filmed at Queenstown. At the time, Olcott was unaware of the explosive content of the material and the controversy that followed its release greatly annoyed the British Home Office.

The film also displeased the local clergy. The Sunday following the completion of the film, the O'Sullivans with Sidney Olcott and some of his crew attended Mass in the local Catholic church. The parish priest of Tuogh, Fr Daly, spoke from the pulpit of the evil element in the village represented by the Kalem Company, whose players dressed as priests and nuns. The village was shocked and a group of local men threatened to 'beat up' the sinners from America. Filming could not continue until Olcott and the American consul in Queenstown met with the local bishop. The bishop instructed the parish priest to apologise for his remarks. Kalem became apprehensive and wanted to recall Olcott, but Olcott admitted his gaffe and promised to stay clear of such delicate subject matter in future. He was allowed to stay in Ireland.

From then on, the O'Kalems, as they jokingly called themselves, and the villagers became firm friends. There was no shortage of villagers willing to play small parts in the films at five shillings per day. Some even played quite important roles: Annie O'Sullivan was one of the female leads in *The Gypsies of Old Ireland*. The bulk of the films were shot in Beaufort, Dunloe and Killarney while much of the travelling was done on sidecars.

Olcott next turned his attention to Dion Boucicault's melodramas and filmed *The Colleen Bawn* starring Brian MacGowan. Olcott himself played the part of Danny Mahon. Then followed *Arrah-na-Pogue* with music specially composed by Walter Cleveland Simon. Other films included: *Robert Emmet, Ireland's Martyr,* starring Jack Melville and Pat O'Malley; *You'll Remember Ellen* (from Thomas Moore's poem); *The O'Neill* (from *Erin's Land*); *The Kerry Gow; A Girl of Glenbeigh; The Fishermaid of Ballydavid; Shaun the Post; The Kerry Dancer; The Shaughraun; Conway* and *Ireland the Oppressed*.

In 1912 Olcott and Gene Gauntier left Kalem and formed Gene Gauntier Feature Players. They returned to Beaufort in 1913, together with Jack J. Clarke, whom Gene Gauntier had married during the making of *From Manger to Cross* the previous year. The people of Beaufort believed that Olcott was deeply in love with Gauntier, and that he would have married her but for the fact that he was a devout Catholic and she had been divorced.

In August 1914, hundreds of Volunteers from all over Kerry and many other parts of Munster marched through the streets of Killarney, which were lined with cheering crowds. The local Killarney company was the centre of attraction but it was the only fully armed group in the parade. Due to the difficulty in obtaining arms the Volunteers had been using dummy rifles for training but the Kerry company was now equipped with rifles and bayonets. Members of the Royal Irish Constabulary were as baffled as the other onlookers as to the source of the arms. The explanation was simple. The rifles and bayonets were props of the Kalem Company. This was Olcott's discreet revenge for the earlier interference by the British authorities. Kalem filmed the competitions in signalling and drilling.

That same year Olcott formed Sid Films and returned yet again to Beaufort to produce a series of films starring Valentine Grant, who later became his wife. They planned to build a permanent studio in Beaufort enabling them to film all year round. He consistently claimed that he found it easy to direct the Irish people, as they were natural actors and actresses.

Gene Gautier and Jack Clarke in *You'll Remember Ellen*.

Kalem's *Rory O'Moore*.

Sidney Olcott's *The Kerry Dancers*.

Unfortunately, the outbreak of World War I put an end to their plans. In his eighteen weeks' stay in Beaufort, he made almost one film per week, each about three reels long and running approximately forty-five minutes. Lewis Jacobs maintains that these films succeeded in killing off the idea of the stage Irishman because they showed people in a realistic setting.

Despite not filming in Kerry again, Olcott and members of the company kept up a long correspondence with the people of the area. Annie O'Sullivan later spoke of how much the Kalem Company loved Beaufort and how they would pretend that their birthdays fell during their visit as an excuse to celebrate.

Alice Hollister recalled how she and Pat O'Malley had got together shortly before the latter's death in 1966, and talked about Beaufort all night. None of the other Kalems are alive today. Valentine Grant died in 1949, Jack P. McGowan died in 1952, Robert Vignola passed away in 1962 and Gene Gauntier in 1967. Following his wife's death, Olcott went to live with Vignola. A few weeks before Christmas of that year, Olcott wrote out his Christmas cards and parcelled up Valentine's jewellery to be sent to individuals that he felt she would want to give them too.

Shortly before Christmas, Annie O'Sullivan found two letters for her in the post. One was from Vignola informing her of Olcott's death. The second was from Olcott and enclosed was a gold braclet belonging to his wife. He had never forgotten Beaufort.

# 2

# THE IRISH PIONEERS

The outbreak of World War I was to remove European competition and establish America's dominance of world cinema. Ireland was to benefit as more American productions began travelling here.

In 1913 an American producer, Walter MacNamara, came to Dublin to make a film on Robert Emmet. He was introduced to an actor/manager, P. J. Bourke, who not only provided him with a shooting script but also made the costumes for the production. Bourke was paid £3 per day for his efforts. The film *Ireland a Nation*, which featured Barry O'Brien, concentrated on the life and times of Emmet and depicted later attempts in the nineteenth century to win Home Rule. It was shot in Baltinglass and Glendalough in Co Wicklow and ran to five reels.

In January 1917 the film had one public showing in Dublin because the British authorities quickly banned it. They felt that it raised contentious issues and interfered with recruitment to the army. The critics were generous in their reviews and found that the editing gave an exciting edge to the film. They explained that only in the courtroom scene was the audience aware of a static camera. Techniques rare for the period were close-ups and the panning shots. However, the film contained some anachronisms, including news of the Act of Union, 1801 being despatched to Father Murphy of Boolavogue fame, two years after his death; and inaccuracies such as Michael Dwyer marrying Anne Devlin and emigrating to Australia (Devlin was his niece). In 1920 the Gaelic Film Company added scenes from contemporary Ireland to bring it up to date. These showed the Auxiliaries, the Black and Tans, and the death of the Lord Mayor of Cork, Terence MacSwiney.

From 1913 onwards, most of the major events and leading figures in the national struggle were filmed. Unfortunately quite a considerable amount of film was either lost or destroyed. Part of what survived was used in George Morrison's two outstanding films, *Mise Éire* (1959) and *Saoirse?* (1961).

Around this period native film-makers, fascinated by this new medium, began to emerge. Many had theatrical backgrounds and some even combined the roles of actor and director. Of course there were also those who saw the possibilities in strictly commercial terms. Setting up a production company was not a difficult task. The initial outlay was on the camera, film, processing facilities and also, possibly, costumes. Actors were readily available, particularly from the Abbey Theatre. Many actors received no payment and others requested only a small remuneration. For most, the excitement of being in a film and seeing themselves on the screen was reward enough.

In 1915 the famed Abbey Theatre actor, F. J. McCormick directed and acted in a film called *Fun at Finglas Fair*, concerning the antics of two escaped convicts. It was written by Cathal MacGairbhigh and starred the Columbian Players. The film was never shown commercially, as British soldiers had broken into the cinema and accidentally destroyed the prints during the 1916 Rising. McCormick appeared in some later films of the Irish Film Company including *Irish Destiny* and *The Life of Michael Dwyer*. These films were primarily shot around Dublin and although there were not many cars in use at the time, an occasional one did accidentally appear in a period setting.

Producers believed that they had a ready market for their films in America, Italy, England, Australia and France, and more companies went into production. In March 1916, just before the Easter Rising, the Film Company of Ireland was established by an American diplomat and lawyer, James Mark Sullivan. Consisting chiefly of actors from the Abbey, this company produced such films as *O'Neill of the Glen* and *The Miser's Gift*, both directed by and starring J. M. Kerrigan. Other titles from this company included *Woman's Wit*, *Food of Love*, *Widow Malone* and *The Eleventh Hour*. In total they produced nine films. Like Sidney Olcott, they intended to show to the world that there was more to Ireland than the stereotypical 'pigs in the parlour'. The company also planned to build a large studio that winter and to install the best equipment available. This plan did not materialise, but they continued in production, chiefly shooting on location.

On 26 October 1916, the Dame Street Picture House showed *The Miser's Gift*, describing it as the first comedy production by the Film Company of Ireland. The same cinema, the following month, showed another of their productions, *An Unfair Love Affair*, directed by Kerrigan and starring Nora

Clancy and Fred O'Donovan. The versatile Kerrigan also directed and starred in *Puck Fair Romance*, co-starring Kathleen Murphy. Another important production in 1916 was Molly Bawn, directed by Cecil B. Hepworth and starring Alma Taylor and Stewart Lowe.

In 1917 the General Film Company of Ireland headed by Norman Whitten, with J. W. Mackey in charge of production and J. Gordon Lewis as cameraman, produced *In the Days of Saint Patrick*. The film directed by Whitten starred a well known Queen's Theatre actor, Ira Allan, in the title role. Alice Cardinall played Patrick's mother, George Griffin was King Laoghaire, Maud Hume the Queen and T. O'Carroll Reynolds played Niall of the Nine Hostages. One of the slaves was a black boxer named Cyclone Billy Warren, a notable character around Dublin for a long time. The main location was Rush, Co Dublin and the ambitious production featured pirate galleys and chariot races. The film took a year of patiently watching the weather and seasons to capture the perfect conditions for filming. The results more than justified the difficult conditions and the critics reviewed it warmly. *In the Days of Saint Patrick* was well received throughout Ireland and England by trade and public alike.

Whitten also ran a newsreel called *Irish Events* for which he had his own laboratory in Pearse Street, Dublin. At that time there were two other film laboratories in Dublin: The Irish Animated Picture Company, also in Pearse Street, and the Gaumont Company in Lord Edward Street. They shot newsreel film of Countess Markievicz and other prisoners and also the surviving leaders of the Easter Rebellion when they left prison in 1917. Other newsreel footage included the Conference of Ireland (excluding Sinn Féin members), which was convened by Lloyd George in Trinity College, and the funeral of Thomas Ashe. These latter films were preserved in the National Library.

This was a busy period with the following films in circulation: *The Upstart*, *Blarney*, *The Byeways of Fate* and *The Irish Girl*, all directed by J. M. Kerrigan, and *The First Irish National Pilgrimage to Lourdes*. The Film Company of Ireland announced their forthcoming films, *Rafferty's Rise*, directed by Kerrigan and a three-act comedy by Nicholas Hayes centring around a policeman, *When Love Came to Gavin Burke*, directed by Fred O'Donovan and starring Brian Moore and Kathleen Murphy. Later that year O'Donovan directed a screen version of Charles Kickham's novel *Knocknagow* in which Cyril Cusack made a fleeting appearance as a five-year old child evicted onto the roadside. Prominent members of the cast included Brian McGowan, J. McCarre and Alice Keating. The film was photographed by William Moser around Clonmel, Co Tipperary where it had its first screening. Other films in production circa this period were a comedy,

The chariot race from *In the Days of Saint Patrick* and opposite an advertisement for the film.

*A Passing Shower*, and two dramas, *A Man's Redemption* and *Cleansing Fires*.

Quite a number of the same names appear in the credits of these films as a repertory group of actors and crews had been assembled. They worked in harmony and moved from film to film. In 1917 the Irish Film Company announced that they had built up a library of 10,000 feet of Irish scenery and had compiled *A Serial of Twenty Irish Scenics*. Whitten's company produced other films of local interest, such as a visit to Patterson's match factory entitled *Matchmaking in Ireland*. He was approached by the Court Laundry to produce a film on their operation and Dubliners saw for the first time how their clothes were cleaned. Ireland's first animated film, 450 feet long, entitled *Ten Days Leave*, was also produced that year. It received its first public showing in the Bohemian Cinema, Phibsboro. Frank Leah was the animator and Jack Warren the director. Warren, an Englishman, was editor of an Irish magazine, *The Irish Limelight*, and Leah one of its regular contributors.

Over forty years before the opening of Ardmore Studios, Bray played a significant part in early film production. William Power, who returned from Manchester with the intention of making films to meet the demand for Irish pictures, was the leading figure in the project. He ran a barber's shop on Novara Road, which was as much a film studio and laboratory as it was a hairdresser's. In 1917 he set up a dramatic society so as to have a recruiting ground for his films. The following year he wrote, produced and directed a short comedy *Willie Scouts while Jesse Pouts*. Power was so pleased with the results and received such support locally that he founded the Celtic Film Company.

Power's second project was a more ambitious two-hour film, *Rosaleen Dhu*, a tale of a Fenian exiled from Ireland who joins the Foreign Legion. He meets and marries an Algerian girl who turns out to be heiress to a vast Irish estate. The film was shot mainly in the Bray area although they did travel as far as Arklow for the desert scenes and to Kilmacanogue for a crossroads sequence.

These early films were shot mainly by a camera in a fixed position but Power, with great foresight, invested in a camera capable of panning, for the princely sum of £88. While the camera and film was expensive the props and cast cost nothing. Extras were selected from amongst the eager onlookers. Frequently the company would neglect to ask permission to use private property. For example, a thatched cottage on Bray Head was used for an eviction scene unknown to the owner, a farmer who was milking his cows in an adjoining field. The hero's farewell took place on a coalboat that had been anchored in Bray harbour for over a week. When Power got word that the boat was about to sail he left a man half shaved in the barber's chair. He gathered his crew, rushed to the harbour and shot the scene.

The film was processed in wooden barrels in a small yard behind the barber's shop and later sub-titled in the tiny laboratory.

*Rosaleen Dhu* was premiered in Mac's, a cinema housed in the old Turkish Baths in Bray. A warm reception from the local audience led to its screening nationwide. An even greater boost came from the offer of £2,000 for it from an American film company.

Greatly encouraged by their success Power planned his second feature, *An Irish Vendetta*, with himself in the leading role. He decided that those taking part in the film would receive shares and thus be fairly rewarded for their efforts. They were filming the story's climax on Leopardstown racecourse when tragedy struck. Power's horse bolted, throwing him onto the railings. Two days later on 6 June 1920 he died in the Mater Hospital. The floods in Little Bray destroyed one copy of *Rosaleen Dhu*. Not a single still or frame of any of William Power's work has survived.

In 1922 Charles McConnell, became chairman of another Irish film company, Irish Photoplays. Other founding members of the company were Fred Jeffs, Senator George Nesbitt and a Londoner, Kenneth Hartley. They financed the making of three films: *The O'Casey Millions*, *Wicklow Gold* and *Cruiskeen Lawn*. The latter concerned horse racing and was directed by Norman Whitten. Harry O'Donovan was property master for the company.

McConnell recalled those days:

We didn't make money from them, but we did cover ourselves. The stars of the films, as we liked to call them, were paid peanuts compared with even small time players of today. The 'extras' were often delighted to work just for the thrill of being in a film.

I remember Jimmy O'Dea quite well. He was very young and shy and mostly played straight parts, like in *The O'Casey Millions* when he was the romantic lead. He revealed great talent even at that early stage and I knew he would have a big future in films. I didn't see him then the great comedian he was later to become, but he had a lively and loveable sense of humour.

We looked upon the film-making as an adventure and great fun. It was grand working with such dedicated people as Jimmy, Thomas Moran, Fay Sergeant, Chris Silvester, Nan Fitzgerald, Fred Jeffs, Kathleen Drago and Barrett McDonnell.

McConnell was proud of the fact that all those early films were scripted, photographed, produced and directed by an Irish team.

I realised at the time that this small country could not compete with the

*Above left*: Jimmy O'Dea, Nan Fitzgerald and Fred Jeffs in *The O'Casey Millions*.

*Above right*: Charles McConnell, chairman of Irish Photoplays Ltd, which had capital of £10,000.

*Opposite*: Frances Alexander in *Willie Reilly and His Colleen Bawn*, which was shot on location in Rathfarnham, Dublin.

Barry Fitzgerald and Maureen Delaney in a scene from *Land of Her Fathers*.

film-makers of Britain and America with all their millions. But our little films – they ran for about an hour – were a success on the cinema circuit in Ireland and were actually shown in America, I must mention John MacDonagh, who scripted and produced *The O'Casey Millions*. He was very gifted.

MacDonagh, brother of the executed Rising leader, Thomas, was a well-known contributor to Radio Éireann and wrote the script for all three films. He later made *Paying the Rent* and *Willie Reilly and his Colleen Bawn* and was involved with other films as writer, director, producer and actor. This latter film was one of the most popular and successful of the Film Company of Ireland's production and starred Brian McGowan and Frances Alexander. The film, based on the 1855 novel by William Carleton, was shot at the height of the War of Independence. The story of a disposed Irish gentleman and his love for the Colleen Bawn made a plea for better understanding between Catholics and Protestants.

From 1922, film-making in Ireland became a regular business as more ambitious projects went into production. In 1924 John Hurley directed Mícheál Mac Liammóir in *Land of Her Fathers* with Phyllis Wakely, Frank Hugh O'Donnell and members of the Abbey Company. The film was made by the Hepworth Company in Enniskerry and Killarney and was shot by one of D. W. Griffith's cameramen. The last print of the film was stolen in New York and was never recovered.

The following year the Jessie Lasky Company filmed exteriors for *Irish Luck* in Killarney. This company, which included Cecil B. DeMille and Samuel Goldwyn amongst its directors, was one of the leading film companies in the world. That same year I. G. Eppel made *Irish Destiny*, a love story set against the background of the Troubles and featuring the burning of the Customs House. Exteriors were shot in Glendalough and Greystones, Co Wicklow and interiors in Shepherd's Bush Film Studio in London. The stars were Denis O'Dea, Una Shiels and Maureen Delaney. The professionals were paid £6 per day and the amateurs in the cast received half that amount.

In 1929 Lt Colonel Victor Haddick from Limerick produced another film about Saint Patrick. It was *Ireland – Rough-Hewn Destiny* with Gearóid Ó Lochlinn, an Irish-speaking actor, playing the saint. Later that year the Muintir Vitagraph Company made *Bunny Blarneyed*, the story of a girl's suitor who forces her father's consent by hanging him over the Blarney Stone. The film starred John Bunny and was directed by Larry Trimble.

Some years after Frank O'Connor's first book of short stories was published

A scene from *Guests of the Nation* directed by Denis Johnston.

in 1931, the playwright, Denis Johnston, made the title story, *Guests of the Nation*, into a silent film. He used actors mainly associated with Dublin's Gate Theatre, including Barry Fitzgerald, Shelagh Richards and Esther Cunningham. Set in 1921, the film depicts the relationship between two captured British soldiers and their IRA captors. When the British authorities refused to trade prisoners, the IRA men reluctantly execute the two soldiers. This was Johnston's first venture into film-making and thereafter he was to concentrate mainly on playwrighting.

# 3

# MAN OF ARAN AND THE DAWN

Some sound films were made from the mid-1920s but the quality of sound was so poor that they were never released. On 6 October 1927 Warner Brothers screened *The Jazz Singer*, starring Al Jolson which changed the history of films.

By 1929 the attendance at picture showings had increased enormously in the USA owing to the popularity of 'the talkies'. In the transition years it appeared as if every second film was a musical with the advertising slogan: ALL TALKING … ALL SINGING … ALL DANCING … ALL COLOUR. Film producers saw the potential of Broadway stars and brought them to Hollywood for screen musicals. Not only were individual performers engaged but entire stage productions. However, many singers were apprehensive of the new genre and were reluctant to leave the stage.

One of the first to be enticed by the attractive salaries was Ireland's John McCormack, then ranked as one of the world's leading tenors. He received $50,000 a week for his ten weeks' work on his sound debut in the Fox musical *Song of My Heart* (for which locations were filmed near Bray). The film, directed by Frank Borzage, also featured the young Irish actress, Maureen O'Sullivan, who was beginning to make an impression in Hollywood. She played the daughter of a family threatened with ruin whose fortunes are restored by a John McCormack fund-raising recital. She was later to gain worldwide fame as Jane in the Tarzan films. Although *Song of My Heart* received good reviews from the critics, the public were not too enthusiastic: they enjoyed McCormack on records and in concert, but were not so keen on him as a stocky leading man.

Some years later McCormack co-starred with Henry Fonda and Annabella in *Wings of the Morning* that was partly filmed in Killarney. Directed by Harold Schuster, it was a melodrama, with a mixture of gypsies, romance, songs and horsemanship. It had the distinction of being the first Technicolor film made in the British Isles. Other notable films produced during 1936 included Brian Desmond Hurst's *Irish Hearts* based on Dr Abrahamson's novel, *Night Nurse*. The cast included Nancy Byrne, Lester Matthews, Sara Allgood and Arthur Sinclair. Hurst followed this with a film version of John Millington Synge's classic, *Riders to the Sea*, starring Sara Allgood, Kevin Gutherie, Ria Mooney and Shelagh Richards filmed in Renvyle, Co Galway. The production sponsored by singer Gracie Fields, was one of a number of films in which companies and individuals invested in return for a percentage of the profits.

On a boat trip from America to Europe, the renowned documentary film-maker, Robert Flaherty, heard a young Irishman describe the Aran Islands off the west coast of Ireland. Life there was so primitive that the islanders had to make soil by hauling seaweed up the cliffs and mixing it with sand to form a topsoil in which to grow their potatoes. The description so impressed Flaherty that he began to research the subject. He saw the region as the ideal location for man's struggle against the elements.

He approached Michael Balcon, production-chief of Gaumont-British, who became interested in the subject. Balcon allotted £10,000 for *Man of Aran*, as a sound film. This was less than the cost of Flaherty's highly praised silent picture *Nanook of the North*, ten years previously.

For *Man of Aran* Flaherty decided to cast islanders in all the roles. In Mikaleen Dillane he found a young boy suitable for one of the main roles. His parents were reluctant to allow the boy to appear in the film and Flaherty had to resort to devious methods to get their consent. Maggie Dirrane was cast as the mother and the most difficult character to cast, the father, was finally found in the person of Colman 'Tiger' King. Flaherty was an intolerable man to work for and in the course of filming, his assistant, John Taylor, was fired twice and quit once but never stopped working.

The islanders, for people who astonishingly could not swim, performed the most amazing feats of bravery, encouraged by Flaherty's unflagging enthusiasm. During filming Flaherty on a daily basis gambled with the lives of people living at starvation level. He was in constant fear that tragedy would strike.

He spent eighteen months filming on Inishmore and shot over 200,000 feet of film, which was processed on the island in a small studio, he had built. The film ran over budget and Gaumont-British felt that Flaherty was shooting the

The dramatic seaweed gathering scene from *Man of Aran*.

same material over and over again. The company suggested that Balcon should stop production. Flaherty did not object, as he was glad to be relieved of the compulsion to continue. The film won the Grand Prix Award at the 1934 Venice Film festival. It has secured a place in the history of cinema as one of the greatest documentaries of all time.

Almost thirty years after Sidney Olcott's pioneering venture in Killarney, filming was resumed in the area by a local garage proprietor, Tom Cooper. With the co-operation of 250 eager amateurs he produced and directed a remarkable picture called *The Dawn*. Cooper himself headed the amateur cast that also included Eileen Davis, Brian O'Sullivan, Donal O'Cahill and Jerry O'Mahoney. Cooper had no formal training or experience in the technique of film other than being a keen film-goer who appreciated the work of D. W. Griffith and Eisenstein.

Originally titled *I am Tainted*, the film took from 1933 to 1936 to shoot as filming was limited to Sunday afternoons and off-peak hours. The consumption of electricity for the indoor scenes equalled the output for the entire Killarney area. There was no basic script and scenes and dialogue were planned only days in advance in local pubs.

As the film was produced on a modest budget, very few members of the company received a wage, but some of the 'stars' received payment in kind for their service. The completed film was cut, edited, printed and developed in an old shed behind the cinema. Converted trawler lights lit the small studio. The only editing implement was a scissors and the one lensed camera did all the shots close up and long range. It was a dramatic sound film, based on IRA activity in the Kerry area during the Black and Tan war. There was an extra degree of realism in the fact that it was actually made by people who took part in that campaign. One critic summed it up as 'too bad to be true and too good to miss'.

Cooper approached the Minister for Defence, Frank Aiken, for permission to use army equipment. The following is the correspondence between Tom Cooper and the Department of Defence:

Hibernia Film Studios, Killarney.

To Frank Aiken Esq.
Minister of Defence
Leinster House
Dublin
5th April 1935

A Chara,

Further to my interview with you in Leinster House some time ago regarding getting from your Department the use of military equipment for the purpose of the production of a film of the Black and Tan days in Ireland, I would be very much obliged if you would kindly arrange to put at our disposal the following:

A quantity of service rifles (war time pattern). A quantity of revolvers, a hotchkiss gun and some machine-guns. Also a small quantity of short, service rifles similar to RIC Carbines, as well as a number of old pattern rifles similar to those issued to the Irish Volunteers in the early days of the Movement. A supply of blank ammunition for the above will also be necessary. I would be obliged also if you could arrange to let us have a number of ammunition belts similar to those used by British Tommies, and two officers uniforms complete with belts similar to British officers dress.

I would also be obliged if you would be good enough to arrange to loan us for a short time two Crossley Tenders and one Armoured Car.

The advice of your Department will also be very appreciated with regard to the correctness of all the equipment and dress outlined above.

I regret having to give you so much trouble but I am sure you will understand that we have no other means of procuring this equipment except through your Department.

For your information I would add that our film will be dated between the years 1918 and '21. A very small portion of the entire film will be dated 1866, and I would be very much obliged for the advice of your Department as to what arms the RIC would carry at about that period.

I am taking up the matter of a permit for the use of the equipment with the Superintendent, Garda Síochána, Killarney, and I would suggest that all arms and ammunition, etc. while here should be under the control of the garda authorities.

I would much appreciate your early attention to this matter, as we are now ready to commence filming the production in question.

Thanking you.

Mise le meas,
T. Cooper

Department of Defence
Dublin
23rd January 1935

A Chara,

I am desired by Mr Aiken to refer to your letter of the 5th instant requesting the loan of certain military equipment and in reply to say that the Department invariably requests payment in advance for services of this nature. The cost involved in this instance will be a charge at the rate of 1 shilling per mile per vehicle used in the transport of the equipment loaned. Any ammunition used must also be paid for and any loss of or damage to equipment arising out of the loan will require to be made good.

With regard to your request for one Armoured Car I am to inform you that it is the custom always to send two of these cars on a journey and these together with other vehicles, guns and ammunition which may be loaned to you will require to be returned to military custody at Ballymullen Barracks, Tralee each night during the period for which they are loaned.

As all the equipment you require may not be in stores the Minister considers it advisable for you to go into this aspect of the matter in detail with the Quartermaster General's staff here and if you will communicate the day and hour which would be convenient for you an interview will accordingly be arranged.

Mise, le meas,
J.J.J.
Secretary to the Minister

Not everything in the filming went according to plan. In an ambush sequence, an IRA unit opened fire on a Crossley tender carrying Black and Tans. It was intended that six of the Tans were to be killed in the exchange and the remainder were to run for cover. In the first take, none of the Tans 'died'. Cooper instructed that six were to die in the next take but this time all twelve were dramatically killed. While Cooper, in desperation, was choosing the six to be killed the next time, a gun was accidentally discharged (the signal to open fire) and the third ambush was enacted without being filmed. There was no ammunition left and filming had to be abandoned for the day.

On its release *The Dawn* proved to be popular with critics and audiences alike and was lavishly praised.

Killarney garage owner and film-maker, Tom Cooper, editing *The Dawn*. Despite his lack of formal training, Cooper had obviously mastered the rules of cinema language. The movie was Ireland's first indigenous sound feature.

Two scenes from *The Dawn*. The first part of the movie opens in 1866 and tells the story of Brian Malone, who is framed as an informer on his Fenian colleagues. The second part is set in 1919, when Brian Malone, grandson of the 'traitor' is a member of the local IRA, despite his brother's opposition. When he in turn is dubbed a traitor, Brian is expelled from the IRA and joins the RUC. The execution of an IRA prisoner by the Black and Tans, causes him to desert and warn his former colleagues of an impending raid.

In 1939 Norris Davidson reviewed *The Dawn* in *World Film News*:

By now the story of its production is fairly well known; short lengths of film developed in a chemist's shop, experiments with more or less home-made sound equipment. The tiny studio is lit by converted trawler lights, the home-made microphone boom squeaked when moved so speakers could not be followed about the studio, the tripod of the Studio Debrie was made in the director's garage, there is not one professional actor in the whole bunch – and with that *The Dawn* began. It began with either blind arrogance or in the courageous spirit of Flaherty returning to the Far North to re-make *Nanook* after the destruction of the first negative. This film is Ireland and the incredible thing is that men who had actually lived a part of the story should not have been too close to it to distinguish between what was important to them and what is important to an audience. The film is not propagandistic, it has no star to create, often its apparent understatement reveals something with dazzling simplicity.

Two films, following in the wake of *The Dawn*, proved a disappointment to those hoping for a successful beginning to an Irish film industry. *Uncle Nick*, directed by Tom Cooper, was a stagy attempt that had all the crudities of his first film but none of the better qualities. The second film was *The Islandsman*, directed by Patrick Heale from a scenario by Donal O'Cahill, who had broken with Cooper. It was badly devised and poorly acted by a cast that included Brian O'Sullivan and Gabriel Fallon and featured Delia Murphy in a singing role.

It was only in the late 1970s that Tom Cooper received a medal from Ardmore Studios in recognition of his contribution to Irish film.

# 4

# IRISH-AMERICAN FILMS

During the 1930s, the Abbey Theatre from Dublin, made several tours of the United States to stage the classic plays of the National Theatre across North America. Film producers began to take notice of their distinctive style of acting.

One of the first directors to tackle an Irish classic was Alfred Hitchcock when he directed Sean O'Casey's *Juno and the Paycock* entirely in the studio in 1930. His stars were Sara Allgood, Edward Chapman, Sidney Morgan and Maire O'Neill. Hitchcock's film was a literal transcription of the Dublin slum play, which the director admitted he could find no way of narrating in cinematic form. The critics lavishly praised it.

In 1934 the distinguished American director, John Ford, directed the film version of Liam O'Flaherty's novel, *The Informer*, for RKO. The film, set in 1922 during the Irish Civil War, was produced for a mere $243,000 and told of a hard-drinking brute who informs on one of his colleagues in order to collect a reward. There was disappointment that the film, featuring Victor McLaglen's powerful performance as the mighty Gypo Nolan, was shot, not in Ireland, but on a Hollywood lot in an artificial mist. Despite this, cinematographer Joseph August captured superbly the atmospheric shadows of a fog-bound 1920's Dublin. Starring alongside McLaglen were Preston Foster, Heather Angel and Margot Graham. Irish personnel in the cast included Una O'Connor, J. M. Kerrigan and Neil Fitzgerald.

Dudley Nichols wrote the screenplay in six days and Ford shot the film in 17 days. *The Informer* proved to be one of Ford's finest films of the period. The film built and maintained a critical and popular reputation and went on to win Oscars for McLaglen as Best Actor, Nichols for Best Adaptation, Max Steiner for Best Musical Score and Ford for Best Director.

In his critique in *The Spectator* Graham Greene wrote: 'Black and Tan patrols through the Liffey fogs, the watching secretive figures outside the saloons as the drunken informer drifts deeper and deeper with his cronies into the seedy night life of Dublin … a memorable picture of a pitiless war waged without honour on either side in doorways and cellars and gin shops.'

The following year when the Abbey Company was touring the States with O'Casey's *The Plough and the Stars*, Ford offered many of the cast roles in his film version of the play. Ford again collaborated with screenwriter Dudley Nichols to transform O'Casey's ironic tragedy into a romantic and sentimental celebration of the struggle for Irish independence. There were an excessive number of scenes with American actress, Barbara Stanwyck – RKO's price for allowing Ford to 'import the Abbey players intact' – as Nora Clitheroe and Preston Foster as her husband, Jack. Amongst Irish actors who accepted roles in the film were Denis O'Dea, Barry Fitzgerald, F. J. McCormick and Sara Allgood.

Barry Fitzgerald is the best example of one who stayed and cornered the market in Irish character roles, culminating in *Going My Way* for which he won a Best Supporting Actor Oscar. F. J. McCormick refused a five-year Hollywood contract and returned to the Abbey. Denis O'Dea appeared in some American films but would not make long-term commitments. In later years Irish actors and actresses including Mícheál Mac Liammóir and Siobhán McKenna made one-off films but refused to be bound by restricting, though tempting, contracts.

1936 saw the shooting of *The Early Bird* under the direction of Donovan Pedelty and starring Richard Hayward, Jimmy McGeehan and Charlotte Teddie. This was the first film produced by Norris Davidson, who had assisted Flaherty on *Man of Aran*. Davidson also collaborated with the playwright, Lennox Robinson on a screenplay for General John Regan, based on a novel by George A. Birmingham. The film was directed by and starred Henry Edwards and co-starred Chrissie White and W. G. Fay.

While Tom Cooper was pioneering in Killarney, another Irishman, Rex Ingram was gaining a reputation in Hollywood. Ingram, the son of a Church of Ireland minister, was born Reginald Ingram Hitchcock in Dublin on 18 January 1893. From an early age he showed an artistic flair and sold many of his drawings. In 1911 following the death of his mother he left for America. A chance meeting with the son of Thomas Edison, a pioneer of Irish film, gave him an insight into this new industry. He began as an actor but later wrote stories and screenplays

Rex Ingram

*Above:* Victor McLaglen in a scene from *The Informer*. McLaglen won an Academy Award for his performance as Gypo Nolan, an Irish rebel, who betrays his friend, Frankie McPhillip, to the Black and Tans. He hopes to start a new life for himself and the girl he loves with the £20 he receives.

Gypo is tormented briefly by his conscience, but doesn't realise the full impact of his actions. As a result he foolishly squanders the bloodmoney. He is finally caught and shot down by the IRA, but makes peace with Frankie's mother before he dies.

and it was not long before he had a comprehensive knowledge of the skills of film-making.

In 1916 Ingram directed his first film, *The Great Problem*, from his own script. Then followed a series of distinguished titles including *Chalice of Sorrows*, *Black Orchids* and *Reward of the Faithless*. It was not until 1920, when he joined the Metro Company and directed *The Four Horsemen of the Apocalypse*, that he became one of the most highly rated and respected directors in Hollywood. This film was responsible for launching Rudolph Valentino as a world star and also Alice Terry, who married Ingram. Many more outstanding films followed – *The Conquering Power*, *The Prisoner of Zenda* and *Scaramouche* – but in 1924 Ingram grew disillusioned with Hollywood and left to open his own studio in Nice. It was here that he directed *Mare Nostrum*, which he regarded as his best film. After making one sound film, *Baroud*, in which he played the leading role himself, he retired from films and devoted himself to sculpting and writing. He died in July 1950. Many regretted that such a talented film-maker had never directed a film in his native country.

Various other schemes were announced from time to time for the production of Irish films during this period, but as budget costs rose, productions became fewer. One project that did get off the ground was *The Voice of Ireland*, directed by the writer, poet and soldier, Colonel Victor Haddick. The film was a rather scrappy musical featuring Haddick himself along with Richard Hayward and Barney O'Hara. Then came *Sweet Inniscarra*, directed by an Irish-American, Emmet Moore, who had made shorts here previously. The cast included Sean Rogers and Mae Ryan. Later titles included *The Luck of the Irish*, starring Hayward, Kay Walsh and Niall McGinnis and *Irish and Proud of It*, produced in 1936 by Haddick, Hayward and Donovan Pedelty and starring Dinah Sheridan and Liam Gaffney.

*Irish for Luck* (1936), directed by Arthur Woods and starring Athene Seyler and Margaret Lockwood, had all the ingredients of films in vogue at the time: a poor duchess, an orphan niece and a busker who wins fame on the BBC. *West of Kerry* (1938), directed by Dick Bird and starring Eileen Curran and Cecil Forde, concerns a girl from the Blasket Islands who falls in love with a visiting medical student.

In 1938 Jimmy O'Dea, Myretta Morven and Ronald Malcolmson starred in *Blarney*, directed by Harry O'Donovan. The plot concerned a salesman who mistakenly took a bag containing stolen gems. Four years previously, Jimmy had appeared in *Jimmy Boy* made by an English company, directed by John Baxter and co-starring Guy Middleton and Vera Sherburne. Jimmy played an Irish bootboy who unmasked a foreign film star as a spy. The only person from this era to continue with production was Richard Hayward, who made *Devil's Rock*, starring himself, Geraldine Mitchell and Gloria Granger under Germaine Burger's direction. Hayward, better known as a writer than a film-maker also produced shorts on aspects of Irish life.

At the outbreak of World War II, the Irish Army co-operated with newsreel cameraman, Gordon Lewis, to make *Ireland's Call to Arms* in 1939 and *Step Together* by Joe Evans. Other indigenous productions of this period included *Kilmainham Jail*, directed by Clifford Marston, a story of the Irish Bastille and *The Life of Michael Flaherty*, directed by John Eldright.

Following the successful screening of several of George Bernard Shaw's plays, the playwright's associate, Gabriel Pascal, came to Dublin to set up a company in Ireland to film *Saint Joan* and a number of Shaw's other plays. Several Dublin businessmen, including Joseph McGrath of the Irish Hospitals' Sweepstake and an influential solicitor, Arthur Cox, were attracted by the enterprise. Shaw favoured the project and aroused the interest of Eamon de Valera's government in the possibility of an Irish film industry. De Valera instructed Dan Breen to travel to see Shaw at Ayot St Laurence and a friendship developed between the two, but the scheme for the filming of Shaw's plays here was not put into effect. The reason was twofold. Firstly, sufficient capital was not forthcoming and secondly, the interest of the businessmen waned when it became evident that the church authorities were reluctant to support the enterprise of a lapsed Protestant.

A letter from Shaw to Dan Breen gives an outline of their plans. It was addressed to 'Dan Breen, Esq. MP Dáil Éireann, Leinster House, Dublin, Eire':

Dear Dan,

Get all this sentimental rubbish out of your blessed old noodle; I have no feeling in business. You can't humbug me; and it grieves me that you have humbugged yourself to the tune of £10,000.

I have given you time to do your damnedest to raise Irish capital. The result is £40,000. For film purposes it might as well be forty brass farthings; a million and a half is the least we should start with, and it would barely see us through two big feature films. The only honourable thing for the company to do is to wind up and pocket its losses.

But after the company has been advertised – as it has been – its failure would be a failure for Ireland. What is the available alternative?

First, to get rid of Pascal and me. The Protestant capitalists will not back me because I am on talking terms with you and do not believe that you will go to hell when you die.

The clergy, now that they know that I will not write up the saints for them, will not back up a notorious free thinker. The Catholic laity will not back up a bloody Protestant.

The capitalists, who have no religion and no politics except money making rule me out as a high brow in whom there is no money. All of them object to Pascal because he is a foreigner who throws away millions as if they were threepenny bits. So out we go with our contracts torn up.

The company must cut out film production from its programme and become a studio-building company, raising capital wherever it can get it from Rank, from Korda, Hollywood, Belfast, Ballsbridge, Paddy Murphy, John Bull and Solomon Isaacs.

The studio would cost two million in two years but when they are ready the company will be an Irish landlord gathering rent from all the producing companies on earth.

I see no alternative to a winding up order except this. I have written it all to Dev; so don't try to gammon him about it; but believe me and face it …

You all thought I was your ace of trumps; I know that I might be a drawback but I thought I might as well have a try. It has been a failure. I apologise and withdraw.

Still, ever the best of friends,

G. Bernard Shaw

Shaw's wishful thinking was confined to verbal exchanges and letter writing but apparently nothing more concrete emerged and their plans faded.

# 5

# HENRY V and ODD MAN OUT

Film producers were never keen to tackle Shakespearean plays. However, Laurence Olivier, believed that these classics had good potential at the box office. His first venture was *Henry V*, a film which might never have been made had it not been for an Italian lawyer, Filippo del Giudice, who had persuaded Noel Coward to make *In Which We Serve* and was now looking for another patriotic vehicle to coincide with D-Day in Normandy.

Olivier planned to cast Vivien Leigh as Princess Katherine but she was under contract to David O. Selznick who refused to allow her to appear in 'insignificant roles'. When he was unable to obtain the services of William Wyler or Carol Reed as director, Olivier was forced to take on the functions of director, co-writer, associate producer and leading actor himself. He performed all roles magnificently.

Film production in Europe at the time was greatly hampered by World War II, but neutral Ireland offered facilities not readily available elsewhere. Extensive exterior filming was virtually impossible in Britain and France. In Ireland it presented no difficulty. Moreover, the absence of blackout restrictions here made it possible to shoot outdoor night scenes. Olivier required an expansive area to stage the Battle of Agincourt sequence of the film. Extras, labourers and horses could also be produced more easily in Ireland than in England.

Olivier who was mustered out of the navy to make the film explained his reason for choosing Ireland: 'The greatest problem of all was finding a spot in England to film the battle. After all this was the spring and summer of 1943 and it was impossible to find anywhere that wasn't buzzing with aeroplanes or covered with modern military defence that would have looked odd in 15th century France. Where could we find a really poetic countryside?'

The ideal location was Lord Powerscourt's estate, twelve miles south of Dublin, which was made available to the film unit. Olivier was enthusiastic about his find: 'A dream layout, exactly the place I had visualised to suit the fantasy of Shakespeare – the little hills, adjacent woods, positions for the French and English camps and a half-mile run for the camera track. Finding it was an absolute fluke.'

Every movement in the battle scene was planned. Olivier and a small team – associate producer Dallas Bower, art director Paul Sheriff and assistant Carmen Dillon, costume designer Roger Furse, musical director William Walton and film editor Reginald Beck – worked closely together. On the walls of Olivier's office were tiny reproductions on 33mm film of meticulous drawings of every shot in the action sequence. Included were scenes of the French knights floundering in a marsh, English archers and foot soldiers behind stakes, long shots of the French charge and a close-up of a cow's head.

The extras were an unkempt and motley crew, as they were not allowed to shave or have a haircut for the duration of their contracts. Consequently, out of costume and dressed in civvies they looked like riff-raff. There were 510 footmen and 164 Defence Force (LDF) from nearby counties. The horsemen were recruited from the twenty-six counties and were paid £1 a day, double that of the other troops. This new source of income, to the unemployed in particular, was most welcome. Horsemen and footmen slept and ate in separate tents but shared the same food and comforts. The general atmosphere was happy and relaxed.

A Dublin archery expert, Horace B. Hammond, instructed the hundreds of mechanics, grocers, clerks, labourers and students in the art of the long bow for the dramatic sequences where the French army faced the hail of English arrows. Horses were removed from under ploughs and milk carts. Even racing stables accommodated the film-makers. Chainmail was knitted in wool by girls from the Institute for the Blind and sprayed with aluminium paint.

The weekly consumption of food was enormous – 20,000 eggs, 500 gallons of milk, 75 gallons of cream, 5,400 pounds of meat and 3,500 cabbages. The camp bar opened three nights per week, but those who had leave passes (issued on alternate nights to footmen, nightly to horsemen) patronised the three pubs in Enniskerry or took the bus to nearby Bray. Both towns profited from this influx of bearded men, whose total weekly salary cheque amounted to over £2,000. Enniskerry, with a population of 370, became a boom town and was unable to cope with the demand for supplies. The village's single taxi, owned by

Joseph Troy, drove visitors several times a day to the location. Fifteen thousand people applied to see the filming but permits were granted sparingly. Security was tight on the gates and all permits were checked.

During filming Olivier appeared to be everywhere at once, instructing, coaxing, and demonstrating how he wanted a scene performed. Often after patiently rehearsing hundreds of horsemen and extras, shooting had to be postponed due to the inclement weather. In spite of the frustrating weather and the onerous responsibility of his first directing job, Olivier maintained an even temper. When rehearsing extended formations of horsemen his voice flowed from a dais in tones of politeness: 'Everybody please halt except section 8 – I'd like you to try it at a steady trot this time, please.' After each day's shooting he ordered a glass of Guinness for every extra. For this and other reasons he was popular with the men.

While he was filming in Ireland, Olivier was unaware that money to keep the filming going was in danger of running out. The production company, Two Cities, had to approach the Rank Organisation for extra funding. Rank financed them to the tune of £300,000 but emphasised that there would be no further payments. The final budget was £475,000. The Battle of Agincourt segment alone cost £80,000 to film and represented fifteen minutes of screen time in a film lasting two-and-a-half-hours.

The acting from the entire cast, including Robert Newton, Leslie Banks and Renee Asherson, Leo Genn and Felix Aylmer and of course Olivier was superb. The credit must also be shared with the director of photography, Robert Krasker and the mood-catching score of William Walton. The actual Battle of Agincourt segment deservedly belongs with the great moments in cinema history. The critical success of *Henry V* encouraged Olivier to make *Hamlet* and later *Richard III* and *Othello*.

A significant new talent to emerge in the British film industry during the war years was Carol Reed. In 1946 he chose Belfast as the location for *Odd Man Out*, a Rank Organisation film with interiors shot in London. In the film an IRA leader, Johnny McQueen, breaks out of jail and plans a payroll robbery on a mill in Belfast to fund their operations. Though he abhors violence, Johnny accidentally kills a man during the hold-up, and is himself critically wounded. Left behind, Johnny stumbles away, descending into a nightmare, as he becomes more delirious from his wound. He encounters an assortment of people who either want to assist him or betray him to the authorities. Reed and Robert Krasker's gritty photography combined to establish a sombre mood in the bleak night-time city where the wounded man seeks refuge. There was a strong

*Above left*: Kathleen Ryan as Kathleen Sullivan and James Mason as Johnny McQueen in *Odd Man Out*. In the movie, McQueen is the leader of the IRA in Belfast and a prisoner escapee, who is helped by Kathleen Sullivan, a young IRA woman who loves him and tries to smuggle him out of the city.

*Above right*: Another scene from *Odd Man Out*.

*Opposite*: Laurence Olivier in Henry V. For the movie, he held the roles of director, co-writer, associate producer and leading actor.

similarity between *Odd Man Out* and Ford's *The Informer*, with the intolerable fate of a man seeking survival.

The film will be long remembered for the stunning portrayal of the dying rebel by James Mason and for the last great screen performance of the Abbey Theatre's F. J. McCormick as the rag-picking bum. Irish actor, Dan O'Herlihy, played his first screen role in the film and soon after received an Academy Award nomination for his role as Robinson Crusoe in the Luis Bunuel film (a role originally intended for Orson Wells). Robert Newton, Kathleen Ryan, Noel Purcell, Robert Beatty, Albert Sharpe and Eddie Byrne played other important roles. Almost painful in its suspense and tragedy, *Odd Man Out* is a drama not easily forgotten. Carol Reed won his first British Academy Award for Best Picture and established him as one of Britain's finest directors. His next two films, *The Fallen Idol* and *The Third Man* were to consolidate his reputation as a major force in world cinema.

During the forties several other less impressive films, many with Irish subject matter, were made here. Frank Launder and Sidney Gilliat Productions shot two films in Ireland in the mid-40s. Their productions frequently suffered from over scripting so that the dialogue tended to slow the pace, as was the case with their first Irish film, *I See A Dark Stranger*, in 1946. The young Irish stage actress, Siobhán McKenna was originally offered the starring role, but turned it down when she was advised by F. J. McCormick that she should remain at the Abbey Theatre for three years and become a real actress. She was replaced by Deborah Kerr, starring as a young Irish girl with red hair, a brogue and a temper who is motivated by her patriotism to spy for Germany. Her co-stars were Trevor Howard, Liam O'Gorman, Liam Redmond, Breffni O'Rourke, Cecil Forde and Eithne Dunne. The film was set during the Emergency (1939-45) and was shot throughout Co Wicklow. The story told of the romance between Bridie Quill, a spy for Germany and Bayne, a British officer on leave. The film proved more popular in the USA than Britain or Ireland.

Launder and Gilliat's next venture, *Captain Boycott*, directed and co-written by Launder and Wolfgang Wilhem was based on the novel by Philip Rooney. The real-life story told of a struggle against tyranny in the Ireland of the 1880s when a wealthy Mayo landowner threatens to evict his tenants, they and the farmers in the district stand up to him – they 'boycott' him. It was a compact historical drama filmed in counties Wicklow, Westmeath and Mayo. The film starred Stewart Granger as the Irish hero, Cecil Parker as Captain Boycott, Alistair Sims as the parish priest, Noel Purcell as a teacher, Mervyn Johns as the bailiff, Kathleen Ryan as a farmer's daughter and the Radio Éireann personality,

Joe Linnane as an auctioneer. Robert Donat played a cameo role as Charles Stewart Parnell.

A unit of the Irish Army was employed for some sequences for which they went under canvas in the mountains. It rained almost continuously and their theme song was 'When it rains, it rains pennies from Denham' (the name of the production company). When the unit moved to Mullingar to film a race meeting, the producers invited local participation. The entire town closed down and turned out in force to be 'in the pictures'. Those in costume were paid twice the fee of those in civvies. The parish priest had to plead with the producers to release the gravediggers to dig a grave.

Brian Desmond Hurst, born in Cork in 1900, began his film-making career in Hollywood in 1925 when he became an assistant director to John Ford. In 1945 he returned to Kerry to do a stint of location work on *Hungry Hill* based on the novel by Daphne du Maurier. The film starred Margaret Lockwood, Dennis Price and Cecil Parker. The Irish members of the cast included Eileen Crowe, Arthur Sinclair and F. J. McCormick. Siobhán McKenna, on holidays from the Abbey Theatre, made her screen debut in a small role. As *Odd Man Out* and *Hungry Hill* were being filmed simultaneously, McCormick moved from one to the other. He was unable for the strain and died less than a year later at the age of fifty-five. Shot partly in Glengarriff, Co Cork, *Hungry Hill* was a rambling Victorian melodrama that chronicled two Irish families, the Brodericks and Donovans, over three generations of feuding and bitterness.

In 1948, British director, Charles Crichton, chose Dublin and Greystones for location work on a mediocre film called *Another Shore*, starring Robert Beatty, Moira Lister and Stanley Holloway. Based on a novel by Kenneth Reddin, it was the tale of a Dublin man's dream of getting away to the South Seas. The following year another British company arrived to make *Saint and Sinners*, starring Cork-born Kieron Moore and Christine Norden, with Noel Purcell and Eddie Byrne in support. Members of the Abbey Company filled other character roles. This was a comedy drama concerning a successful businessman who returns to his native Irish village to find that many things have changed. Direction was by Leslie Arliss from a screenplay by Paul Vincent Carroll.

Other feature films made in Ireland during the forties include *Crime on the Irish Border* (or *The Voice Within*), a tale of smuggling on the border (1946), directed by Maurice J. Wilson and starring Kieron Moore, Barbara White, Shaun Noble and Breffni O'Rourke. In 1947 Desmond Leslie directed *Stranger at My Door*, also called *The Iron Staircase*. Four years later, Leslie returned to Dublin to direct a thriller, *At a Dublin Inn*, the story of an ex-convict who becomes a burglar

Michael Scott and Deborah Kerr in *I See a Dark Stranger*.

Brian O'Higgins, Jack McGowran, Noel Purcell and Michael Gough in *No Resting Place*.

to help a blackmailed girl, featuring Joseph O'Connor, Valentine Dyall and Agnes Barnhill. In 1948, Patrick McCrossan directed two films. The first, *My Hands Are Clay*, with a weak plot and unimaginative direction, starred Shelagh Richards, Bernadette Leahy and Cecil Brook, and was partly filmed in Dublin and Enniskerry. The second production, *Dublin's Fair City*, was never completed.

The highly respected team of Michael Powell and Emeric Pressburger shot sequences for *Black Narcissus* in Killarney and Tipperary in 1946. The film, starring Deborah Kerr, Sabu and David Farrar, was a sentimental melodrama concerning a group of nuns who open a school and hospital in a hill village in India. That same year also saw the arrival of another leading British director, Herbert Wilcox, to film a segment for one of his highly successful films of the period, *The Courtneys of Curzon Street*. The film starred his wife, Anna Neagle, as an Irish maid, with co-stars Michael Wilding and Gladys John. It was a musical spanning the years 1899-1945 that followed the saga of the family of a nobleman and became the top money-making film of that year in the British Isles. In 1947 Richard Massington directed a children's story entitled *The Greedy Boy*, starring Síle Nic a Bháird, Joyce Sullivan and Terry Wilson. This film, which was made in Wexford, won an award at the Venice Film Festival. That same year, American stars Gene Kelly and Betsy Blair came to Shannon Airport to film a sequence for *Transatlantic Flight* under the direction of Joseph Ryle.

The 1950s began with a number of insignificant films starting in 1951 with a drama, *The Strangers Came*, directed by Alfred Travers, and starring Seamus MacLocha and Gabriel Fallon. The following year *The Promise of Barty O'Brien*, directed by George Freedland, described how Marshall Aid was put to use in Ireland. The writer, Frank O'Connor, wrote the screenplay that featured such veteran players as Eric Doyle, Harry Brogan, Eileen Crowe, Doirin Ní Mhaidin and Philip O'Flynn. One of the most famous and popular lord mayors of Dublin, Alfie Byrne, made a guest appearance. The plot concerns Barty O'Brien's determination to become an electrical engineer and his father's opposition to it. *La Jeune Folle* was a French production set during 'The Troubles' and was partly filmed in Dublin in 1952 by director Ives Allegret. In 1953 Gerald Healy directed two films, *Cosc an Gadaí* and *Turas Tearnaimh* featuring the Abbey players.

In 1950 Paul Rotha, an authority on the cinema, having written many books on the subject, produced a sensitive film about Wicklow tinkers titled *No Resting Place*. The grim story concerns a group of itinerants, the Kyles, and particularly one, Alec Kyle, who is forced to become a fugitive with his family when he accidentally kills a gamekeeper in retaliation for an attack on his young son. One guard becomes obsessed with tracking down Alec for murder. The film staring Michael Gough, Noel Purcell, Eithne Dunne, Brian O'Higgins and Jack McGowran proved once again that an artistic film could be produced on a modest budget. It was the first feature by Rotha and also the first British film made entirely on location.

Another small, yet distinguished film that cannot be overlooked is *A Jack of All Maids*, about a man who loved women, starring Jack McGowran. It was directed by Abbey Theatre director, Tomás Mac Anna, in the café of the old Abbey in the summer holidays of 1951. Mac Anna had previously directed two other films – a documentary called *Wicklow Gold* and an uncompleted documentary about Maynooth College. He then came to the juncture where he had to decide between the cinema and the theatre. Fortunately for the Abbey and its audience he opted for the latter.

The participation of the Irish defence forces in film-making began in 1943 with the LDF in *Henry V*, and continued successfully on a regular basis with Irish soldiers doubling as British, German and French troops in a number of major films. Whenever possible, depending on the availability of manpower, the Department of Defence has acceded to requests for the deployment of troops in films. It was the department's policy to scrutinise scripts to ensure there was no propaganda or other element that would cause embarrassment before making a commitment. Generally the film companies made payment directly to the Department of Defence and they in turn decided the sum to be paid to the respective ranks.

6

# THE QUIET MAN

One of the most successful films ever made in Ireland was produced in 1951 when John Ford moved into counties Galway and Mayo to direct *The Quiet Man*. The eye-patched American director (real name John Feeney), the son of an Irish immigrant, wished to take a break from filming westerns – *She Wore a Yellow Ribbon*, *Wagonmaster* and *Stagecoach* – which had established him as the supreme master of the genre. The story of *The Quiet Man*, which Ford termed 'a mature love story', may have attracted him because it concerned an Irish-American returning to the 'ould country'. Characters and acting combined to make *The Quiet Man* the most autobiographical film he had ever made. Previously Ford had regularly included a stage-Irish character in his films; following *The Quiet Man* this practice became more apparent.

Ford, whose family came from Spiddal, Co Galway, had discussed the possibility of making the film with his friend, Lord Killanin, as far back as 1936. The war intervened and it was not until fifteen years later, when producer Herb Yates provided the finance, that filming began in Connemara in locations chosen by Killanin. *The Quiet Man* was based on a short story entitled *Green Rushes* by the Kerry writer, Maurice Walsh. Ford asked Welsh author, Richard Llewellyn, who had written *How Green was my Valley*, to expand it into a novel and set the story in 1922 at the time of The Troubles. The original draft featured the Black and Tans, but Ford felt that the scenes of violence destroyed the mood and they were eliminated. Frank S. Nugent wrote the screenplay.

The cast was led by John Wayne in what for him was an unusual role, Maureen O'Hara in character as the fiery redhead, Mary Kate Danaher; Barry

John Wayne and Maureen O'Hara in *The Quiet Man*.

Fitzgerald outstanding as Michaeleen Óg Flynn, a match-making jarvey, and Victor McLaglen giving a likeable performance as the burly villain of the piece. Having cast the main roles, Ford auditioned actors from the Abbey Theatre to make the film as authentic as possible. Many Irish character actors appeared in the credits including Eileen Crowe, Jack McGowran and May Craig. Ford filled the other supporting roles with his stock players: Ward Bond as the priest, Mildred Natwick as the widow, Arthur Shields as the Protestant clergyman and Francis Ford as Old Dan.

It was the first Republic Picture made outside America and the most expensive feature they had produced at $1,175,000. Wayne was paid $100,000 and waived his usual percentage. Shooting commenced in June 1951, in the village of Cong, Co Mayo where many locals from the surrounding areas were employed as extras. Despite careful preparations it was a difficult film to shoot. The vagaries of the Irish weather during the six-week Irish schedule made it difficult to match the lighting. Yates was determined that it should remain within budget and scrutinised the spending of every cent. While filming in Ireland Ford received his highest military honour, by being named an admiral. To celebrate the occasion John Wayne pushed Ford into Galway Bay.

Wayne played Sean Thornton, a successful boxer in America, who accidentally kills an opponent in the ring. To forget the tragedy he returns to settle in his native Innisfree. Soon he falls in love with a fiery girl, Mary Kate Danaher, but her brother Red Will, the local squire, refuses to allow him to marry her. All is settled in the end but not before Thornton, overcoming his fear of killing another man, challenges Danaher to a fight – which results in what must be the longest, toughest, most memorable screen fight of all time.

*The Quiet Man* was an instant box office success. For Bord Fáilte it proved one of the most valuable publicity pieces ever, attracting thousands of foreign visitors, particularly Americans. They travelled to the bleak west coast to visit the tiny village of Cong, to see the breath-taking beauty of Lough Corrib and to find the cottage in the wilds of Mamm Valley which was Wayne's house in the film.

While in Ireland the film raised many belly laughs, in America it raised the hackles of Irish people living there for its 'stage Irishness'. The film won Ford his sixth Academy Award and Best Cinematography Award for Winton C. Hock. The film also brought international fame to songwriter, Dick Farrelly, a Dublin-based detective for his composition, *The Isle of Inishfree*, that featured as the film's theme tune under Victor Young's musical direction. Another positive side effect of the film's success was that it made Republic Studios solvent following a bad period with *The Masked Marvel* and other cliff-hangers.

Later Ford, Lord Killanin and Brian Desmond Hurst were involved in setting up an Irish film company, Four Provinces Productions. They intended to establish an Irish film industry to bring to the screen some of the classics of Irish literature, including works by James Joyce, Liam O'Flaherty and Sean O'Casey. They planned to make their headquarters in a provincial town – preferably one like Galway that had a variety of locations within easy reach. Unfortunately, owing to his commitments with the International Olympic Committee from 1952, Killanin had to curtail his involvement in film-making.

In 1952 *The Gentle Gunman* was shot on location in the Dublin Mountains and Wicklow area by the successful British team of director Basil Dearden and producer Michael Ralph who later went on to revolutionise British cinema with such wide-ranging films as *Victim*, *Violent Playground* and *League of Gentlemen*. *The Gentle Gunman* starred John Mills and Dirk Bogarde, both then at the height of their popularity in Britain. In support were Robert Beatty, Gilbert Harding, Michael Golden, Joseph Tomelty, Elizabeth Sellars and Barbara Mullan. Set in 1941, the plot concerned a small group of IRA men engaged in planting bombs in London. The film was, in essence, a plea to the Irish not to blow up London. Bogarde and Mills played Irish brothers with the latter replacing the former as an activist when he deserts the IRA on realising the futility of violence. The original play by Roger MacDougall may have been a serious study of pacifism and the moral ironies of war but it lost much of that in its transformation to the screen.

In 1953 Hilton Edwards, who, with his partner, Mícheál Mac Liammóir, was a founding figure of the Gate Theatre in Dublin, directed a short film, *Return to Glenascaul*. The film received widespread cinema release and was nominated for an Academy Award. The script, written by Edwards and based on a well-known Irish ghost story, told of strange happenings to a man one winter's night. At the time of making the film Edwards was in Rome making *Othello* with Orson Welles. He asked Welles, who had encouraged him to direct films, to play in the prologue and epilogue and he agreed. This section Edwards directed in the Scalera Studio in Rome before returning to Dublin with cameraman George Fleischmann to shoot the remainder of the film in the Phoenix Park and in an old house in Milltown, near Dublin. The only difficulty he encountered was in matching the car he used in Dublin with the one he had already used in Rome, but this was effectively done by the addition of a Mercedes radiator cap. Welles was in fact returning a favour: he had made his first major stage appearance at the Gate Theatre under Edwards' direction in 1931. Welles played a character who is told a ghostly personal adventure by a man to whom he gives a lift one night as he drives near Dublin. It was a chilling ghost story, expertly produced and photographed. A local theatre owner, Louis Elliman, who was dabbling in film production, financed the film.

Once again it proved that a wholly Irish-made film could become a reality, given the right facilities and the necessary financing. While most European countries established viable film industries, an indigenous feature film still remained a once-in-a-decade undertaking in Ireland. Hilton Edwards was later to attempt a second film entitled *Stone in the Heather* (changed to *Cross My Heart*) using an early Irish myth as his theme. Louis Elliman was producer and Edwards wrote the script with the assistance of George Morrison and filmed it in the Dublin Mountains. Unfortunately it did not achieve the same results as his first venture. Although it produced some interesting scenes it did not satisfy Edwards in the editing. In a frank interview he admitted that he did not have enough money to finish it to his liking. Another short film he directed, also with George Fleischmann as cameraman, was a record of the Gate Company preparing for their trip to Elsinore in Denmark where Mícheál Mac Liammóir and company played *Hamlet* at the invitation of the Danish Government. Edwards learned much from Orson Welles and whenever people mentioned that Welles was responsible for the direction of his films, he would express pleasure before modestly admitting they were his own work.

# 7

# HUSTON'S MOBY DICK

The next major film unit to visit Ireland was for location work on the screen version of Herman Melville's classic novel *Moby Dick*. John Huston transformed Youghal, Co Cork, into the waterfront of New Bedford, Massachusetts, in 1840, when it was the world's foremost whaling station. Huston could not use the real New Bedford as it was too modernised. Youghal was Sir Walter Raleigh's first landfall after his 1551 voyage of exploration to the Americas, when, in return, a grateful Queen Elizabeth gave him Youghal and land in Co Cork amounting to 40,000 acres. A major problem confronting the film-makers was to find an authentic whaler of the period. This problem was solved by buying the 'Hispaniola' – the ship Walt Disney built specially for *Treasure Island*. They converted her into a three-masted schooner – the whaling ship 'Pequod'. The harbour at Youghal had to be dredged to take the ten-foot draught of the 'Pequod' and other craft. Though outwardly the ship appeared authentic to the last detail, internally it had make-up rooms, wardrobes, hairdressing rooms, and kitchens to feed the unit while on location at sea.

Ray Bradbury co-wrote the screenplay with Huston that centred on the peg-legged Captain Ahab's maniacal chase for the giant white whale that had torn off his leg and scarred him for life. To capture the powerful adventure Huston and cinematographer Oswald Morris employed a muted Technicolor process. What *The Quiet Man* had achieved for Connemara three years previously, *Moby Dick* was to do for this small, south coast fishing resort. Visitors flocked to see the company at work, view the buildings camouflaged with false fronts and catch a glimpse of the stars. The stellar all male cast was led by Gregory Peck as the sadistic Captain Ahab and supported by Richard Basehart, Leo Genn, Noel Purcell, Bernard Miles, Harry Andrews and the well-known Dublin journalist, Seamus Kelly. Orson Welles made a short but dramatic appearance as the hell-fire preaching Father Mapple.

Filming at sea proved hazardous for both cast and crew but the end result was a tribute to Huston's determination and leadership. The film was visually stunning, especially the whaling scenes and deservedly won Huston the New York Critics Best Director Award. Many anecdotes are still told about the production, particularly about boats avoiding dummy whales in the shipping lanes. Older residents will not forget the filming of *Moby Dick*.

In 1953 Powerscourt demesne in Co Wicklow was again to hear the pounding of hooves and the clanging of steel when the crew of *The Night of the Round Table* moved in. Other scenes were filmed in Luttrelstown Castle. This was a straight version of the later Richard Harris musical *Camelot*, and the epic *Excalibur* (made in the same location almost three decades later), all based on the Arthurian legend. The film perceived the tale of Lancelot, Guinevere and King Arthur through the eyes of Hollywood. Starring Robert Taylor, Ava Gardner and Mel Ferrer, it was directed by Richard Thorpe. Local men again grew beards and repeated the film experience they had with Olivier. Out came the horses and everything else that could be hired to the film-makers.

Another costume drama, *Captain Lightfoot* was shot on location in counties Louth, Dublin, Wicklow and Meath. Strongly featured in the film were the Four Courts, the beach at Clogherhead, a chase at Slane Castle, and inevitably Powercourt estate. This was a swashbuckling story in the true Errol Flynn/Douglas Fairbanks tradition about a legendary Irish highwayman during the redcoat era. The script took many liberties with Irish history. Hollywood star, Rock Hudson played the title role with Barbara Rush as his leading lady. Jeff Morrow, Finlay Currie, Denis O'Dea and Kathleen Ryan headed the supporting cast. The film was directed by the cult American director, Douglas Sirk, a greatly underestimated figure in film literature. As he displayed in this film, he was a master of creating and sustaining mood and in handling actors, exposing depths in their performances with a consistency that few other directors have been able to achieve.

Four years after *The Quiet Man* John Ford returned to Ireland to make *The Rising of the Moon*, also known as *Three Leaves of Shamrock*. This film was a trilogy based on the works of Irish writers. The first episode, an adaptation of Frank O'Connor's story, *The Majesty of the Law*, was a comedy of pride, which featured Noel Purcell as Old Dan, the last survivor of a noble family, now alone in his

Maureen Potter as the barmaid and Jimmy O'Dea as the amorous railway porter in the second part of *The Rising of the Moon.*

Geoffrey Golden as Andrew Boyd and Vincent Dowling as John Haslett in *Boyd's Shop.* Haslett wants to open a new grocers in a closely-knit village, but faces a challenge from popular Boyd's shop. The plot thickens when Haslett falls in love with the daughter of his competitor.

John Gregson, Eddie Byrne, Jack McGowran and Noel Purcell in *Rooney.*

crumbling ancestral tower. He is arrested for assaulting a seller of bad poteen. The central episode was based on Michael McHugh's one-act play, *A Minute's Wait*. The comedy derives from the manner in which the Dublin train's brief halt at a country station is extended into an hour of jollity and general chaos. Lady Gregory's one-act play provides the basis for the final episode from which the film takes its title. Set in 1921, it describes the rescue from jail of a condemned IRA man.

The three stories contrasted immensely in content. In a departure from his usual practice, Ford used no star names (except an introduction by Tyrone Power) and instead relied on established actors to fill the roles. The line-up was impressive, containing names such as Noel Purcell, Donal Donnelly, Frank Lawton, Cyril Cusack, Denis O'Dea, Jack MacGowran and Maureen Potter. The main locations were in counties Clare and Galway. Unlike *The Quiet Man*, this was one of Ford's less successful films, but he did manage to recreate an authentic atmosphere of the period for the Black and Tan episode. One of the main criticisms was that he attempted to condense too much into too short a time.

*Jacqueline*, made in 1956 by Roy Baker, was based on a screenplay by Liam O'Flaherty and Patrick Kirwan with additional dialogue supplied by Patrick Campbell and Catherine Cookson. The plot concerns a Protestant family, the McNeils, living in Belfast. Mike, the father, works in the shipyards and when he becomes ill he begins drinking heavily. Fired from his job, with his wife despairing of his alcoholism, his situation seems hopeless. However, all is made right by his young daughter, Jacqueline, whose charms persuade the shipyard owner, Mr Lord, to give Mike a better job, on a country farm far from the shipyards. British actor, John Gregson played Mike McNeil and Kathleen Ryan his long-suffering wife. The film was the screen debut of young Dublin actress, Jacqueline Ryan and her performance won much praise; however, her fame was short-lived and she faded after this single film. Among the cast were Noel Purcell, Cyril Cusack, Liam Redmond and Marie Kean. The film gave some dismaying insight into how the Rank Organisation portrayed life in Northern Ireland in the 1950s.

In the same year *The March Hare*, directed by George More O'Farrell, came to Ireland for location work in the Enniskerry area. It was a comedy about horse-racing, starring Terence Morgan, Peggy Cummins and Cyril Cusack, which did little more than give employment to bit-part players. In 1958 a second feature thriller entitled *Dublin Nightmare* was filmed in the capital under the direction of John Pomeroy. The plot describes how a photographer, while visiting Ireland, is drawn into political conflict and violent of which he has no real understanding.

The stars were William Sylvester, Marla Landi and Richard Leech.

In the late fifties, producers turned to popular Abbey Theatre plays in the hope that they might prove a success on the big screen. Two such plays, filmed as low budget second-features, were George Shiels' *Professor Tim* and *Boyd's Shop*, both produced by Emmet Dalton and directed by Henry Cass. The principal scenes were filmed around the village of Enniskerry and interiors were shot in London. *Professor Tim* starred Ray McAnally and Maire O'Donnell and *Boyd's Shop* starred Eileen Crowe, Geoffrey Golden and Aideen O'Kelly. The supporting cast in both films read like a Who's Who of the Abbey Theatre, with the National Theatre shaping up as quite a repertory company for visiting film productions. Hardly a film was produced in Ireland without the names of several of their players appearing in the credits. Neither of the above films did anything to enhance the reputation of the National Theatre or to encourage the foundation of an Irish film industry. They did point, however, to the need for the setting up of a film studio in Ireland. Why should films with an Irish setting, Irish actors and Irish producer have to move to England to complete the production in a studio?

The majority of films with Irish settings were criticised for dwelling too much on the proverbial 'stage Irishman' with his exaggerated gestures and expressions. A prime example of this paddywhackery was the Rank Organisation's *Rooney*. Dublin was the setting for this enjoyable comedy centring on a Dublin dustman, who, to avoid the attentions of his amorous landlady, takes a room in the O'Flynn household. However, he is rejected when the family discovers the nature of his work. His only friends are the old grandfather and a young cousin, Máire. Later Máire inherits the grandfather's money and Rooney proposes to her. A parallel plot is told of Rooney fulfilling his ambition to play in the All-Ireland Hurling Final.

George Pollock, best known as director of the *Miss Marple* series of films in the 1960s directed this lightweight comedy. Dublin locations included Ringsend, Rathmines, the quays, Mount Street and Croke Park, where scenes were shot during an actual All-Ireland Hurling Final. Interiors were filmed at Pinewood Studios in London.

John Gregson, again cast as an Irishman, played the leading role and was ably supported by Noel Purcell, Eddie Byrne, Jack McGowran, Muriel Pavlow, June Thorburn, Pauline Delaney and Máire Kean. Barry Fitzgerald stole the film as the loveable grandfather. Some critics argued that the Dublin binmen depicted in the film were far too polite and mannerly, thus diminishing the reality of the plot.

# ARDMORE STUDIOS

Since 1914, when Sidney Olcott dreamt of operating his own permanent studio in Killarney, numerous attempts had been made to build one. In the late 1930s George Bernard Shaw and his associates planned to erect a studio near Dublin in which all his plays would be filmed but as sufficient capital was not forthcoming the project collapsed.

Finally in 1958, Ireland got its own film studio –Ardmore Studios in Bray, Co Wicklow – which was officially opened in May that year by the Minister for Industry and Commerce, Seán Lemass. Up to that time film-making in Ireland was confined to location shooting which, while expensive to the producers and lucrative to the local communities, represented only a small proportion of the completed film. The heavy cameras, massive arc lamps and cumbersome sound equipment, all required that interiors be shot in a studio. With the opening of Ardmore, producers could come to Ireland and carry out the full process of film production.

Most previous efforts to establish a film studio had collapsed through lack of finance. That obstacle was surmounted when the Industrial Credit Company advanced £217,750 by way of a debenture loan, with an additional grant of £45,000 from the Industrial Development Authority – a total investment of £262,750 towards Ardmore Studios.

Many factors contributed to the establishment of the studios. In 1954 an enquiry was set up by the government to examine film-making in Ireland. Lord Killanin and film director, Brian Desmond Hurst, headed the group. While this body achieved little, a move by Fred O'Donovan was indirectly responsible for the setting up of the studio. He made a deal with an American film company to produce thirteen films in Ireland based on Irish classics and in the main to employ Abbey actors. O'Donovan went as far as signing up the entire Abbey Company for the project, but the plan collapsed through destructive criticism, indifference and lack of interest in Ireland. However, the idea was not entirely lost as Major General Emmet Dalton, an important figure in the foundation of the State and now a film producer, saw the scope for such an undertaking and pursued it on a smaller scale. His productions of *Professor Tim* and *Boyd's Shop* served as trial runs for shooting a film entirely in Ireland.

The enterprise, which led to the setting up of Ireland's first feature studio, was one of the proposed industry's greatest events. The joint managing directors were Emmet Dalton and impresario Louis Elliman. The other directors were A. B. Elliman and C. P. McGrath. The studio manager was Captain Justin Collins, a son-in-law of Dalton. It was a completely self-contained film centre, on ten acres, on the outskirts of Bray, above Ardmore Valley. The studio was suitable for building a wide range of interior and exterior sets, and extended to a second lot of twenty-seven acres in the valley, through which the River Dargle flows.

An experienced crew of technicians was recruited to operate the studio. They consisted of key personnel with many years' experience in the film industry at home and abroad. Many Irish technicians were glad of the opportunity to return home. The company also had available a large pool of skilled craft workers plus make-up, hairdressing, wardrobe and construction workers.

Stage A and B in the studio were capable of accommodating major productions. The smaller Stage C was suitable for medium-sized films. This was what Ardmore, one of the most modern studios in Europe, with the newest equipment and latest techniques had to offer to film-makers. The studio operated on a rental basis – the rental was £1,000 a week for one of the larger stages, with the use of the workshops, dressing rooms, projection theatre and a certain allocation of equipment. Stage C rented at £500 per week.

The studio got off to an encouraging start with a series of traditional films produced by Emmet Dalton. The first film to go into production was *Home is the Hero*, a screen adaptation of Walter Macken's stage success. Macken, one of Ireland's leading playwrights and novelists, played the title role opposite American star, Arthur Kennedy. Maire O'Donnell and Harry Brogan headed the supporting roles. Veteran American director, Fielder Cooke, directed the film in which Macken returns home after completing a prison sentence following the death of a man in a public house brawl. The story traces the consequences for his family and friends.

The pattern was similar to pre-Ardmore productions of 'from stage to screen' scenarios such as *Professor Tim* and *Boyd's Shop*. Much of the acting was exaggerated, with some of the cast not yet familiar with the intimacy of screen acting. However, these films were released as second features of approximately sixty-minutes duration.

British director, George Pollock, must have been fascinated by Irish themes because he directed the next two films at the studio based on Abbey comedies – *The New Gosson* by George Shiels, retitled *Sally's Irish Rogue*, and *The Big Birthday* by Hugh Leonard, retitled *Broth of a Boy*. Pollock had been in the business for thirty years, having worked as an assistant to directors such as David Lean. Pollock had high praise for the Irish actors and stated that any type of film, from science fiction to westerns, could be produced at Ardmore.

*Sally's Irish Rogue* starred Julie Harris, a graduate of the Strasberg School of Acting, where classmates had included Marlon Brando and Montgomery Clift. She captured beautifully the blarney of the country lass but an English actor, Tim Seely, was far less convincing as the restless young man. The film was well received but showed no great returns. Harry Brogan, Philip O'Flynn, Eddie Golden and Marie Kean played strong character roles. The film described how a young man revolts against his family a few days before he was to come into possession of his late father's farm. He even breaks his promise to marry Sally, the daughter of a wily poacher.

*The Big Birthday* was a light comedy about a television producer who discovers the oldest man in the world in an Irish village and tries to entice him onto television. Such players as Harry Brogan, Marie Kean and Dermot Kelly outshone Tony Wright, as the English producer. Barry Fitzgerald played the leading role in what was to be his last screen appearance. One amusing scene of Barry Fitzgerald and his son Harry Brogan cycling a tandem was particularly memorable. The principal location for both films was the village of Kilcoole.

It was now apparent that it was producer's policy to use big star names in every film, whatever its size and budget, and to employ Irish actors in the lesser roles. This policy was understandable to a neutral observer who could understand the desirabilily of a big name to sell the film abroad and make it a commercial proposition. Irish actors were not pleased at being merely 'glorified extras'.

Dalton and Elliman travelled to America to sell studio space. As a result many leading producers came to see for themselves the high standards on offer. They were enthusiastic and began their bookings.

The Black and Tan era in Ireland was a recurring theme for film-makers. Executive producers George Glass and Walter Seltzer selected one such subject

Harry Brogan as Cassidy, Don Murray as Kerry O'Shea and James Cagney as Sean Lenihan in *Shake Hands with the Devil*.

Robert Mitchum and Dan O'Herlihy on the set of *A Terrible Beauty*.

for their big budget film to be shot in Bray; *Shake Hands with the Devil*, adapted from the novel by Reardon Conor. Young British director, Michael Anderson, with a number of successes to his credit (including *The Dam Busters*, *Around the World in Eighty Days* and *Yangtse Incident*), was producer/director. Anderson was a stickler for perfection and periodically, on the set, his temper flared, striking fear into cast and crew. He gathered an impressive array of stars led by James Cagney, Don Murray, Dana Wynter, Glynis Johns, Dame Sybil Thorndike and Sir Michael Redgrave. The Irish reliables filled the minor roles, led by Cyril Cusack, Harry Brogan, T. P. McKenna, Richard Harris, Noel Purcell and Ray McAnally.

The film centres on an Irish-American, Kerry O'Shea, a medical student in Dublin in 1921. Although his father has been one of the early leaders in the republican movement, Kerry refuses to become involved. When an IRA classmate of his is killed, Kerry discovers that his professor of surgery, Sean Lenihan, is an IRA leader. Ultimately Kerry changes his mind, joins the movement and helps kidnap the daughter of a senior officer and hold her hostage.

The IRA general informs Lenihan that a compromise peace treaty is to be signed, but Lenihan will settle for nothing short of unconditional victory and, in a frenzy of anger, breaks with the movement. The death in prison of Lady FitzHugh, for whom the IRA had hoped to exchange their hostage, sends Lenihan, now an unqualified fanatic, out to kill the English woman. Kerry, who has fallen in love with her, reasons in vain. In a final effort to halt the senseless killing he draws his own gun. Both men fire simultaneously, thus bringing the story to a violent climax.

James Cagney, giving one of his best performances, played Lenihan, the IRA leader. Don Murray was the young medical student torn between loyalty to his friends and to his country. He gave a brilliant performance as the strong-willed pacifist. Both American actors made a good attempt at the Irish accent. Dana Wynter and Glynis Johns supplied the love interest. Richard Harris, in another small role, went on to achieve international stardom. Sir Michael Redgrave played the small but nevertheless important, role of the general – thereby supporting Stanislavsky's theory that there are no small parts, only small actors. This black and white production captured the contrast between the claustrophobic back streets of Dublin and the open, rugged landscapes of Co Wicklow to exquisite effect.

While in Bray, James Cagney was casual and relaxed and could often be spotted strolling with his wife along the promenade or on one of the river walks. He took daily tap-dancing lessons from a local dancing teacher, who also ran a fishmongers. They became such good friends that Cagney insisted that all fish used in the studio during his stay were to be purchased in her shop.

Emmet Dalton chose yet another stage adaptation, *This Other Eden* by Louis Dalton, for his next production. Emmet's daughter, Audrey, then gaining quite a reputation for herself in Hollywood, played the female lead opposite British comedian, Leslie Phillips. The film was reasonably well produced and displayed the most fruitful returns so far for a medium budget film shot in Ireland. It combines ingredients of comedy and drama, with the shadow of a dead Irish hero of the Troubles in the background. Outstanding in his first big screen appearance was Norman Rodway from the Globe Theatre, playing an angry young man.

The next major film to be shot in Ardmore was *A Terrible Beauty*, directed by veteran American, Tay Garnett, and the first of a number of films to be shot by producer Raymond Stross at Ardmore over the next few years. Robert Mitchum, Anne Heywood, Dan O'Herlihy headed the cast with Richard Harris gradually climbing up the credits. Noel Purcell, Cyril Cusack, Eddie Golden, Joe Lynch and T. P. McKenna were also in the cast. Mitchum was miscast in the main role and simply played Robert Mitchum.

The film concerns the activities of the IRA in a border town in Northern Ireland in the mid 1940s. Led by their club-footed leader (O'Herlihy) they intend to blow up the local RUC station. Mitchum, on learning that the sergeant's wife and family are in the barracks, strongly objects. He threatens to expose the plot unless O'Herlihy and his colleagues rearrange their plans. Subsequently Mitchum is branded a coward and traitor. In a farcical ending the hero cum-pacifist sails to a self-imposed exile in England.

The village of Rathdrum in Co Wicklow was the focal point of the film. Many shops had false fronts attached and names added. Although set in the same period and area as Reed's *Odd Man Out*, it would do a grave injustice to the latter to attempt a comparison. The film received very critical reviews and Richard Harris remarked that it was one of the six worst films ever made.

# 9

# GORGO AND ROBIN HOOD

In the winter of 1960 the King Brothers' horror film, *Gorgo*, starring Bill Travers, William Sylvester and Vincent Winter moved into Coliemore Harbour in Dalkey, Co Dublin. MGM transferred tons of equipment from England to accommodate the crew on their one week's location.

Under Eugene Lourie's direction much of the proceedings were improvised and the Irish lines had to be written on the set with the assistance of helpful locals, as the scriptwriter seemed unable to provide appropriate dialogue. The plot concerned a sea-monster, which is captured off the west coast of Ireland and put on display in London. Its parent comes after it to wreak havoc on the city. Locals were deprived of the pleasure of seeing the actual monster that was only inserted later by the special effects team.

On the last day's shooting the entire unit was marooned for several hours at the end of Dún Laoghaire pier, as a thunderstorm with mountainous waves lashed the coast and blocked their retreat. A high proportion of the scenes shot during their stay in Dalkey was cut from the film.

Up to this period Ardmore had produced films with a strictly Irish provenance, consisting of a natural story set locally. In 1961 this policy was to change when the English producers, Roy Baker and Monty Bergman, attempted to film *The Siege of Sidney Street*, concerning the activities of the anarchist movement in London in 1911.

The film challenged the resources of the studio but also those of the producers who faced the problem of acquiring costumes and authentic props of the period. The location manager had quite an array of sites to choose from in

Dublin that were suitable because they resembled where the actual action actually took place. The main reason for not shooting in London was the fact that skyscrapers now replaced the East End haunts of Peter the Painter. Dublin's narrow lanes and Georgian houses resembled London of the period. An advantage Ireland offered foreign film-makers was the availability of exteriors dating to the latter half of the nineteenth century and its comparative freedom from air pollution and smog.

The climax of the film is the siege which developed into one of the bloodiest battles in the annals of British crime. When this sequence was being re-enacted in Wellington Street in Dublin, large crowds gathered to watch the filming. However, this portion of the film was executed brilliantly and showed the director's thorough research into the actual incident. The end result was an exciting, fast-moving thriller.

Starring in this non-fiction film were Donald Sinden, Nicole Berger, Kieron Moore and Peter Wyngarde. Screenwriter Jimmy Sangster, bearing a striking resemblance to a young Winston Churchill, then Home Secretary, who personally supervised the final battle, made a walk-on appearance. Equity turned out actors and extras by the score to fill the minor roles and crowd scenes. Major roles went to Godfrey Quigley, Joe Lynch, Christopher Casson and T. P. McKenna. Extras doubled as poorly clad Londoners, Scots Guardsmen and members of the London constabulary.

*The Siege of Sidney Street* was one of the first films to receive financial assistance from the Irish Film Corporation. This state-sponsored body, a wholly owned subsidiary of the Industrial Credit Company, was incorporated in 1960, when it became apparent that the absence in Ireland of an organisation to provide risk capital for producers wishing to film in Ardmore Studios retarded the development of the studio's facilities.

In 1960 a production company from the Bavarian Studio in Munich came to Ireland to make two feature films based on the popular G. K. Chesterton character, Father Brown. The company hired equipment from Ardmore but filmed on location in Howth and Galway. The director and leading actors were German and the Irish members of the cast, although speaking in English, later had their voices dubbed into German. A German actor, Heinz Ruhman, popular in his native country for his Fernandel style comedy, played Father Brown.

Bill Luckwell, producer of the successful *Maigret* television series, made four second-feature films in Bray in a two year period: *Ambush in Leopard Street*, *Enter Inspector Duval*, *A Question of Suspense* and *Murder in Eden*. All were run-of-the-mill thrillers with English settings, which Max Varnell directed. They began shooting on Ardmore's small Stage C but when the larger stages became available they utilised them. Luckwell had initially only intended making one film, but when the opportunity of gaining priority in a top studio arose, he took advantage. Hence the films were churned out in rapid succession.

These films were a major disappointment when one considered his achievements with the Simenon series. They were more comparable with episodes of popular television series of the period such as *No Hiding Place* and *The Saint*. Although British actors such as Peter Reynolds, Bruce Seton and Anton Diffring played leading roles, these films did bring Irish actors to prominence, most notably Norman Rodway and Ray McAnally. In *Murder in Eden* McAnally gave a credible performance as a detective investigating an art gallery murder. These productions, with budgets ranging from £4,500 to £20,000 merely maintained employment at the studio.

Many of these films were shot on the streets of Bray where residents found their lack of continuity amusing. One instance, guaranteed to bring howls of laughter in local cinemas, was a scene where an actor turns from one street into another that was obviously in an area miles away.

With film-making at an all times high in England during the early sixties, Ardmore benefited from the overflow. One of the busiest periods was when three productions with star casts were in progress simultaneously. They were Nigel Patrick's *Johnny Nobody* with Patrick himself, Aldo Ray, Yvonne Mitchell and William Bendix on location in Dublin; Richard Fletcher's *The Big Gamble*, starring Stephen Boyd, Juliette Greco and David Wayne; and Terence Fisher's *Sword of Sherwood Forest* with Richard Greene, Sarah Greene and Peter Cushing. *The Sword of Sherwood Forest* had all the ingredients of the earlier Robin Hood films and the only touch of originality was in the choice of actors. The landscapes and waterfall of Powerscourt again offered a picturesque backdrop for the film. Produced by Michael Carreras and directed by Terence Fisher for Hammer Films this was the first costume drama to be shot at the studio. Many locals were recruited as extras to play some of Robin's men or soldiers of the villainous Sheriff of Nottingham. Richard Greene brought to the big screen the role he had played for many years on television. Following this film he went into semi-retirement in Wexford. Peter Cushing, taking a break from horror films, played the sheriff, Sarah Branch was Maid Marion, Nigel Green was Little John and Niall McGinnis played Friar Tuck.

*The Big Gamble*, from a script by Irwin Shaw, told the story of an Irishman (Stephen Boyd), his wife (Juliette Greco) and a meek cousin (David Wayne) who sought their fortune on the Ivory Coast. The only memorable part of the film was

An action scene in Wellington Street, Dublin for *The Siege of Sidney Street*.

Peter Cushing on the set of *The Sword of Sherwood Forest*.

Stuart Whitman, director Guy Green and Donald Wolfit on the set of *The Mark*.

the opening sequence which was shot from the bridge of a ship sailing up the Liffey. For the first time colour photography captured the red-bricked heart of the city to best advantage. Other Dublin scenes were shot on the quays and at an old crumbling house in Kilmainham. Stock Irish actors including Philip O'Flynn and Marie Kean played character roles. When the action transferred to Africa the film developed into a second rate melodrama.

Nigel Patrick's film was an off-beat thriller concerning an atheist writer being shot dead in an Irish village by a mysterious stranger and becoming famous as Johnny Nobody. The villagers claim the act to be a miracle. The local priest is mistaken for the killer and goes on the run. The village of Enniskerry was the focus of the story with other scenes shot in Kilquade, the old railway line at Carrickmines, Mountjoy Jail and the Wicklow Mountains. American actor, Aldo Ray, who played the title role, persistently complained about the size of his role. He declared that it was the smallest part he had ever played, with only three short appearances, in the beginning, the middle and the end. Jimmy O'Dea made one of his rare screen appearances as the postman. Other Irish actors in the cast included Noel Purcell, Eddie Byrne and Joe Lynch.

Up to this time Julie Harris was the only graduate of the Strasberg Acting School in New York to work at Ardmore. This academy was famous for its method style of acting. The second graduate to hit Ireland was cast in the lead role in the next Emmet Dalton production, *The Webster Boy* (or *The Middle of Nowhere*). This was the versatile actor/director, John Cassavetes, who in later years achieved fame, as one of America's most important and original directors. In this drama, he played an American who had been divorced many years before and returns to his ex-wife, now happily remarried with a growing son. She cannot resist his charm and they fall in love again. Understandably friction erupts as the wife finds herself suddenly with two husbands. Her son warmly admires the American and the plot progressed in sentimentality. Clients of the Royal Hotel in Bray were frequently treated to spontaneous rehearsals as Cassavetes performed. Elizabeth Sellars, David Farrar, Seymour Cassel and Richard O'Sullivan played other roles under Don Chaffey's direction.

*Lies My Father Told Me*, a second feature drama, came from the same production team of Dalton and Chaffey. The story centred on a Dublin Jewish family and starred American actress, Betsy Blair, making one of her rare film appearances. Harry Brogan led the supporting players. The film literally vanished following its initial screening at the Cork Film Festival where it received good notices. Most people who saw the film regarded the performance of Harry Brogan as one of the best in his career. Brogan felt that the film was regarded as being anti-Semitic in some quarters and this was the reason it was shelved.

The next film to go before the cameras in Ardmore was a controversial film, *The Mark*, produced by Raymond Stross with a star cast. Originally Richard Burton was to have played the leading role as a man who seeks to re-establish himself in society after a prison sentence for kidnapping a ten-year old girl in order to molest her. American actor, Stuart Whitman was cast as the man, with Rod Steiger as an Irish psychiatrist and Maria Schell as a young mother with whom Whitman falls in love. Donald Houston played the reporter who shadows the ex-convict, endeavouring to secure a sequel to his first story.

The film's strength lay in its remarkable dialogues between Steiger and Whitman. Their scenes together were directed with great firmness by Guy Green and acted with convincing sensitivity and good humour.

Not surprisingly, with its controversial subject matter, *The Mark* was banned in Ireland. In England it was generally cold-shouldered and received a limited showing. In America it was a top box-office draw and reviewers referred to it as 'a first rate psychological drama,' 'a masterpiece' and 'an absorbing, memorable film'.

For his performance in the film Stuart Whitman was to receive an Academy Award nomination but lost out to Gregory Peck for *To Kill a Mockingbird*. Following the success of *The Mark* the number of enquiries about the studio's availability increased.

The next three films to go before the cameras in Ardmore did little to enhance the reputation of the studio. The first two were *Freedom to Die* and *Stork Talk*, both of which received grants from the Film Finance Corporation. The former, a second feature thriller directed by Francis Searle, was similar to the Luckwell series. The latter brought Anne Heywood back to Bray to co-star with Tony Britton in this saucy comedy set in a hospital and directed by Michael Furlong. The film was banned in Ireland and little was heard of it elsewhere after its completion. The third film, made in 1962, was a mediocre thriller, *A Guy Called Caesar*. It was also directed by Searle and starred Conrad Phillips, George Moon and Philip O'Flynn. Former RTÉ newsreader, Charles Mitchel, featured as one of the crooks. The film involved a policeman who poses as a crook to join a gang of jewel thieves and unmasks their leader.

In 1962 an MGM unit under the direction of American Robert Stevens moved into the county Cork village of Crookhaven for location work on *I Thank a Fool*. The screenplay was by John Mortimer, based on the best-selling novel of the same name by Audrey Erskine Lindop. The story tells of a doctor (Peter Finch) who employs a repentant murderer (Susan Hayward) as a companion for his mentally ill wife (Diane Cilento). While they are visiting the wife's drunken father (Cyril Cusack) in Ireland, she dies and the companion believes she has been set up. Cusack in particular was praised for his fine performance.

# 10

# COPPOLA AND LOW BUDGETS

The next large-scale production to take the floor at Ardmore was *Term of Trial*. Initially it was announced that Hayley Mills would play opposite Laurence Olivier but was later replaced by an unknown actress, Sarah Miles. At the helm were producer James Wolfe, director Peter Grenville and director of photography, Oswald Morris. Other members of the cast included Simone Signoret, Hugh Griffith and Thora Hird and Terence Stamp making his screen debut. No Irish actors featured prominently in the credits.

In *Term of Trial* Miles plays a 15-year-old schoolgirl infatuated with her middle-aged teacher (Olivier). At first it seems nothing more than a harmless adolescent attraction for an older man, but on a school outing to Paris she schemes to be alone with him. Owning to a delay on the return journey the party are forced to stay overnight at a London hotel where her true motive is revealed when she tries to entice him to make love to her. He maintains his fatherly pose and sends her back to her room. At home, following his degrading rebuke, she tells her parents he assaulted her. The film concludes with a dramatic court room sequence.

The subplots are neatly interwoven with the main one – the teacher's nagging wife in whose eyes he must damn himself to regain her affections; the amorous mother who only had time for her male companion, and ignores her impressionable son and the bully who makes life unpleasant for all.

All shooting, with the exception of one week's location in Paris, was undertaken in Ireland. The film-makers transformed Quinsboro Road in Bray into a market with stallholders and fishmongers. Various schools throughout the

COPPOLA AND LOW BUDGETS

country supplied children for the classroom scenes. *Term of Trial* served as a springboard to international stardom for two young unknowns – Sarah Miles and Terence Stamp, who played the young thug.

*The Very Edge*, a Raymond Stross production, was less impressive. Had it not been for its star names it could have been from the Luckwell stable or a British television series. Areas of Co Dublin duplicated for an English town where the story was set. It told how a housewife (Anne Heywood) is menaced by a stranger who attacks her, causing her to have a miscarriage. He is arrested and jailed but to stretch the storyline to ninety minutes he conveniently escapes. The second half of the film is almost a repetition of the first as he sets about his sinister deed again. The film concludes when the stalker falls from the roof of a block of apartments. The cast was sadly wasted with Anne Heywood wearing appropriate expressions of shock and fear, her husband, Richard Todd, displayed a constant frown, Jack Hedley was the plodding detective and Jeremy Brett was not the least bit menacing as the intruder. Cyril Frankel directed this insipid thriller.

The same year a British second feature, *Dead Man's Evidence*, directed by Francis Searle was shot on location in counties Dublin and Wicklow. The film starring Conrad Philips and Jane Griffith told of a secret agent investigating the death of a frogman who is exposed as a traitor.

Another film unit found that Dublin's streets offered good period locations for another detective film about Conan Doyle's famous sleuth: *Sherlock Holmes and the Deadly Necklace*. This was a German-English production directed by Terence Fisher with Christopher Lee in the title role, supported by Senta Berger and Thorley Walters. Holmes and his faithful aide, Watson were again locked in combat with the evil Moriarty, who was in pursuit of a valuable diamond necklace.

The last film under the Emmet Dalton banner to be made at Ardmore was *The Devil's Agent*, one of the most disappointing of Dalton's films. It concerned spying at the United Nations and was a complicated and stilted production. The story relates how Draste meets his old friend, Von Straub, who subsequently invites him to his home for the weekend. He is tricked by Von Straub's sister into acting as a secret agent and from there is inveigled into becoming a double agent. John Crowley, a household name in RTÉ's television series, *The Riordans*, played an important role. The unit found it necessary to move to Vienna for concluding scenes when Trinity College refused permission to shoot within its grounds. The film, under John Paddy Carstairs' direction and starring such talented players as Peter van Eyke, McDonald Carey and Christopher Lee received poor reviews.

It was inevitable that an enterprising producer would attempt to bring John

Millington Synge's *The Playboy of the Western World* to the screen. In 1961 Brian Desmond Hurst directed a version with Siobhán McKenna as Pegeen Mike and Gary Raymond as Christy Mahon. Niall McGinnis and Liam Redmond played other leading roles. The actual plot, about a young stranger who becomes the idol of a small village, was less important than the soaring, poetic language of the play. McKenna gave a marvellous performance, although her age – she looked too old to be Gary Raymond's girlfriend – was a weakness in the production. Two of the highlights of the film, which was principally shot on Inch Strand in Co Kerry, were the score by Seán Ó Riada and the cinematography of Geoffrey Unsworth.

Brendan Behan was the first contemporary Irish literary figure to have his work produced at Ardmore Studio. It was his outstanding prison drama, *The Quare Fellow*, which was based on his own prison experiences. His play traces the final hours of a condemned man and the effects on the other prisoners. Fundamentally it was an anti-capital punishment statement but the film did not do justice to the original. The glorification of the new warder and the love affair between him and the condemned man's wife, were departures from Behan's original text that diffused the impact of the whole.

Two British stars, Patrick McGoohan and Sylvia Syms headed the cast, with Walter Macken, Pauline Delaney, T. P. McKenna, Harry Brogan and Dermot Kelly heading a large contingent of Irish players. The direction of the American Arthur Dreyfuss was evenly paced. Kilmainham Jail provided a perfectly dank environment for the prison scenes. Irish cinematographer, Vincent Corcoran, made an impressive debut in feature films with a documentary-like introduction that was screened behind the credits.

A short film made at Ardmore around this period entitled *Meet the Quare Fellow* was a straight face-to-face interview between Eamonn Andrews and Brendan Behan. Although by no means as sensational as the Malcolm Muggeridge television interview, it did manage to convey a great deal of the warmth and humour of the Dublin writer. Fred O'Donovan directed the fifty-minute film for the extraordinary low figure of £500.

Within months of each other, two renowned directors of the old school – John Huston and Carol Reed returned to Ireland for location work on their latest films, *The List of Adrian Messanger* and *The Running Man*, respectively. Both productions were modern-day thrillers, with Huston's productions winning by a short head, but both proved unsatisfactory.

Huston's film, based on a novel by Philip MacDonald, opened with a writer handing a detective a list of twelve men who died accidentally during the previous five years. Later, he himself dies in a plane crash but manages to babble a few delirious words to the only survivor, a friend of the detective's. Patching together the clues, the detective – a retired intelligence officer – realises that the 'accidents' in fact were perfect crimes. Following many tense atmospheric scenes, the detective interprets the clues with almost Holmesian powers of deduction before apprehending the killer.

Each new venture by Huston was a challenge. His film characterisations varied enormously, from the sadistic Captain Ahab to the young Yankee soldier's conflict in *The Red Badge of Courage* to the rugged portrayals of Bogart. The impression could have been gleamed that Huston, after the rigorous experience filming Freud, was inclined to relax with this genial thriller. His fox-hunting scenes will long be remembered, with the blazing red jackets and tally-ho of the riders on their sturdy mounts, attuning with the melodious yapping of the pack. Huston, who had been Master of the Galway Blazers, made a fleeting appearance during this sequence.

George C. Scott and Dana Wynter were the stars of the film but many other big names including Kirk Douglas, Robert Mitchum, Burt Lancaster, Tony Curtis and Frank Sinatra made cameo appearances. Most of the Irish scenes were shot around Cabinteely House in Co Dublin. The film was made during Huston's love affair with Ireland when he had set up home in Craughwell, Co Galway. He took every opportunity to do a stint of location work in Ireland even when the film did not warrant an Irish setting.

Sir Carol Reed returned to Ireland for location work on his thriller, *The Running Man*. The plot relates how Rex and Stella Black defraud an insurance company of £50,000. Rex presumed killed in an air crash, remains in hiding until the claim has been paid to his wife. He sets out to join Stella in Spain and stumbles across an assurance agent who has accidentally blundered into the situation and fallen in love with Stella. This lights the fuse on a chain of events that ends in tragedy.

Reed shot his interiors at Ardmore, where a plane crash was simulated on the back lot. Locations were filmed at Bray, although Ireland does not feature in the plot. His stars were Laurence Harvey, Lee Remick and Alan Bates. Irish actors Eddie Byrne, Noel Purcell and Joe Lynch filled supporting roles.

Lack of finance was the principal reason given by Irish film-makers as to why feature films could not be successfully produced here, but in 1963 one small film made at Ardmore challenged this conventional notion. An American company owned by producer-director Roger Corman made the *Haunted and the Hunted*, retitled *Dementia 13*. It was made cheaply and quickly, with a small cast and crew and a minimum of sets. A twenty-three-year old American, Francis

Laurence Olivier and Terence Stamp in *Term of Trial*.

Francis Ford Coppola, director of *Dementia 13*.

Rita Tushingham in *Girl with Green Eyes*.

Pat Boone filming *Never Put it in Writing* in Dublin.

Ford Coppola, from the University of California film school, who had worked in other capacities on Corman films, was given his big chance with this claustrophobic horror story. Corman was serving as soundman on Corman's *The Young Racers* when he dashed off a screenplay in three days for a quickie gothic chiller and persuaded the producer to finance the film. Corman supplied $22,000 and several of his stars including William Campbell, Luana Anders and Bart Patton. Irish actors, Patrick Magee and Eithne Dunne were added to the cast.

Coppola shot the film in three weeks, two weeks in the studio and one week on location in the village of Newtownmountkennedy in Co Wicklow. A crew of fourteen, ten of them Irish, worked on this production and cut the crewing level by approximately fifty per cent.

On some films the total budget would not even have covered the construction of sets. The entire studio work was undertaken on the small Stage C at Ardmore. Every day Coppola gathered his technicians and artists together to discuss each scene in depth. The result was a minimum of takes on each sequence and the saving of film or an actor fumbling his lines.

The plot of *Dementia 13* was simple. As an eccentric Irish family squabble over a vast inheritance in an isolated mansion, a mysterious axe murderer kills them off one by one. The setting is a sinister Irish castle with a neurotic family dominated by a widowed mother, Lady Haloran. When one of her sons dies from a heart attack his wife dumps his body in a lake and pretends that he is still away on a business trip. To further this plan she attempts to drive her mother-in-law insane, but is hacked to death by a mysterious figure after a midnight swim.

The contrived material was lifted to a higher level by Coppola's clever editing and obvious flair for composition. Over the years *Dementia 13* developed a cult following and hinted at the originality of Copploa who went on to direct the Godfather films and *Apocalypse Now*.

Comparatively low budget films had been produced successfully over a number of years by the veteran American director, Andrew Stone and by the British Woodfall Films. The two companies shot films in Ireland, in the Dublin/Wicklow area within a six-month period. Both had, for the early sixties, a revolutionary method of operating by filming entirely on location. Many established directors frowned on this form of filming but both Stone and Woodfall were justified by their list of credits – the former with *The Last Voyage* and *The Password is Courage*, and the latter with *A Taste of Honey* and *The Loneliness of the Long Distance Runner*. Like the remainder of the Woodfall productions they were frank, provocative dramas, pioneering a new trend in realism.

Woodfall's Irish production was *Girl with Green Eyes*, adapted from Edna O'Brien's *The Lonely Girl* and starring Peter Finch, Rita Tushingham and Lynn Redgrave. Desmond Davis, who had started his career as a 16-year-old, clapperboy, directed the film. He had worked as a camera operator on all Tony Richardson's films since *A Taste of Honey*, and now had the opportunity to direct his first feature film. The story concerns a quiet and rather philosophical English writer who drifts into a transitory love affair with an Irish girl much younger than himself. A memorable sequence, perfectly modulated by Davis, was their long conversation that sustained a logical train of thought while the visuals shifted from one setting to another – tea-shop, book shop, pub and seashore – indicating a passage of time and a growing rapport. The device was not new in cinema, but it has seldom been employed to better effect. Overall it was a skilful and touching film.

*Girl with Green Eyes* was part of a remarkable renaissance in the British cinema. This began in the late fifties with a return to films of reality e.g. *Room at the Top* and *Look Back in Anger*. The cinema had turned to successful new novels and plays of authentic regional and working class life for its raw material.

The second film was Andrew Stone's *Never Put it in Writing* which told the plight of a young executive who must retrieve a letter of resignation before it reaches his boss. American singing star, Pat Boone, played the young man, supported by Milo O'Shea and Fidelma Murphy. The scenes focused mainly on the trio rushing in and out of buildings in pursuit of the letter. The result was little more than a sub-standard slapstick with a few funny moments. In the credits was a long list of Irish supporting players headed by Colin Blakely, Eddie Golden and Harry Brogan.

A number of misfortunes struck the film. On the first day's shooting at Shannon Airport a small Proctor plane crashed into a camera truck injuring five people including the director, though none seriously. At a later stage in filming the production was informed by the Department of Transport and Power that permission for further flying sequences over Dublin had been refused. Subsequently the unit had to transfer to London for concluding scenes.

# 11

# THE TRIALS OF ARDMORE

From the early 1960s Ardmore Studios was to experience a number of problems. They came under the headings of distribution, finance and industrial disputes. Independent producers, many of whom had received loans from the Irish Film Finance Corporation, experienced problems with the distribution of their films. After participating in the financing of fifteen films to the extent of £385,000 in the period 1960-62, the Corporation was reluctant to back any further projects. Many of these films had failed to recover their costs and the Corporation, therefore, incurred heavy losses which were only marginally offset by profits on a series of successful second features in which they participated. The main reason for the losses was the failure of the films to secure a release on either of the British circuits, J. Arthur Rank Organisation or ABC. In some cases this might have been due to the indifferent quality of the product but it was obvious that at that time (and the same is mainly true today) neither circuit was keen to take films by independent producers.

When Ardmore was established no provision was made for the training and staffing of Irish film technicians and the resultant vacuum was quickly filled by British technicians. In fact Ardmore became an extension of the British film industry. Irish carpenters and plasterers, canteen staff were casually employed from the local work force whenever the studio was in operation, but the crewing of film technicians was arranged in London by whatever company had hired the studio. Also, by a quirk of film tradition, electricians were regarded as film technicians and it was at that level that one saw most clearly the paradox of British film employment at Ardmore. In 1962 a conflict flared between the Irish

Electrical Trade Union and its British counterpart, which bedevilled the studio until the end of 1964.

The Irish union claimed that, as it was Irish government money that built Ardmore they should supply the electricians for productions there. The British union counter-claimed that as it was British Government money that subsidised films made at Ardmore, they that should enjoy the employment opportunities. The British Federation of Film Unions closed ranks behind the electricians and threatened to stop all future productions at Ardmore. The arrangement, resulting from long deliberations between the unions, was that a meeting would take place before each film to be shot at Ardmore to decide the ratio of English and Irish electricians employed on that particular film.

The next film to encounter problems at Ardmore was a remake of Somerset Maugham's classic novel, *Of Human Bondage*. The Irish Electrical Union claimed a breach of agreement on the crewing of the film and placed a picket on the studio. Members of other unions employed there passed the picket and filming proceeded but the production was plagued by many other problems.

Laurence Harvey and Sophia Loren were originally cast as the stars but Kim Novak replaced Loren as Mildred before shooting began. Soon after filming commenced, Novak had a row with the director, Henry Hathaway, over her characterisation and he resigned. One of the cast, Bryan Forbes, became temporary director until Ken Hughes took over as the third director. Kim Novak had another disagreement and flew to London, refusing to finish the film. Elizabeth Taylor was named as a replacement. Following negotiations Novak returned and filming resumed. When students threatened to kidnap Novak as a rag-day prank she received a garda escort. An American film unit flew in to make a film on this much publicised production. Bryan Forbes had to leave the film owing to prior commitments and was replaced by Jack Hedley. His scenes had to be reshot.

Ironically the final scenes were shot in a make-shift cemetery in the shadow of the gasometer in Bray. The previous week carpenters had transformed the over grown field into a diminutive cemetery. On a call of 'action' by director, Ken Hughes, Laurence Harvey strolled from the cemetery towards a waiting cab where he spoke to Nanette Newman. In the background gravediggers filled in Mildred's (Kim Novak's) grave as an old steam engine shunted to and fro on the line above to add a period touch. By 7.30 p.m. Hughes had called 'cut' for the final time on the set of *Of Human Bondage*.

For the next twelve months the stages of Ardmore lay idle. Potential customers were put off by the rows behind the Maughan remake. Finally in November 1963 William Sandys was appointed receiver. The studio closed and

Kim Novak in *Of Human Bondage*. This was the third screen adaptation of Somerset Maugham's novel about the destructiveness of sexual obsession. Laurence Harvey played the role of Philip Carey, an unsuccessful club-footed artist who falls in love with a waitress, Mildred Rogers (Novak). That love remains despite her infidelity and her even becoming a prostitute.

An interrogation scene starring Richard Burton from *The Spy Who Came in from the Cold*. Burton played the role of Alec Leamas, a burnt-out British MI6 secret agent stationed in Berlin.

A scene from *The Blue Max*.

the managing director, Justin Collins, resigned. An advertisement appeared in an English trade magazine stating that the studio was for sale.

Almost unnoticed, a major production slipped into Ardmore and was announced officially only a few days before shooting commenced. The film was *Ballad in Blue*, the straight acting debut of American jazz musician, Ray Charles. Paul Henreid, once a Hollywood heart-throb, was chosen to direct this sentimental weepie. One of the highlights of the film was a concert in Dublin's Gaiety Theatre. Charles' international co-stars included Tom Bell, Mary Peach, Dawn Addams and eight-year-old Piers Bishop.

While unable to find a buyer the receiver promoted the studio and was responsible for enticing Paramount to film *The Spy Who Came in From the Cold* at Ardmore. Richard Burton took on one of the year's most demanding and coveted roles as Leamas, a seedy British agent in the screen adaptation of John Le Carre's bestseller. The story reveals how the spy (Burton) is recalled for one more mission in East Germany – to eliminate the head of the espionage service there. Claire Bloom, Oscar Werner, Peter Van Eyke, Sam Wanamaker, George Voskovec and Cyril Cusack played other leading roles.

Producer/director Martin Ritt moved into Ardmore for a seven-week shoot before the unit moved to Holland and Germany for concluding scenes. He regarded the overcast conditions, which prevailed during the winter schedule in Ireland ideal as they reflected the atmosphere of the plot. Even Dubliners found it difficult to identify the city locations, which were so skilfully transformed into English and East German settings. The Checkpoint Charlie – the official crossing point between communist East Berlin and the American sector – set erected at Smithfield in Dublin was built to the most exacting details. A fifty-man construction team spent a month building the set, which included West Berlin shops, barbed wire barriers and 25-foot high guard towers.

Ritt, who was making the $3 million film for his own company, Salem Films, was no stranger to controversial themes. He spoke of his reason for filming in Dublin. 'It is because of the cold grey climate. The predominantly overcast sky was a particular asset, as a gloomy background was required throughout the film. Then the studio cost, with that of labour and materials, is considerably less than in Britain or on the continent. Many of the Irish settings appeared more realistic than Berlin at the time of the action [1961].'

Richard Burton was a likeable and friendly man with a wry sense of humour. He was approachable, signing autographs and posing for photographs. His then wife, Elizabeth Taylor, was more elusive and avoided the press. Burton's performance earned him a well-deserved Oscar nomination but the award eluded him. The film itself lived up to expectations and was regarded as a masterpiece, receiving almost unanimous praise from the critics.

When 20th Century Fox set out to make *The Blue Max*, they found that there was little similarity between how the site of the original Battle of the Somme appeared in World War I and how it looked in the mid-sixties. They began a search for a location similar to the Somme, which they found in Kilpedder, Co Wicklow. The unit was based in Ardmore and the aerial sequences were shot at Weston Aerodrome.

The production team, headed by producer Christian Ferry and director John Guillerman recreated the era with painstaking authenticity. The nine fighter planes featured in the film were exact replicas of the aircraft used by both the Germans and the Allies. The Department for Defence permitted the film-makers to use several hundred troops in the battle scenes, the troops doubling as both Allied and German soldiers. The FCA's traditional opposition to the regular army made for such a high degree of realism in the battle scenes that there were several casualties, though none fatal. During the shooting of the war scenes, seven tons of explosives were used each day. To unleash the power under strict control, while simulating battle conditions with intensive gunfire and bombardment, twenty-five miles of electric charge wire and two-way radio sets linked the sixty-man team.

The producers assembled a top cast headed by George Peppard, James Mason, Ursula Andress and Jeremy Kemp. The film depicts the evolution of air power during the Great War and the emergence of determined pilots whose field of honour was the sky. They fought and died by a gentlemen's code that was never to be known again. The film centres on one such pilot, Peppard, who combined all that was best and worse in that breed of men. It was glory rather than love that he sought – the ultimate glory crystallised in a few inches of blue enamel and silver known as the Blue Max and achieved by shooting down twenty planes.

George Peppard, a rather passive actor, allowed the character's inner determination to be so deeply soured as to be barely visible, but he gave a competent performance in a difficult role. Bruno was far from being a hero and the film failed to bring him to life. Ursula Andress was not impressive as the Countess (wife of the German air commander – the James Mason character), a part developed out of box-office consideration, but she made the most of a one-dimensional character.

The other locations, which included Christ Church, Trinity College and Powerscourt, were so meticulously camouflaged that they were almost impossible to identify. The film was superbly photographed and the staged aerial battles were regarded as some of the best ever filmed.

# 12

# JOHN HUSTON AND THE IRISH FILM INDUSTRY

John Huston found in Ireland, a tranquillity that allowed him to recharge his batteries between the rigours of film-making. From the late 1950s he lived in St Clearans, a Georgian mansion at Craughwell, Co Galway. The house was adorned with mementoes of his travels to film locations in many continents. In his home he entertained many celebrities, from Arthur Miller to Marlon Brando and Montgomery Cliff. He became so immersed in the Irish way of life, as country squire, Master of the Galway Blazers, recipient of an honorary degree from Trinity College, that he became an Irish citizen in 1964.

One long-term ambition of Huston's was to produce a film on the most dramatic few days in modern Irish history – the Easter Rising of 1916. He began preliminary work and assigned Thomas M. Coffey's novel, *The Agony at Easter*, for the screen. He received the Government's backing and their commitment to allow him all facilities and the use of hundreds of troops. Even the rebuilding of Nelson's Pillar was on the agenda. Unfortunately, owing to the escalating Northern troubles and the sensitive nature of the subject, the production had to be postponed. Despite this setback, the number of films Huston wholly or partially shot in Ireland during the period of his residency here increased substantially.

One of these was *Casino Royale* (1966), a lavish, big budget spoof on the James Bond spy adventures, produced by Charles K. Feldman. Wolf Mankowitz wrote the screenplay from the Ian Fleming novel in which he introduced the original Bond character. The £4 million film, which took ten months to shoot, was divided among five directors – John Huston, Val Guest, Joseph McGrath,

Robert Parrish and Ken Hughes, although a substantial amount of footage was shot by the 'action director,' seventy-year-old Richard Talmedge. A host of stars including Orson Welles, George Raft, Peter Sellers, Woody Allen, Peter O'Toole, Charles Boyer and William Holden added their lustre to the extravaganza.

Even though the film had no Irish connection, Huston came to Ireland to shoot part of his quota. He brought stars, David Niven, Deborah Kerr and a bevy of beauties to romp around the wilds of Glencree and Killeen Castle. Huston attempted to persuade Charlie Chaplin to take the role of 'M', Bond's boss, and when Chaplin declined, he played the role himself, with a carroty red wig, fated to be blown to kingdom come. Deborah Kerr played a lusty secret agent named Mimi, masquerading as Lady Fiona McTarry, a Scottish chieftain who planned to seduce Niven and failed. She got uproariously drunk and set her teenage daughters to accomplish the task that had proved beyond her. She then renounced the world and entered a convent. She reappears at the end of the film in a wimple to give Niven a valuable clue (and a wink that implied that the holy lady had not entirely forgotten her earlier self). The sequence was an endearing touch of Huston at his most irreverent.

The plot and continuity of the film were a disaster and the film looked as if several different scripts had got mixed up. One of its most impressive aspects was the sets designed by Michael Stringer. Originally assigned to design thirty sets he ended up, designing over fifty, constructed at three different studios as three units were filming simultaneously. Another redeeming facet of the film was the special effects and the gambling finale in the casino of the title was well staged.

Not long after the Bond fiasco, Huston was back in Ireland for his next production, *Sinful Davey*, the story of Davey Haggard, the son of Scotland's most notorious highwayman. In 1821 Haggard deserts the King's army and sets out to outdo his father's legend, at first pick pocketing, then robbing graves for which he is thrown into jail. He endears himself to the Duke of Argyle and during a grand ball he robs the Duke's guests of all their jewellery. He is caught and sentenced to hang but of course he escapes.

John Hurt, Pamela Franklin, Nigel Davenport and Robert Morley headed his cast and amongst the strong Irish contingent were Fidelma Murphy, Donal McCann, Mickser Reid, Eddie Byrne and Niall McGinnis.

The best aspect of the film was the photography of Ted Scaife, who captured magnificently the soft lights and dewy mountains of Co Wicklow. The craftsmen did a skilful job of transforming Glencree Reformatory into the period Scottish town of Stirling. The sets, costumes and locations were chosen with great care and were a joy to watch. The film turned out to be nothing more than a romp in

David Niven as Sir James Bond in John Huston's *Casino Royale*. The score for the movie was by Burt Bacharach and included the Oscar-nominated 'The Look of Love'. Huston and William Holden also feature in the above photo.

John Huston directing Pamela Franklin in *Sinful Davey*.

the Walt Disney tradition. One expected more from a Huston film but was redeemed by the energetic performance of John Hurt in the title role.

In 1967 during the course of filming, Huston took the opportunity of expressing his opinion on the need for an Irish film industry. He invited the then Taoiseach Jack Lynch and some of his ministers to the location where he expounded his views. He pointed out that the only reason this film was being made in Ireland was that he himself liked to work there and his associates humoured him. Huston suggested that a board should be set up to decide on a programme of six modest budget films.

The Government took up his suggestion and the Minister for Industry and Commerce set up a committee to examine the problems involved in the establishment of an Irish film industry. John Huston was elected chairman. Included on the committee were Patrick Carey, Dermot Doolin, Wilfred Eades, Lord Killanin and Louis Marcus. Within a year the body had produced a Report of the Film Industry Committee. They drew up recommendations on how an Irish film industry could be established and, more importantly, how it could function.

Some examples of film-making practices in other countries were listed:

The present artistic and commercial success of countries such as France, Poland and Czechoslovakia in low budget feature films stems directly from the short story films of these countries. Their technicians such as French cameraman, Raoul Couterd, the Polish director, Roman Polanski and the Czech director, Jan Nemac, all began as makers of short fiction films. As the skills and techniques required for this type of short film are similar to those required for features there is obviously no better training ground and no clearer indication as to the feature-making potential of the various sectors involved...

The Board should engage in the following activities:

(a) DISTRIBUTION AGREEMENTS to advise on or assist producers in the making of agreements for the marketing of films.

(b) CO-PRODUCTION AGREEMENTS to assist in negotiating arrangements between Irish film-makers and those of other countries with a view to the sharing of resources and facilities in specific ventures.

(c) TRAINING FACILITIES to provide the opportunity and financial assistance to writers, musicians, directors, artists, designers, craftsmen and technicians to be trained in film-making either at home or abroad.

(d) THE PROVISION OF OTHER FACILITIES NECESSARY FOR FILM PRODUCTION to provide to any producer contemplating the making of a film in Ireland advice on location, technicians, extras and any aspect of film-making in Ireland including finance.

(e) To make recommendations from time to time to the Government which it might consider necessary to advance the Irish film industry.

(f) NATIONAL FILM ARCHIVE to establish a national archive.

These were the main proposals that the Government and other interested bodies had to consider.

While the backroom boys sat down to discuss Huston's proposals the veteran director continued his output. In 1973 he found another opportunity to bring a big budget production, *The Mackintosh Man*, into Ireland. On this occasion a section of the storyline was set in Ireland along with Malta and England. Huston lined up an impressive cast headed by Paul Newman, James Mason, Dominique Sands, Harry Andrews and Ian Bannen. In one pub scene, set in Roundstone in Connemara, the cream of Irish character actors were present – Noel Purcell, Eddie Byrne, Joe Lynch, Joe Cahill and Donal McCann. The mandatory car chase also came in the Irish segment – across the bogs and along the rugged roads of Connemara, ending in a spectacular crash with a Mercedes hurtling over the Cliffs of Moher.

*The Mackintosh Man* was a complex spy thriller – Mackintosh of the title is a mystery man who hires Reardon (Newman) to stage a diamond robbery. Reardon is arrested and sentenced to twenty years imprisonment. Here, for the umpteenth time, Kilmainham Jail doubles as an English prison. Also in prison is a convicted Russian spy named Slade, played by Ian Bannen. For a large sum of money, both men are freed, and smuggled out of England to Ireland, where the plot becomes more intricate. Although not a Huston classic, the film did manage to keep the action and suspense well balanced.

# 13

# JOYCE AND THE CINEMA

The Irish writer, James Joyce had a keen interest in the progress of the cinema since its inception by the Lumière brothers in Paris in February 1896. The medium had a strong influence on his novel, *Ulysses*, and to an even greater degree on *Finnegans Wake*.

In 1909 Joyce was living in Trieste when his sister, Eva, a regular cinema-goer pointed out that it was unusual to find a city the size of Dublin without a cinema. Joyce saw this as both a challenge and an opportunity. Any mention of Dublin normally fired his imagination and he immediately set about planning a cinema for his native city. However, his intention was to make money rather than to bring a novel artistic experience to Dubliners.

Joyce convinced a number of businessmen in Trieste to finance the venture. He found no difficulty in acquiring suitable premises, the necessary licences, the staff and the films. The cinema, which he named the Volta, was situated at 45 Mary Street. The majority of films screened there were continental with Italian titles. The opening programme consisted of a number of one-reelers, *The First Paris Orphanage*, *La Pouponniere*, *Devilled Crab*, *The Bewitched Castle* and *Beatrice Cenci*.

The venture proved successful and people flocked to see each new film. Joyce enjoyed his role as a prosperous businessman and even planned to expand and open cinemas in Cork and Belfast. However, on his return to Trieste the business declined through mismanagement and had to be sold.

In 1930 Joyce was visited in his Paris flat by the renowned Russian director, Sergei Eisenstein, best known for his production, *Battleship Potemkin*. The latter believed that cinema, and cinema only, could combine and synchronise the senses of sight and sound, yet he was so taken with *Ulysses* that he declared Joyce had done for literature what he was attempting to do for cinema. The two men formed a common bond: both were aspiring to create new forms of expressing the inner processes of thought and emotion, and Joyce hoped that if anyone was to film his writings it would be Eisenstein. Joyce read passages of his work to the Russian and despite his growing blindness, expressed a desire to see *Battleship Potemkin*. In his film school in Moscow, Eisenstein used to set his pupils passages from *Ulysses* to be turned into film format.

Eisenstein did, in fact, endeavour to set up a film production of *Ulysses* but he did not succeed. He was only the first of many film-makers, including John Huston and Hollywood producer, Jerry Wald, who tried unsuccessfully to bring the complexities of the book to the screen. Wald in fact, bought the film rights and came to Dublin to scout for locations and a possible cast, but he was too preoccupied with his successful television series, *Peyton Place*, to proceed with the filming. 20th Century Fox, the company in which Wald was involved, were plagued by financial difficulties, not least from the mounting expenditure on *Cleopatra* and *Ulysses* had to be shelved. It is worth noting that such names as Rod Steiger and Marilyn Monroe were mentioned for the parts of Leopold and Molly Bloom.

The American director, Joseph Strick bought the film rights for $75,000 and planned to make the film as a trilogy: the first part, the day of Stephen and Bloom; the second, every word of Nighttown; and the third, every word of Molly. The bankers were not enthusiastic and forced him to turn it into one film. Most American and British producers turned him down before Walter Reade, who was associated with British Lion, decided to back him. Strick's next problem was discovering that the banks were insisting on Reade and himself putting up personal sureties of £50,000 as insurance against the film being turned down by the British censor. Determined to make the film, Strick raised some of the cash by directing a play, *Gallows Humour* by Jack Richardson, at the Olympia Theatre for the Dublin Theatre Festival and making a documentary on the British general election for the BBC.

Eventually after surmounting most of the problems, the film went into production on a budget of $450,000. Strick had a ground rule that there would be no new writing, no additions or corrections, and no play narrative. Every pound of expenditure had to be examined closely. On occasions they were fortunate, as when they procured a circus free of charge.

Strick directed it entirely on location in Dublin, in many of the places

James Joyce

Joseph Strick

Volta Cinema, Mary Street, Dublin.

depicted in Joyce's classic: the Irish House, Martello Tower, Sandymount Strand and Howth Head. He gathered a fine cast, albeit virtually unknown outside Ireland headed by Milo O'Shea as Bloom, Barbara Jefford as Molly, Maurice Roeves as Stephen Dedalus and T. P. McKenna as Buck Mulligan. In the supporting cast were Joe Lynch, Fionnula Flanagan, Martin Dempsey and Anna Manahan. None of the crew or actors was paid more than a £100 per week but everyone received a percentage of the profits.

Overall the film was a disappointment but Strick did manage to convey some interesting images. The main criticism was that the period was transferred from its original 1904 to the present day (1965). Strick was forced to agree but argued that he could not afford a period film. In technical terms some extremely old-fashioned techniques were employed and a number of performances were inadequate while other were exaggerated. Although the film was to establish Milo O'Shea as an international star, many interpreted his portrayal as nothing more than the antics of a dirty old man. Barbara Jefford beautifully delivered Molly's soliloquy in language hitherto unheard in cinemas in the British Isles.

Even before its release, *Ulysses* had a stormy passage. In Britain, Strick had many confrontations with the Board of Censors and its secretary John Trevelyan, both while scripting and on completion of filming. The censor demanded cuts amounting to two scenes and 400 words. The film was banned from some cinemas in Britain but it did enjoy a long run in the West End of London. In America it opened simultaneously, uncut, in 150 cinemas from coast to coast for a limited run of three days and was acclaimed by the public and critics alike. Back in Joyce's native Dublin, the film was banned and the Lord Mayor of Dublin, Seán Moore, wanted it known publicly who had financed the film.

Strick, by now obsessed with the works of Joyce, returned to Dublin to film *Portrait of the Artist as a Young Man* in 1975. This book chronicled the childhood memories and emerging manhood of Stephen Dedalus, Joyce's alter ego, and examined the struggle of the artist in the Dublin of the 1890s. The story follows Stephen Dedalus through many segments of his life – the famous Christmas dinner scene, life at Clongowes Wood College and later Belvedere and University College, Dublin. It also depicted his gradual disenchantment with religious and political life in Ireland.

Again Strick shot the film entirely on location in Dublin, this time in period costume and used an almost entirely Irish cast headed by Bosco Hogan in the title role. Supporting him were T. P. McKenna, Maureen Potter and Rosaleen Linehan, the latter two playing very much out of character. Sir John Gielgud made an impressive cameo as the preacher who delivers the hell-fire sermon. The production, less complex than *Ulysses*, captured more successfully the essential elements of the book and its characters and lent itself more satisfactorily to treatment on film. *Portrait* fared better with the censor and was released in Ireland.

Strick's ultimate goal was to film all of Joyce's major works. Joyce himself during his lifetime cherished the thought that if by some act of fate the city of Dublin was destroyed that it could be rebuilt simply by reference to his books. Many buildings, filmed by Strick for Ulysses, have since then been demolished and this film may well serve as a pictorial record of the places so beloved of the writer.

In 1964 Mary Ellen Bute skilfully brought Joyce's *Finnegans Wake* to the screen in a black and white adaptation of the Mary Manning play on which it was based. It took seven years to raise the modest budget of £85,000 and the final segment from a subvention from the University of Minnesota in the United States. The film was shot in a small New York studio and on location in Dublin. Bute, in consideration of the non-Joycean student, included subtitles – a most unusual practice for an English-speaking film shown to an English-speaking audience. The cast of twenty-three Irish and Irish-Americans included Martin J. Kelly as Finnegan, Jane Reilly, Peter Heskell, Page Johnson, John V. Kelleher and Ray Flanagan. Before filming commenced, many of the cast had just finished a run of Brendan Behan's *The Hostage* on Broadway.

In 1987 John Huston was to film his last project, a screen adaptation of James Joyce's short story 'The Dead' from his collection, *Dubliners*. Since the 1940s Huston had been unsuccessful in his bid to bring Joyce's *Ulysses* to the screen but this production was to be a family affair for the Hustons, with his Oscar-winning daughter, Anjelica, playing the female lead in a screenplay by his son Tony. The original plan was to shoot the film in Ireland but John Huston was too ill to travel and interiors were filmed in America, directed by Huston from his wheelchair. Huston was deeply disappointed that he could not travel to Dublin, but a second unit under Séamus Byrne shot link-up scenes in Dublin at Number 15, Usher's Island, which featured in the actual story and at Glendalough.

Set in Dublin in a January night in 1904 the film takes place at the home of spinsters Kate and Julia Morkan during their post-holidays party. The party scene is full of choreographed movement of chat and laughter. The most powerful scene is the final one between Gretta and Gabriel Conroy as she reveals the strong memories of her long dead love.

Anjelica Huston apart, the cast consisted entirely of Irish players headed by

Donal McCann, Dan O'Herlihy, Donal Donnelly, Helena Carroll, Rachel Dowling, Catherine Delaney and tenor Frank Patterson. The film received two Academy Award nominations, for Best Adapted Screenplay and Best Costume Design. *The Dead* proved to be a beautiful, mature film and a worthy tribute to conclude the distinguished career of John Huston.

In 2002 the young Irish director, Seán Walsh brought a long-term project on James Joyce to fruition. Since 1993 Walsh had been dogged in his determination to direct a new version of *Ulysses*. Finally the low budget film, *Bloom*, was shot on location in Dublin with Stephen Rea and Angeline Ball playing the Blooms.

# 14

# ON LOCATION

Producer Harry Alan Towers bought the film rights to Sax Rohmer's novels on the exploits of the oriental menace, Fu Manchu. He announced that he would produce five films on the infamous character, with Christopher Lee, most noted for his portrayals in Hammer Films, cast in the title role. The first Fu Manchu book was written in 1911 by Rohmer, pseudo name for Fleet Street journalist, Arthur Sarsfield Ward. Between 1915-35, four feature films were produced with Warner Oland and Boris Karloff playing the 'plotter-of-evil'. In the first of the new productions, *Face of Fu Manchu* (1964), Tsai Chin played his daughter, Howard Marion Crawford was the British Home Office pathologist and Nigel Green was Fu's stalwart adversary, Nayland Smith.

'A most unconventional film-maker' was how producer Towers had been described. In a two-year period he made twelve films on location in such varied places as South West Africa, Mozambique, Marrakesh, Beirut, England and Ireland. Most of his films had been made as co-productions with German companies and featured a mixture of German, English and American actors.

He chose Ireland to film *Face of Fu Manchu* although the plot was set in China and rural England. The deserted Kenure House in Rush, Co Dublin was the main location. Other scenes were shot in Skerries, Dublin docks and Kilmainham Jail. There was an excellent sense of atmosphere which period cars, horse-drawn carts and cobbled streets helped to create. Under Don Sharp's direction the film became a fast-moving thriller.

Immediately on its completion, Towers commenced production on another film in Ireland with relatively no advance publicity. It was based on an Agatha

Christie thriller, *Ten Little Niggers*, discreetly retitled *Ten Little Indians*. This book had been filmed some years previously with Barry Fitzgerald and called *And Then There Were None*, but this second outing lacked the suspense of the Rene Clair version. Towers assembled a top-line cast including Hugh O'Brian, Shirley Eaton, Stanley Holloway, Wilfred Hyde White, Fabian, Dennis Price and Leo Genn. George Pollock directed the entire film in Kenure House. Valuable props insured for £40,000, were shipped from England to add authenticity to the set. They included Edwardian ornaments, Tudor furniture, glittering suits of armour and valuable paintings.

The action takes place in a large house in the Austrian Alps, cut off by a raging blizzard. The only access is a cable railway that has been wrecked, severing all means of escape. Ten people are forced to take shelter in the eerie atmosphere of the mansion. One by one they are murdered, with everyone held under suspicion. Finally, there are only two people left and at that point the audience are given an intermission to puzzle it out for themselves.

Towers explained why he had been so keen to make a second film in Ireland: I'm so pleased with conditions in Ireland that I intend to make many more films here. We can film in the heart of Dublin and still not cause much disruption to traffic. This is utterly impossible in London where one has enormous problems working away from the studio. The only minor difficulty we have encountered here so far is that outdoor locations attract large crowds. At times this can become quite annoying. Film-making is still a novelty here and people travel miles to watch a film in production.

In 1965 John Ford returned to Ireland to direct a third project, *Young Cassidy*. John Whiting wrote the screenplay based on playwright, Sean O'Casey's autobiography, *Pictures in the Hallway*. It had long been an ambition of Ford's to direct a film on the life of the Dublin playwright. O'Casey's permission for this film had been given because he was friendly with the film's two producers – Robert Graff and Robert Emmett Ginna. Graff had previously directed a television film for NBC called *A Conversation with Sean O'Casey* and Ginna with Gjon Mili, had produced a feature for *Life* entitled *The World of Sean O'Casey*.

For the title role of the rebel playwright, several big names were considered, including Richard Harris and Peter O'Toole. Eventually Sean Connery was cast as the young O'Casey but before filming commenced Connery had received the role of James Bond in *Dr No*, which set him on the way to becoming an international star.

He was replaced by Australian actor, Rod Taylor and two actresses who were later to become international stars, were cast as the loves of his life, Julie Christie as the Dublin girl, Daisy Battles, and Maggie Smith as Nora, a bookshop assistant. Others in the distinguished cast included Flora Robson as his mother, Sian Philips as his sister, Sir Michael Redgrave as W. B. Yeats and Dame Edith Evans as Lady Gregory. Irish actors appearing were Philip O'Flynn, Jack McGowran, Pauline Delaney, Donal Donnelly, T. P. McKenna and Joe Lynch. Almost every actor and extra of Equity's books was on the film's payroll.

Ford (who was paid $50,000) and the producers had a difference of opinion as to how the film should be approached. They felt that the Dublin of 1964 bore little resemblance to that of 1911, and wanted to work in a less developed town. Ford insisted that if they were to make the film in Ireland it must be Dublin. Ford got his way and the film was shot entirely on location in Dublin with two weeks interior work at MGM Elstree Studio.

The story begins in Dublin in 1911 where Johnny Cassidy, a working class lad, works as a navvy. He writes and distributes propaganda sheets, and during a riot between strikers and police he rescues young Daisy Battles. When the Easter Rising of 1916 erupts, Johnny is a member of the Irish Citizen Army and escapes capture. The joy when a publisher accepts his first book is short-lived as his mother dies soon afterwards. Later he falls in love with Nora but she recognises the rebel and dreamer in him. Although the Abbey Theatre rejects his first play, he perseveres and eventually they stage *The Shadow of a Gunman*. It is a moderate success and Lady Gregory and W. B. Yeats befriend Cassidy. His next play, *The Plough and the Stars*, causes a riot in the theatre. Following a row with his friend Mick he leaves Nora and goes to England.

Ford preferred to shoot in sequence and began filming in mid July 1964 at the King's Inns on Henrietta Street. During the course of shooting several accidents befell the unit. Blow number one was when Rod Taylor and several other actors were thrown heavily from a sidecar and could resume work only after medical attention. The next mishap occurred when Julie Christie was rushed to hospital to undergo an emergency operation for acute appendicitis. She returned to the set following a few days convalescence. The greatest misfortune, however, came after thirteen working days when John Ford fell seriously ill with viral pneumonia. His doctor advised him to retire from the film and he was flown back to Los Angeles for hospital treatment. He lost 38 pounds during his illness.

Production came to a standstill for some days while a substitute was sought. Jack Cardiff flew to Dublin to replace him. Cardiff made an even greater effort to capture the atmosphere and flavour of Dublin and its characters. He had tried for many years to secure support for a film on the most celebrated of all literary

Hugh O'Brian and Shirley Eaton in *Ten Little Indians*.

Rod Taylor and Julie Christie in a scene from *Young Cassidy*.

A dramatic scene from 1967's *Rocket to the Moon*, directed by Don Sharp.

records of Dublin life, *Ulysses*. Having failed to obtain the necessary financing for the latter, he was determined to put Dublin on film with *Young Cassidy*. He succeeded remarkably well, although the film did tend to be marred by its episodic nature.

The next film to go into production in Ireland saw the return of Desmond Davis and Woodfall Productions to make *I Was Happy Here*. It had a great deal in common with his previous Irish venture, *Girl with Green Eyes*. Both had Irish settings with young Irish girls as the central characters and both were adaptations from the works of Irish novelist, Edna O'Brien. His new production was based on her short story, 'Passage of Love' and starred Sarah Miles, Cyril Cusack, Sean Caffrey and Julian Glover. The Irish scenes were shot in the environs of the attractive Co Clare town of Lahinch. The film, produced by Ray Millichop and photography by Manny Wynn, was the first to be financed under the new National Film Finance Corporation and the Rank financing scheme for independent producers.

The heroine (Miles) comes from her Irish village to a London bedsit and marries a Wimbledon doctor (Glover) who seeks to mould her to his upper middle-class ways. Fleeing from a marital quarrel, she returns to her village and the fisherman she once loved (Caffrey). There she realises that she fits neither world and must painfully work out her own salvation. The theme reflected the social change occurring in the conservative society of the times.

The love scenes on Ireland's Atlantic coastline in mid-winter were powerfully evocative. Photography and editing were a delight for the student of cinema: tracking shots into tracking shots, jump-cuts that far from simply jumping had a clear editorial continuity – a seagull's provocative cry that jumps to a shot of brakes screeching in a loud street – and a virtuoso 6 x 360 degree hand-held shot of Sarah Miles cycling around a London courtyard. If her playing occasionally hovered between winning innocence and King's Road frivolity, the deepening of her character gradually impressed. Both the male characters were seen through the girl's eyes and accordingly were less rounded, though the character of the spoiled doctor was established with deft, strong strokes. Cyril Cusack was the quiet, sensitive, cagey Irish publican whose presence dominated all his scenes and were to win him international fame.

In 1966 Harry Alan Towers returned to Ireland to shoot his next film, *Rocket to the Moon*. Dave Freeman wrote the screenplay, inspired by the writings of Jules Verne. Don Sharp was again assigned to direct the $3 million comedy featuring some of the most talented international stars. From America came Burl Ives and Troy Donohoe, from Germany came Gert Frobe, from Israel Daliah Lavi and from Britain Terry Thomas, Lionel Jeffries, Dennis Price and Jimmy Clitheroe. The cameras began to roll in Kenure House, Tower's improvised film studio. Later, the unit moved into a variety of picturesque and historic locations, including Dublin Castle, the Botanic Gardens, Avoca, Brittas Bay, Powerscourt and the Curragh. At least eighty per cent of the film was shot outdoors. Once more it proved that Irish locations could substitute for countries as diverse as Germany, England and France.

The story was an amusing piece of Victorian science fiction about the launching in 1875 of a moon-bound spaceship. A strange assortment of characters was involved. Leading the adventure was Phineas T. Barnum (Ives), assisted by Tom Thumb (Clitheroe), a French balloonist, some rival inventors, a dim-witted lord, Queen Victoria and a few delectable girls. It was, in fact, a pedestrian production with more that its fair share of tedious segments. The starry cast literally tripped over each other as they made their entrances and exits. Many talented actors were wasted.

It was inevitable that a film would be made about the Great Train Robbery of 1963 and three years later, Stanley Baker starred in, and produced, *Robbery*, based on the event. His co-stars were Joanna Pettit and James Booth. Although the film outlined in great detail the planning and execution of the raid on the London night mail-train, it also examined carefully the personal lives of the gang, thus distracting from the central theme. A German film on the same subject was far more successful. Most of the Baker film was shot in England but the prison sequences, involving a daring jailbreak, were filmed at Kilmainham and Arbour Hill jails. The film will be best remembered not so much for its robberies – there were two, a £75,000 jewel heist to finance the big job – as for its exciting car chase at the beginning, a forerunner to director Peter Yates' high powered car chase in *Bullitt*.

The next offering from Ardmore was an action adventure, *The Viking Queen*, in colour and wide-screen, starring Don Murray, back in Bray in a greatly diminished part, with new discovery Carita, his co-star. Others in the cast included Donald Houston, Andrew Keir, Niall McGinnis and Adrienne Corri. The film was produced by John Temple-Smith and directed by Don Chaffey, an Ardmore regular. Exteriors were shot in a variety of locations in the Wicklow Mountains with vast crowds of extras. A large contingent of the Irish army worked in the big-scale action scenes in Powerscourt. *The Viking Queen* is the story of a Boadicea-like queen of ancient Britain (Carita), who is forced to take arms against the Roman occupation forces commanded by the man she loves (Murray).

The successful team of producer Harry Alan Towers, director Don Sharp and stars Christopher Lee, Tsai Chin and Douglas Wilner returned to make another Sax Rohmer yarn, *The Vengeance of Fu Manchu*. They did a short stint at Ardmore and the remainder around the quays and Dublin's back streets. Sharp was notable in that he attempted, whenever possible, to introduce new faces in his Fu Manchu films, including many Irish actors:

> I think that goes back to my days as an actor of being given opportunities by people and also when I was directing in the theatre working with completely new people. I find it very exciting. I don't think you can mix too many new people in the film and you can't always give a person new to film techniques a prominent role. You can have somebody with all the natural characteristics in himself that the character requires but because of the lack of film technique he may not be able to bring these characteristics out as clearly as you would wish.

# 15

# THE LION IN WINTER TO O'TOOLE

While the background boys sat down to discuss Huston's proposals, Ardmore was kept busy. When it was decided to bring James Goldman's excellent Broadway play, *The Lion in Winter*, to the screen, one man was an obvious choice for the role of Henry II: Peter O'Toole. For O'Toole, who had already excelled in *Becket* opposite Richard Burton, it was his first film, not alone in Ardmore but in Ireland and it was at his suggestion that the film moved to the Bray studio. The interiors were filmed on elaborate sets on the stage at Ardmore and location work was undertaken in France and Wales.

The producer Martin Poll and director Anthony Harvey signed up a top cast including Katherine Hepburn as Eleanor of Aquitaine, Jane Morrow, Anthony Hopkins, John Castle and Timothy Dalton. John Barry composed the musical score. The film takes a look at the politics of the Middle Ages and examines the ruthless power play among England's royal family – and their three sons – in choosing a successor to the crown.

It is set at Christmas 1183 when the all-powerful Henry, summons his politically ambitious family to a reunion. They include his wife, whom he has kept in a remote castle and his three sons – all coveting his kingdom. Over the course of the film the members of the tempestuous family squabble and jockey for position.

The luminous Rosemary Harris had dominated the Broadway stage hit of the play. In the screen version Hepburn is stunning as the scheming and shrewd Eleanor and deservedly won her third Oscar.

Hepburn was popular with the locals in Bray as she cycled around the town and swam daily in the wintry sea. O'Toole spent much of his free time in the Harbour Bar, where the proprietor was appropriately named – O'Toole. During the course of this production the company employed a system agreeable to late risers – they did not commence work each day until 10 a.m.

The film proved a worldwide box-office success and was nominated for seven Oscars winning three, Hepburn as Best Actress, James Goldman for Best Adapted Screenplay and John Barry for Best Original Score.

One of the *Casino Royale* directors, Joseph McGrath, came to Dublin to film a segment of *30 is a Dangerous Age, Cynthia* in 1967. Heading his cast was Dudley Moore, Suzy Kendall, Patricia Routledge and Eddie Foy Jr. The film concerned the efforts of a piano player (Moore) to attain success and marriage by his thirtieth birthday – in six weeks' time. Moore, one of England's most versatile comedians, gave this uneven production moments of inspired lunacy with his virtuoso musical parodies. In the course of the film Moore comes to Ireland to research his subject. He could be seen walking through many picturesque locations in Dublin, running around the gasometer and doing weird things on Sandymount Strand. There is a disappointing OTT cameo featuring Mícheál Mac Liammóir telling a story as he lies in a four-poster bed in a Martello tower.

The streets and buildings of Kilkenny so closely resembled eighteenth-century London that it was chosen as the location for *Lock Up Your Daughters*. The castle, narrow streets and laneways ideally suited the period setting. The film was a rehash of the stage play, *Rape upon Rape*, by Henry Fielding that became a stage musical and finally the basis for a screenplay by Keith Waterstone and Willis Hall. The film has a confused plot about lusty sailors whose amorous pursuits entangled them with Lord Foppington and Sir Tunbelly and his daughter, Hoyden.

Some difficulty arose when the film-makers were unable to persuade local girls to play buxom wenches in low-cut gowns and they had to bring young women in from England. One of the highlights of the film was a custard-pie throwing battle. The film directed by Peter Coe attracted an all-star cast including Christopher Plummer, Susannah York, Ian Bannen, Tom Bell, Glynis Johns and Roy Kinnear.

Counties Clare and Galway saw a considerable amount of filming during the summer of 1968. One film was a £500,000 Walt Disney production, *Guns in the Heather*, a quintessential Disney yarn about two boys, one American, one Irish, who become involved in mystery and intrigue, directed by Robert Butler. American, Kurt Russell, and Bray boy, Patrick Dawson, play the boys. Peter Vaughan, Alfred Burke and Godfrey Quigley play the crooks. The script did not call for any of the actors to overtax themselves but it was enjoyable escapist entertainment.

Filming simultaneously in Galway, on a bigger budget and longer schedule was MGM's *Alfred the Great*. This was an epic tale of the bloody battles between the Vikings and settled Saxons, and studied the character of the king who tried to impose order not only on his country but also on himself. British actor, David Hemmings played King Alfred and was supported by Michael York, Prunella Ransome and Colin Blakely. Clive Donner, whose past work included *Nothing but the Best* directed what was his first outdoor epic. The area around Loughrea represented Alfred's Wessex and where a village was built. Replicas of Viking ships sailed up the River Shannon. Hundreds of local men and students were hired for the summer months and were required to grow beards and their hair long. Under stunt men they practised hand to hand combat. The producers built their own studio close to the area in which they were filming. They were too far from Ardmore, and, moreover, Irish weather conditions being so unreliable, it was sensible to have a base nearby where they could construct sets and store equipment.

Also shooting that summer was *The Prince and the Pauper* produced by Professional Films of New York. Director Elliott Geisinger and producer Ronnie Saland brought a cast of unknowns to an old farm in Navan that was the main location for this Mark Twain story. The film was aimed at a young audience and was released nationwide in the United States.

In 1967 Ardmore Studios changed hands and was bought by an English company, New Brighton Enterprises. An Englishman, Lee Davis, became the new studio chief. He was the nearest thing to a Hollywood mogul that the studio had ever experienced and he seemed to aspire to the mantle of Louis B. Mayer. Davis went to America to sell the studio's services and brought back some big contracts, including *Darling Lili* and *The Violent Enemy*. To the flamboyant Davis, money appeared to be no object and he had his office panelled in expensive wood, with concealed lighting, sumptuous seating and a huge desk. He drove a Jaguar with a crest on the door, the letters A.S. for Ardmore Studios and L.D. for his own initials.

*Darling Lili* brought to Dublin the combined talents of Julie Andrews and Rock Hudson under the direction of Blake Edwards, who had made the Pink Panther films. It was a return to Ireland for Hudson who had made *Captain Lightfoot* here, some fourteen years previously. Jeremy Kemp, Lance Percival and Michael Witney co-starred, with Doreen Keogh, the only featured Irish artiste. This was a big budget, glossy comedy in which Julie Andrews played a seductive

Katherine Hepburn and Anthony Hopkins in *The Lion in Winter*.

David Hemmings in the title role of *Alfred the Great*.

Rock Hudson and Julie Andrews in the Blake Edwards-directed *Darling Lili*.

singer who was also a Mata Hari-like German spy and moved in glittering social circles during World War I.

The opening sequence was shot in Dublin's Gaiety Theatre, transformed into a music hall. The audience of socialites, with a sprinkling of khaki-clad soldiers on leave from Mons and Cambrai, are enjoying themselves at a concert given by Julie when suddenly air-raid sirens sound and the audience jump to their feet. She immediately bursts into morale-boosting songs of the period such as 'It's a Long Way to Tipperary' and 'Roll out the Barrel' and the entire audience, forgetting the danger, join in the singing.

Other Irish locations include Heuston Station, Powerscourt, Carton House and Trinity College. The many flying sequences were filmed near Weston Airport where the producers were able to utilise the planes and pilots from *The Blue Max*. The latter film had served as a dummy run and many of the aerial problems had been resolved.

The film proved a commercial failure at the box-office as musicals were then out of vogue.

For the film *Where's Jack?* director James Clavell set about transforming the old Glencree Reformatory once again from the remains of Huston's Scottish city into a slice of Hogarth's London. The film tells the tale of Jack Sheppard, a locksmith's apprentice in eighteenth-century London, whose only crime is that of poverty. He meets with Jonathan Wild, a notorious and unscrupulous thieftaker (bounty hunter). Wild, however, tricks Jack into crime. Eventually he breaks free of Wild and, spurred on by his love for Edgeworth Bess, he rampages through London, looting. His fame reaches the royal court and the king himself. He becomes the darling of society and soon it is fashionable to be robbed by him.

The film had a good deal in common with *Sinful Davey* but was a far superior production. Clavell's direction was crisp, full of action and colour, and he sought to pack every frame with details from Hogarth's paintings. The inn scenes, in particular, were alive with movement and atmosphere. Singing star, Tommy Steele was suitably heroic as the hero, Stanley Baker (who also produced) was treacherously villainous as Wild and Fiona Lewis was decorative as the buxom wench. Noel Purcell, minus his beard, plays a mute.

The *Italian Job* film unit came to Dublin for location work at Kilmainham Jail and Arbour Hill. Kilmainham was receiving so many visits from film-makers that it could have doubled as a film studio. Both jails figured prominently in the film, as Sir Noel Coward, who was incarcerated within, was mastermind of a number of highly successful robberies. Michael Caine plays the leading crook on the outside. It was an amusing, exciting film with most of the acting honours going to Coward but even his performance was overshadowed by the stunt drivers who did some spectacular driving in the Italian locations. The film brought back to Ireland Peter Collinson who had worked in RTÉ in the early days and had now carved out quite a lucrative career for himself as an international director.

In the same year, 1968, the studio manager at Ardmore, Wilfred Eades, produced a taut thriller, *The Violent Enemy*, at the studio with exteriors around Dublin. A regular visitor to Ireland, Don Sharp, again directed. English actor, Tom Bell, whose acting ability was often underestimated, played the main role of an IRA man who breaks jail, as his expertise in explosives is needed in Ireland. Veteran American actor, Ed Begley co-starred, and Susan Hampshire, from the television series, *The Forsythe Saga*, switched to modern dress to supply the love interest. Noel Purcell and Philip O'Flynn were well placed in supporting roles.

Around this period several works of Dublin best-selling author, Lee Dunne, were filmed in Ireland. First came a screenplay in which he was co-author called *I Can't, I Can't*, during production but released as *Wedding Night*. The film was directed by Piers Haggard and starring Dennis Waterman and Tessa Wyatt with Eddie Byrne and Marie O'Donnell in support. The low-budget drama revolved around the difficulties of a young married couple and recouped its production costs in America alone.

Next followed a short film, *The Girl with the Pale Face*, in which Dunne was closely involved – he wrote much of the screenplay and also played a cameo role as a bus conductor. It concerns a young man who meets a girl at a dance and takes her off to a lonely beach, hoping to have his way with her. It starred Fidelma Murphy and Kevin McHugh and was directed by Paul Gallico Jr.

Dunne's third film, *Paddy*, was the most ambitious of all his projects. It was the screen adaptation of his best selling novel *Goodbye to the Hill*. The story follows the trials and tribulations of young Paddy Maguire from a Dublin slum, and his sexual pursuit of various females. The film gave young Abbey actor, Des Cave, his first screen role as the active youth. Maureen Toal and Dearbhla Molloy played two of the females in his life. The film under director Daniel Haller was shot entirely on location in and around Dublin with a small crew and on a budget of $100,000. Hallier had intended to make an Irish version of the classic French film, *A Man and a Woman*. To achieve this end the same French camera crew worked on this film, but they fell short of their goal. Like Dunne's book the film was banned in Ireland.

*Underground* was the first of two World War II films to be shot at Ardmore, with exteriors in the surrounding counties, by producers Jules Levy and Arthur

Gardner. The film tells of a group of French Resistance fighters and the guerrilla warfare they wage against the Germans. Enniscorthy, Co Wexford, with a little camouflaging, served quite well as a French town of the period. The film was directed by Arthur Nadel and starred American singing star Robert Goulet, Daniele Gaubert and Joachim Hansen. It maintained a fast rate of action and was average for this genre.

The second Levy-Gardner production, *The McKenzie Break*, gave a new twist to the prisoner of war theme, with German prisoners in a British camp in Scotland the ones seeking to escape. The film-makers built a complete prison camp, consisting of huts, guard towers and barbed wire at Ballymoney, Co Wicklow. Members of the Irish army, by now experts at the business, acted as both British and German troops. The film will be remembered for the rugged performance by the American actor, Brian Keith as one of the camp's officers. He was well supported by Ian Hendry as the camp commander and the leading German actors, Helmut Griem and Horst Janson, who gave first class performances.

In 1969, Peter O'Toole took a break from epics to bring another film, *Country Dance*, also known as *Brotherly Love*, into Ardmore. This MGM production was produced by Robert Emmet Gina and directed by J. Lee Thompson from a screenplay by James Kennaway. In the unusual love story set in Scotland, Susannah York plays O'Toole's sister and Michael Craig her husband in a three cornered relationship with O'Toole having more than brotherly feelings towards his sister. He plays the part of an eccentric landowner of a stately mansion in the Highlands quite sensitively. Cyril Cusack and Harry Andrews play other important roles. Much of the filming was done around the environs of Enniskerry, with interiors in Ardmore.

# 16

# FILMING RYAN'S DAUGHTER

One of the biggest films to be shot in Ireland, on a par with John Ford's *The Quiet Man*, was *Ryan's Daughter*. The veteran director, David Lean conducted an extensive search throughout Ireland for the ideal location for his epic love story. He discovered that location in the Dunquin area of the Dingle Peninsula in Co Kerry, where he shot the entire film except for a short sequence in South Africa. Lean undertook this project in the same meticulous style that had made his previous films such as *Dr Zhivago*, *Bridge on the River Kwai* and *Lawrence of Arabia* so memorable.

For *Ryan's Daughter*, which took an entire year (1969) to complete, Lean again teamed up with Robert Bolt, who had scripted his two previous films. On this occasion Bolt wrote an original screenplay set in a remote coastal village on the west coast of Ireland shortly after the 1916 rising. It centres on a local girl, married to the village teacher who has an affair with a British officer, and the local reaction that arises from her action.

As in all Lean's films, a top-line cast was assembled, headed by Robert Mitchum, Sarah Miles, John Mills, Trevor Howard, Leo McKern and Christopher Jones. Mitchum took some persuading before accepting the role of the gentle teacher who marries a former student. The gamble of the tough guy playing against type paid off. The role of the unfaithful wife was specially written by Bolt for his wife, Sarah Miles, who had played her screen debut in *Term of Trial* at Ardmore seven years before. Alec Guinness was offered the role of the priest but turned it down because he felt it was not significant enough.

The West Kerry region, particularly around Dingle, reaped the benefits from the protracted visit of the film-makers. Every available room in hotels, guest houses and farm houses was completely booked out for the duration of filming. All aspects of local trade and industry felt the generosity of the big spenders from Hollywood. Locals were employed as extras and in many other capacities. Tradesmen were engaged in set building which included the erection of an entire village complete with church, pub, shops and houses.

Lean chose his other locations wisely and featured most of the finest beaches on the peninsula including Inch, Barrow, Castlegregory and Coumenole at Slea Head. On many occasions he patiently waited for hours for the exact shadow or cloud effect for a particular scene. In one ten-day period only one minute of screen time was shot due to the inclement weather.

Many Irish Equity members were employed as 'special extras' earning £50 a week in what amounted to non-stop employment. Leading performers for the Dublin Theatre Festival that year were scarce as players such as Marie Kean, Des Keogh, Arthur O'Sullivan, Niall Toibin and Emmet Bergin were contracted on the film. Author Bryan McMahon was assigned as technical advisor for the school sequences but unfortunately broke his leg the night before filming commenced and had to withdraw.

Robert Mitchum relished the fact of taking over the Milltown House Hotel. He answered the phone to unsuspecting callers and attempted to book guests in. There have been endless reports of his parties and antics during his stay there. It is reputed that the first pub grub ever served occurred in Dingle during the making of *Ryan's Daughter*. Some of the crew were taking a break in Nora Ashe's pub when the aroma of an Irish stew cooking in the kitchen reached their nostrils. They asked the proprietor if they could have some and she served the first pub grub in Kerry.

During filming an accident occurred in which Trevor Howard and John Mills almost lost their lives. The two actors were manning a currach when it overturned in the rough sea and they were flung into the water. Only for the quick action of a rescue team there could have been a serious or fatal accident.

One of the biggest delays David Lean encountered was waiting for a storm for the film's dramatic climax. The west coast, particularly the Dingle Peninsula, is noted for having more than its fair share of atrocious weather throughout the winter months, but when a storm was required it did not materialise. Lean had to wait months until he got conditions ferocious enough for his liking and then it was in Kilkee, Co Clare. The actors and extras that participated in this scene worked under perilous conditions to gain the dramatic effect.

*Ryan's Daughter* can best be summed up in the words of Robert Mitchum:

Robert Mitchum and Sarah Miles in *Ryan's Daughter*.

A magnificent beach shot from *Ryan's Daughter*.

I loved every minute of it. Robert Bolt had written an excellent, literate script. The film emerged as David Lean's love affair with Ireland. A costly love affair it might be added – fourteen million bucks worth. I felt for him at times. The trouble with David is that he shoots four versions of a film and then chooses the best.

The completed film which ran to 3 hours 26 minutes won two Academy awards, although nominated for four – one for Freddie Young for his magnificent photography and the other to John Mills for his faultless performance as the village fool. Only a few seconds of cloud effect behind the credits was all that remained of the effort of Irish director, Patrick Carey, who spent months shooting thousands of feet of second unit footage.

The music of Maurice Jarre, whose association with the Lean films, *Lawrence of Arabia* and *Dr Zhivago*, had earned him Academy Awards, was most effective, particularly 'Rosy's Theme' where the haunting score seemed to glide over the windswept beaches.

On completion of the film the producers presented the village to the locals. There was a dispute of what should become of the site and it was decided to demolish the buildings. All that remains of the set of *Ryan's Daughter* is the schoolhouse, which is in a bad state of repair.

A film with the strange title *Quackser Fortune has a Cousin in the Bronx* was filmed in a six-week shoot in Dublin in the late 1960s. The shoestring budget production starred two then unknowns, Gene Wilder and Margot Kidder. The Irish supporting cast headed by May Ollis, Seamus Forde, David Kelly and Martin Crosby were over-shadowed by Wilder's likeable personality. His Dublin accent was surprisingly authentic and far more true to life than attempts by other bigger stars. He was ably supported by Kidder who played an American student at Trinity College. Hardly a street or landmark in the city was omitted from Quackser's wanderings. Next to *Young Cassidy* this film best captured the flavour and character of Dublin. Director Warris Hussein managed his players to the best advantage.

*Quackser* tells the tale of a Dublin man from a working class background and his fight against the establishment. Instead of taking a conventional job in the foundry he tours the city with his barrow, collecting horse manure and selling it to women for their gardens and window boxes. He meets an American girl who introduces him to a whole new middle class world where he feels out of place and returns to his roots. Although a simple idea, it was a humorous film with sharp moral overtones. The film was well received, particularly in America, where it developed a cult following. It told a wholly Irish tale with a simple story line.

*Sitting Target*, the next production shot in Ireland, was a fast-moving thriller about a convict who breaks jail in order to kill his wife for her infidelity. Oliver Reed plays the vengeful husband with his usual brooding expression and Jill St John looked decorative as his wife. They were supported by Ian McShane and Edward Woodward under Douglas Hickox's direction. Once again Kilmainham Jail and Arbour Hill were the locations for the prison scenes.

American actor, Cliff Robertson, who had won an Oscar for his performance in *Charley*, spent two weeks at Weston Airport using their World War I fighter planes for a spoof film he was attempting to get off the ground, entitled *Where Were You the Night the Baron Was Shot Down?* Robertson was both star and director of this comedy. When the Irish sequence was completed Robertson put the film into cold storage, as he sought backing to complete the project which emerged some years later as *Ace Eli and Rodgers of the Skies*.

The play, *Philadelphia, Here I Come* by Brian Friel was staged on Broadway and won worldwide acclaim. The stars of the stage production, Donal Donnelly and Patrick Bedford were replaced in the film version by Donal McCann and Des Cave, both members of the Abbey Theatre. Others in the cast included Siobhan McKenna, David Kelly and Eamonn Morrissey. True to the stage play the script was wise, witty and full of compassion.

The story of *Philadelphia* concerns the last night at home of a young man about to emigrate to America from a small town in Donegal. It was a difficult play to transfer to the screen as the bulk of the action takes place in one setting. Englishman, John Quested, who had served as assistant director on several previous films made his directorial debut. He managed to be flexible with the camera and opened out the story from its claustrophobic setting. Baltinglass, Co Wicklow stood in for the Donegal setting. Friel had employed the theatrical device of an inner and outer self, which Quested used to good effect. McCann and Cave gave brilliant performances as the two sides of the central character.

With the exception of the director and cinematographer the film was made entirely by an Irish cast and crew. Following its completion it encountered distribution difficulties and it was not until 1974 at the Cork Film Festival that it was screened publicly.

Powerscourt and Ardmore saw several weeks' activity with yet another remake of Anna Sewell's classic tale, *Black Beauty*, from the screenplay by Wolf Mankowitz. Director James Hill, noted for his animal films, in particular *Born Free*, filmed this classic in Ireland and Spain. Some of the film's best moments were the photography of the second unit under Patrick Carey. The film starred

Jack Wild in a scene from
*Flight of the Doves.*

John Philip Law as *The Red Baron.*

Mark Lester, Walter Stezack, Patrick Mower and Ushi Glass.

Also shooting around this time was *The Sky is Blue* which was no more than a suitcase French production starring Alexander Stewart and French actor, Frederico Du Pasquale. It told of a bittersweet romance set in Ireland of a girl working in the American Embassy in Dublin who meets a French sports journalist covering the Ireland-French international rugby match. Scenes for the film were shot during an international match between the two countries.

Two films by top American directors were shot simultaneously in Ireland during the summer of 1970. The first, *Flight of the Doves*, under the control of producer/director Ralph Nelson was based on the book of the same name by Irish author, Walter Macken. It was the first film to be filmed in Ardmore that year following a decline after several bumper years. The film covered many counties from Dublin to Galway in the chase for two runaway children. It brought together such talented performers as Ron Moody and Jack Wild, (Fagin and the Artful Dodger respectively in the hit musical film, *Oliver*) the satirist, William Rushton, American actress Dorothy McGuire and the veteran of the English stage, Stanley Holloway. Noel Purcell, Tom Hickey, John Molloy, Brendan O'Reilly and Barry Keegan led the supporting cast of Irish players. Ireland's Eurovision Song Contest winner, Dana, made her screen debut as a tinker girl.

The second film was *The Red Baron* directed by the horror film director, Roger Corman. This was his most ambitious project to date and he painstakingly recreated the exploits and ultimate fiery death of Germany's fabled World War I flying ace, Baron Von Richthoften, known as The Red Baron. John Philip Law played the baron and Don Stroud the pilot in the British Air Force who shoots him down. Corin Redgrave, Tom Adams and David Weston played other important roles. In contrast to the Nelson film, few Irish actors were employed; among these were Des Nealon and Martin Dempsey.

The main shooting for the film, which was referred to as a mini *Blue Max* with a budget of one million dollars, took place at Weston aerodrome, which doubled for both the German and British airstrips. Some of Ireland's most scenic locations were secured for additional scenes with sections of Powerscourt House used as the German officers' club. Other locations included Leinster House, George's Hill, Baldonnel and the drawing rooms of Dublin Castle.

Only a matter of days before the completion of filming, a British stunt pilot was killed at Weston. Ten planes were engaged in the scene when one of them spun to the ground hitting a truck. The pilot, Christopher Boddington, had only arrived at the location the previous days to take part in the dogfight sequences. When another less serious accident occurred the next day involving Don Stroud,

Corman called off the rest of the aerial scenes.

Shortly afterwards another film with a World War I setting, *Zeppelin*, was also struck by tragedy as it was shooting dogfights off Wicklow Harbour between five bi-planes. The scene was being filmed from a helicopter and four dummy runs had already been completed to get the timing correct. The other four were chasing one plane, it swept below the helicopter and when it rose out of the dive it struck the helicopter at a thousand feet. Both craft fell into the sea and four men were killed. The bulk of *Zepplin* was filmed in England and only the aerial scenes were shot in Ireland.

The film was a variation of the war theme seen through German eyes with the introduction of the Zepplin – their new flying machine. The film was directed by Etienne Perier and starred Michael York, Elke Sommer, Anton Diffring and Andrew Keir.

# 17

## ALTMAN AND MORE RECEIVERS

The distinguished American director, Robert Altman, who made his reputation with such hit films as *M.A.S.H.* and *Brewster McCloud*, came to Ireland in 1971 to film *Images*. With the exception of a few days filming at an isolated house in Glencree and at Powerscourt, the film was confined to the stages of Ardmore. Susannah York, in one of the highlights of her screen career, played a woman gradually descending into madness. It was a film of shadows that trembled on the uncertain line between fact and fantasy. It worked as much through John William's remarkable musical score as it did through the fractured pictures Altman created.

The plot concerned Cathryn (York) and her husband Hugh, who divide their life between a luxurious city apartment and a house in the country. She confuses Hugh with a previous lover, Rene, now dead, and talks to him, mocks him and finally eliminates him from her memory. Her confusion is heightened when a friend of her husband's, Marcel, visits their country house with his daughter Susannah who bears a striking resemblance to Cathryn. She finds reality frightening, as characters become interchangeable and does not know whether she is speaking to her husband, her dead lover or the friend, her would-be lover.

A disturbing film, it hinged almost entirely on Susannah York's performance, which was first-rate. There were no Irish actors in the cast that comprised mainly of unknowns – Rene Auberjonis, Marcel Bozzuffi, Hugh Millias and Cathryn Harrison. An unusual aspect of the production was that the characters used their own Christian names for their screen roles. The film was entered as Ireland's first official entry at the Cannes Film Festival and won Susannah York the Best Actress Award. The cinematography of Vilmas Zsigmond was also highly praised.

Italian director, Sergio Leone, was the best non-American interpreter of westerns – having found a successful formula that produced such box-office hits as *A Fistful of Dollars*, *The Good, the Bad and the Ugly* and *Once Upon a Time in the West*. Leone, a beefy, bearded man with a strong aversion to violence – although violence figured prominently in his work – came to Ireland for a short spell of location work on his film, *Duck, you Sucker*, retitled *A Fistful of Dynamite*, with his crew and two stars, James Coburn and Rod Steiger. He chose Toners pub in Dublin and some rich pastures in Glendalough, Co Wicklow for his IRA flashback segment, which was effective in the finished film.

For *A Fistful of Dynamite*, the Italian director switched from a spaghetti western to a turn-of-the-century revolutionary story. Coburn plays an exiled IRA man whose knack with explosives almost wins the Mexican Revolution for Pancho Villa. Steiger is a Mexican bandit.

Leone said of his work:

Movie-making is my life, my hobby and my food. It never bores me. My fascination with physical violence and the philosophy behind it will always play an important part in my work. In this film the violence is not a personal one between individuals but rather between the individuals and the state.

A strange film called *Act Without Words*, assembled by producer Richard Denypont, brought Rod Steiger back to Dublin to star in what was to be a one-man feature based on a mime work by the Irish writer, Samuel Becket. Originally the film was to be shot entirely in the Eamonn Andrews Studio in Dublin under the direction of Tom Blevins but problems arose over insurance. The equipment was being flown in from Britain and the insurance company stipulated that it could be insured for £1,000 a week in Belfast but would cost £5,000 per day in Dublin. The reverse would have been easier to understand. Despite guarantees from Fred O'Donovan of the Eamonn Andrews Studio that the equipment would be under strict security at all times, the figure remained. The film then transferred to Ardmore but soon afterwards the production broke up – and the film was never completed. There was an unconfirmed report that a row had developed between Steiger and Denypont.

The tenure of the New Brighton Enterprise and Lee Davis, one of the most colourful characters to ever operate the studio, lasted until 1971 when another receiver, Alex Spain, was appointed. In July 1972 the studio was again put up for

Susannah York in a first-rate performance in Robert Altman's *Images*.

Rod Steiger as a Mexican bandit in *A Fistful of Dynamite*.

sale and there was keen interest shown in the property. A group headed by George O'Reilly, were the highest bidders at £265,000 and they became the new owners. O'Reilly became chairman and general manager. On the board of directors were such notables as John Huston, Bing Crosby, John E. Nolan and Thomas Farmer. O'Reilly went abroad to sell studio space at Ardmore and in the intervening weeks he lined up quite a number of films, but they were never to materialise. The new owners began to disagree over policy and several resigned from the board. Soon O'Reilly was left as the sole director. The group was in business only four months before another receiver, Thomas Kelly, was appointed.

It was a costly gamble for O'Reilly:

I lost my home and my money over Ardmore. I had a vision of the studio as a really top-class international centre to make films. But I did not get the time to realise my dreams. The trend was towards doing films on location in the streets of San Francisco or New York using the natural backdrop. This was bad for studios throughout the world. My plan was to make not only major films at Ardmore but to cash in on the rapidly growing television film market.

The formation of the Dublin Film Co-operative was the first really practical step taken to set up an entirely Irish-made film. The co-operative embraced many technicians who had gained experience at home and abroad. The members intended to work for a nominal wage and take a share of the profits when production costs had been recouped. Their first film, *The Hebrew Lesson*, ran for thirty minutes and was intended as a pilot for a series that they hoped to sell worldwide but the series never materialised.

Behind the camera it was literally a one-man project as it was written, produced and directed by the veteran film-maker, Wolf Mankowitz. He had settled in Cork and had taken a keen interest in trying to foster a film industry in the country. The film was shot in ten days on a small set at Ardmore. The story is set in Cork in 1921 and starred Milo O'Shea and Patrick Dawson. O'Shea plays an old Jew who shelters Dawson, an idealistic young IRA man on the run from the Black and Tans. The film relates the interplay between the two as they expound their philosophies of life. Playwright Alun Owen makes a fleeting appearance as a Black and Tan.

A new dimension in film-making that originated in the United States was the 'telemovie'. Films in this category fell somewhere between a television series and a full-length feature film whereby the end product could be screened on either medium. The first of these productions to be made in Ireland was *Alive,*

*Alive O* which later became *And No One Could Save Her* starring American actress, Lee Remick, and Milo O'Shea. Remick spends the duration of the film trying to trace her missing husband, played by Frank Grimes. O'Shea plays a stage-Irish solicitor and the supporting cast includes a host of Irish actors.

Director Kevin Billington who produced the film aimed at appealing to an Irish-American audiences appeared to do no more than position his actors before some famous Dublin landmarks and have them spout their lines. A cedar-wood bungalow built overlooking Brittas Bay was the setting for the American sequence of this below-standard thriller.

A film with the unusual title of *Mother Mafia's Loving Fold*, was one of a series of Italian films which chose, rather surprisingly, Dublin as their central location. Little was known about the Italian group except that they gave employment to a handful of Irish actors including Liam O'Callaghan and Arthur O'Sullivan. The crew appeared in a street with a minimum of equipment, usually two minibuses holding their entire stock, and set up their camera and small arc lamp. Following a quick rehearsal they shot the scene and quickly moved to the next location. *Mother Mafia's Loving Fold* was one of the low budget productions that hoped to cash in on the success of *The Godfather*. The producers believed that they could best reproduce this yarn of the Mafia in the New York of the 1920s in the dockside streets of Dublin. The production caused a furore when they attempted to import prop-guns. They engaged in much discussion with customs officials at Dublin Airport before the matter was resolved. Later there was some question of harassment as the company pulled out of Dublin with their film unfinished.

A telemovie produced in Ireland by Harlech Television entitled *Catholics* was based on the novel by Brian Moore. The setting is a remote island off the coast of Ireland where an order of monks defies the Vatican and retains the Tridentine Mass. The story tells how a young priest (Martin Sheen) is sent from Rome to rectify the matter. The strong cast is headed by Trevor Howard, giving one of his best performances, Cyril Cusack, Raf Vallone and a host of Irish character actors. Jack Gold directed at an even pace with a balance of humour and pathos.

Two films set against the Northern Troubles were shot secretly in Dublin, within months of each other. The two productions maintained a low profile during their spell in the capital and neither was prepared to issue press releases. In fact, neither revealed its true theme until much later.

The first, by an American company under the direction of George Schaffer, was *A War of Children*, with many Dublin streets standing in for areas of Belfast. The producers felt it would be too dangerous to shoot in the strife-torn Northern capital. The original report – that it was a story of the relationship of two children

– was far from the truth as it depicts a tale of bigotry and hatred between the two communities. Some locals did become suspicious when they observed a British Army Saracen and British Tommies running along Camden Street in the early hours of the morning, but the film-makers managed to get in and out without any interference. It was difficult for Dubliners to accept that such recognisable places as Westland Row and Blackrock College could be passed off as areas of Belfast, even CIÉ buses doubled as Ulsterbus vehicles. British actress, Jenny Agutter, and Vivien Merchant headed the cast and among the Irish names were Aideen O'Kelly and Patrick Dawson. Although the film caused raised eyebrows in Ireland when it was screened at the Cork Film Festival, it was a big success in America and won an Emmy Award.

The second company, from Canada, slipped into Dublin to film 'a television film'. Only on their return to Toronto did they announce that they had produced a feature film set against the Northern Troubles. Once again areas of Dublin, particularly around Smithfield, doubled for Belfast in *A Quiet Day in Belfast*, under Milad Basada's direction. The producers claimed it was non-political and non-partisan, a dubious claim since the hero is a British soldier killed in the street by an IRA sniper. The stars, Barry Foster and Margot Kidder, were no strangers to filming in Ireland – Foster now playing the British soldier had the contrasting role of the IRA leader in *Ryan's Daughter* and Kidder had fallen in love with Quackser Fortune.

The story line was kept so secret that even the twenty Irish actors employed on the production were unaware of its true purpose. During the filming of one scene, where Margot Kidder, tarred and feathered, is thrown from a moving car, local women came to her assistance with tea and blankets, unaware that it was a scene from a film.

*Steve McQueen … I am Not* also known as *Horowitz of Dublin Castle*, was a medium-budget thriller set in Dublin, directed by William Kronick. A press release referred to it as 'a cops and robbers drama with touches of humour'. The film starred American actor, Harvey Lembeck, whose main claim to fame was in the popular *Sergeant Bilko* television series. On this occasion he plays an American cop who comes to Ireland and becomes involved with crooks, finally solving the crime more by accident than design. His character had a strong resemblance to the later Colombo. He is ably supported by Cyril Cusack, his daughter Sinéad and Martin Dempsey. Writer, Michael Judge, gives an example of how unorthodox the production proved to be. He was placed in a hotel room and told to write a few pages of dialogue. At the end of each day the pages were taken away and he was given a handful of money.

18

# EXIT MR KUBRICK

Early in the summer of 1973 one of the greatest masters of the craft of film-making, Stanley Kubrick, arrived in Ireland to scout locations for his next film, *Barry Lyndon*. He chose Ireland because he feared interference from pressure groups in England following a UK High Court judge's opinion that his last film, the highly controversial *A Clockwork Orange*, had inspired two killings. He set up base in a Waterford hotel and inspected areas in Killarney, Cork and Waterford itself. Kubrick, a self-made genius, was reluctant to talk about his work to the press but gradually information about the film leaked out – the film was tentatively titled *The Luck of Barry Lyndon* and based on a novel by William Makepeace Thackeray.

If Kubrick remained true to form, this was expected to be one of the most significant films ever made in Ireland. Besides *A Clockwork Orange*, he had an impressive list of films to his credit, including *Lolita*, *Spartacus*, *Dr Strangelove*, *Paths of Glory* and *2001: A Space Odyssey*. Each film differed completely in content but possessed the Kubrick stamp of originality.

For *Barry Lyndon*, which he was making for Warner Brothers, he cast Ryan O'Neal as the Irish rogue, gambler and womaniser and Marisa Berenson as the leading lady. Hardy Kruger headed the supporting cast that included Steven Berkoff, Godfrey Quigley, Patrick Magee, Leonard Rossiter, Marie Kean, Arthur O'Sullivan and Patrick Dawson.

*Barry Lyndon* is an Irish rogue who falls in love with Nora who is in a match with an English officer. Her family trick Barry into leaving. His subsequent adventures involve him joining and deserting from two warring armies, wooing a widowed aristocrat and playing many card games for high stakes.

Ryan O'Neal said of Kubrick:

Stanley is an amazing man. He uses his camera like an old gunfighter with his six-shooter… I'm too tired when I get back to the hotel to even have dinner, but it's worth it working with someone like Stanley Kubrick. Even if he did make me do a scene forty-eight times, in which I had to carry a man up some stairs, and at the end said 'it doesn't work, we'll scrap it.'

Filming commenced in the Waterford area amidst a veil of secrecy. Quite an amount of employment was given locally and those involved found Kubrick to be a hard taskmaster. Kubrick, a stocky man with a bushy beard, in an oversized waterproof supervised every aspect of the production, even choosing the extras himself from their photographs. He chose the actors from videotape auditions. To ensure absolute control, Kubrick had as few people around him as possible and then only those that he trusted implicitly. He overshadowed every inch of the film personally – from the casting and selection of the locations, right through the shooting, deciding the musical score (provided by the Chieftains and Schubert), to the final editing.

He wrote the screenplay himself which he rewrote constantly during filming. Many scenes were improvised in his caravan on the set on the actual morning of filming. Entire sections of completed film were scrapped and new characters were written in while others were written out. There were many sackings on the set and this inevitably led to bad feelings.

In another innovation, Kubrick endeavoured to recreate the look of the eighteenth century canvasses by resolving to shoot the film wholly without artificial lighting. With cinematographer John Alcott, he pioneered the indoor use of ultra-high speed colour film and lit some scenes only by candles. On more than one occasion Kubrick left the set because he was not happy with the location – some small detail irked him. He wanted total perfection and would settle for nothing less. When the unit moved to Dublin he encountered a major snag – they were to film in some stately homes but the families concerned were not too happy at the film-makers taking over their homes at Christmas. The cameras did not roll again until January in such picturesque settings as Powerscourt House, Dublin Castle and Carton House, which were transformed into gaming houses.

On the day when Dublin was hit by a spate of bomb hoaxes the unit was lining up a shot in the Phoenix Park. Kubrick heard the news and immediately left the set and returned to his house in Leixlip and refused to leave. It was late afternoon before his associates could persuade him to return to a new location in

Rousing battle scenes from *Barry Lyndon*, which was based on a novel by William Makepiece Thackery.

Dublin Castle but not until he got a garda escort and an assurance that civil war had not broken out. He had constant fears of the IRA and wanted armed guards on the set. It was reported that he kept a double-barrelled shotgun in his bedroom. It was ironic that a man who had depicted so many violent scenes in his films would seem to recoil from the reality of violence.

Rumours began filtering through that the film was encountering major problems. Ryan O'Neal was reported to have had a row with Kubrick after appearing on the *Late Late Show* to discuss the film. Another report stated that Kubrick was running over budget and Warner Brothers were concerned. These reports were denied but matters soon came to a head when Kubrick suddenly pulled the unit out of Ireland at a few hours' notice.

During a lunch-break at Dublin Castle the cast waited to be recalled to the set but Kubrick had quietly slipped away to his base in Leixlip. It was reported that a phone call purporting to be from the IRA had ordered him to leave the country or else. A press report from the company stated that the reason for his departure was that he had completed his shooting schedule in Ireland and was finishing the film in England.

For whatever reason, he left many puzzled people and at least five more weeks' filming, including two large ballroom scenes to be shot in Powerscourt House, which would have employed 500 extras at about £10 a day. Also cancelled was Barry's wedding in the chapel of the disused King's College School which craftsmen had transformed into a church. Kubrick did not appear behind the camera again until the following week in Salisbury, England.

The film opened to mixed reviews with the acting, particular of O'Neal and Berenson regarded as being wooden and the plot as lacking lustre. There was no disputing the fact that the visual effects were some of the most stunning ever put on film. Although *Barry Lyndon* was nominated as Best Film and Kubrick as Best Director and for Best Adapted Screenplay it was the cinematography of John Alcott, Art Direction, Costume Design, and Musical Score which all deservedly won Academy Awards.

# 19

# ENTER JOHN BOORMAN

One film-maker who has always been a good friend to Ardmore is English director, John Boorman. He has been living with his family in Annamoe, Co Wicklow since the end of the sixties. He began his career as a producer with the BBC before making a number of important films, each distinctive in style and content, including *Catch Us If You Can*, *Hell in the Pacific*, *Point Blank* and *Leo the Last*.

His first encounter with Ardmore came in 1969 when he was engaged in post-production work on *Leo the Last*. In the Wicklow countryside he found an ideal retreat from the rat race of film-making when casually one day he wandered into an auction in Dublin and bought himself an old rectory in Annamoe and his Irish sojourn began. It was not long before he, like John Huston, became committed to the realisation of an Irish film industry.

In 1973 on the crest of his success with *Deliverance*, which had been nominated for three Oscars, Boorman approached Warner Brothers and Columbia with his proposal for *Zardoz*. He gave them a ten-minute synopsis, but not the script, demanded a free hand at all stages of production from casting to final editing, and gave them one hour in which to make up their minds. They each turned him down, but 20th Century Fox accepted his offer. Boorman returned to Ardmore and set the wheels in motion.

When others were avoiding the Bray studio he set about bringing this extraordinary film, *Zardoz*, with a futuristic setting in the year 2293. American actor, Burt Reynolds, one of the stars of *Deliverance* was set for the leading role but was struck down with double hernia before filming commenced. Boorman

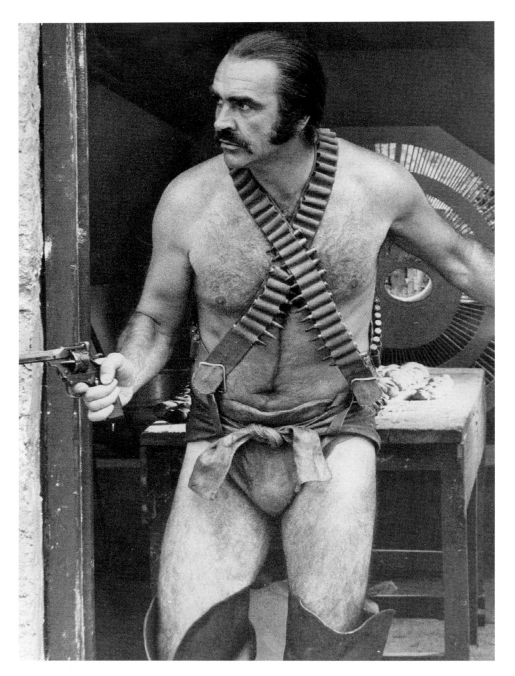

Sean Connery as Zed, in attacking mode, in the John Boorman-directed film, *Zardoz*. In this complex movie, Boorman had to create an entirely new world for his characters.

sent Sean Connery the script, which he read and accepted immediately. Charlotte Rampling, Sara Kestleman, John Alderton and Irish actor, Niall Buggy, filled the other main roles. On the $1.5 million film, he assembled a strong team, led by director of photography, Geoffrey Unsworth.

Behind the camera, it was virtually a one-man show with Boorman serving as writer, producer and director. He had conceived the idea, brought it through the planning stages and into production in barren Ardmore, then in the hands of the receiver. Everything was against him – the equipment was run down and badly in need of overhauling and there was few of the permanent staff still in residence. He persevered regardless and the interior scenes were shot on some highly imaginative sets at Ardmore and the exteriors in Glencree and the rugged surrounding countryside. Boorman even used the grounds of his own house at Annamoe for some sequences.

The title *Zardoz* was derived from *The Wizard of Oz*. In the film the world as we know it has disappeared but a small group of scientists, intellectuals and the rich and powerful have formed a new perfect society called 'The Vortex'. In the Outlands beyond the sheltered cocoon live the remnants of the war-torn world, polluted old world and from that chaos emerges a new breed of man, physically perfect, to launch nature's counter attack. When their leader Zed (Connery) invades the ordered world of the Vortex there is a dramatic and resounding clash.

*Zardoz* is a complex film and Boorman had to create an entirely new world for his characters. He succeeded in bringing in the film on budget. Although it received mixed notices in England and the United States it did show the beauty and diversity of the Irish landscape to an international audience.

Since 1970 production companies in Ireland had sought finance from the government. The Minister for Industry and Commerce, George Colley, introduced a Film Industry Bill in the Dáil but the government was in no rush to implement the Huston Report. A general election intervened which brought a coalition government to power. Colley was replaced by Justin Keating who was more committed to establishing a native film industry.

In July 1973, when receiver Thomas Kelly put Ardmore up for auction, a new group calling themselves The Irish Film Workers Association was formed. The members of the association covered every aspect of the film industry and included such people as Robert Monks and Kieran Hickey. They petitioned the minister to save Ardmore and to encourage and promote the growth of the film industry. They argued that the studio was a viable proposition – not only would it provide employment for members within the industry but it would attract revenue into the country by encouraging feature films to be shot here. At this period building speculators was showing a keen interest in the prime building land at Ardmore. There were growing fears that the property would become a shopping centre or housing estate.

On the day of the auction, 25 July, in an unexpected move, RTÉ on behalf of the government bought Ardmore Studios for £390,000. RTÉ were to manage the studio in a caretaker capacity pending the establishment of a body to be created by the Minister for Industry and Commerce. The government's intention was to safeguard the employment of skilled Irish personnel and to ensure the continued existence of those facilities for the Irish film industry. It was also their wish to set up a film school, in association with the studio, to train Irish technicians.

In the interim the studio was managed by Dermot O'Sullivan of RTÉ whose first task was to give the camera and lighting equipment a badly needed overhaul. Much of the equipment was by then obsolete. In the first six months the studio showed a profit of £22,000 which primarily accrued from the production of commercials and the short visit by Stanley Kubrick.

Following a degree of re-structuring, a new board was appointed and Ardmore became a state-sponsored company known as the National Film Studios of Ireland (NFSI). John Boorman was appointed chairman and senior RTÉ producer Sheamus Smith became managing director. Other members of the board included film director, Vincent Corcoran, and trade union chief, Ruairi Roberts. Boorman reiterated the government's dual intention of maintaining both an on-going film centre and a film school.

Justin Keating had hoped to re-introduce the Film Bill but a general election resulted in the defeat of the coalition government and Fianna Fáil's return to power. There were numerous calls both inside and outside the Dáil for the introduction of the Bill but this did not occur for another six years. During the intervening years animosity grew between the two groups – the NFSI and the Irish independent film-makers who claimed they constituted the core of an Irish film industry and that any finance available should be channelled in their direction.

# 20

# UNCERTAINTY

There followed a depressed period in film production worldwide, particularly in Britain where the decline was drastic. This automatically had an adverse effect on Ireland that depended so much on its neighbour's fortune. The reason for the decline was manifold: escalating film budgets, the ever-present influence of multi-channel television and the growing threat of video. Some major studios were forced to close and the property sold. Those remaining were utilised to a greater degree by American companies; the completed films were classed as 'American' and the profits remitted to the USA. Two prime examples of this were *Star Wars* and *Superman*. The output of actual British films fell to an all-time low, with producers relying almost entirely on film versions of successful series or soft-porn comedies.

Kubrick's sudden departure and the bombs in Dublin in May 1974 together with the continuing Northern Ireland conflict and anti-British slogans were contributing factors to the fall-off in film-making in Ireland. Amongst the losses was a John Huston film that he insisted should be made here but the producers were resolute and said no. There was a strong possibility that the screen version of the internationally acclaimed play *Equus* by Peter Shaffer would be produced at Ardmore but producers Lester Persky and Elliot Kastner shied away and transferred the production to Canada. *Equus* had an impressive cast list which Ireland could ill afford to loose: Richard Burton, Peter Firth and Jenny Agutter, under the direction of the highly rated, Sidney Lumet.

Despite the recession, films continued to be shot here, albeit at irregular intervals. Some productions maintained a low profile and it was only following their departure that their visit became public. One such example was *McVicar*, starring Roger Daltry and Adam Faith. Two of the main locations were Arbour Hill and Kilmainham Jail which were in constant demand by film-makers, because it was virtually impossible to obtain permission to film inside an English prison. Kilmainham Jail Restoration Fund was greatly boosted by the revenue that accrued. The inconsistencies of film settings, as exemplified in *McVicar*, proved amusing for Dublin audiences – the opening sequence showed a police escort leaving St Patrick's Institution, North Circular Road, and travelling what was supposedly several hundred miles before entering the gates of Mountjoy Prison, a mere hundred yards from its starting point.

Other films of the mid-seventies included the umpteenth remake of Mary Shelley's classic *Frankenstein*. This Swedish version, directed by Calvin Floyd and starring Per Oscarsson and Leon Vitali, was filmed in many atmospheric locales. *Seamarks*, a ninety-minute telemovie, directed by Ron Maxwell, was also made at the National Film Studio. Ireland was one of a variety of worldwide locations for a $4 million oil thriller, *The Next Man*. Director Richard Sarafian brought stars Cornelia Sharpe and a bearded Sean Connery, as a peace-making Arab, to the National Stud and Castletown House in Kildare before moving to such exotic destinations as Nassau, Austria, London, Munich, Nice, New York and Morocco.

In 1976 two contrasting star-studded films went into production almost simultaneously. They were Yves Boisset's *Purple Taxi* and Marty Feldman's *The Last Remake of Beau Geste*. Boisset's film was based on the book by French author, Michel Deon, and featured Charlotte Rampling, Peter Ustinov, Fred Astaire and Philippe Noiret. The ageing Astaire, as the village doctor, drives the brightly-painted London taxi of the title, manipulating the fate of everyone around him. The unit travelled about 2,000 miles, covering counties Dublin, Wicklow, Galway, Kerry and Mayo during its twelve-week schedule. The film serves as a perfect showcase for the windswept scenery of the West.

For the first time the National Film Studio agreed to provide facilities, personnel and finance (to a maximum of £270,926). There have been conflicting estimates of the proportion of this figure that has since been recovered.

Yves Boisset summarised the film: 'It's not specifically a love story or great action. It's about justice, man's search for the true meaning of his life. His relationship with others is a universal theme. It reflects a slice of life.'

Director Feldman gave his reason for filming the Wren classic in Ireland: 'My original intent was to make *The Four Feathers* but I inadvertently gave the wrong title and was stuck with it. I wanted a simple low-budget film and they gave me millions and a string of stars. They told me Hollywood was too

An aging Fred Astaire as the village doctor in *Purple Taxi*.

Donald Sutherland as the pick-pocket and Sean Connery as the brains in *The First Great Train Robbery*, which was directed by Michael Crichton.

expensive and I was to film in Spain and Ireland. So here I am.'

And what an array of stars – Ann Margaret, Peter Ustinov, Trevor Howard, Michael York and Spike Milligan. The only Irish name to feature prominently in the credits was Sinéad Cusack. Following a countrywide search for a look-alike, Feldman signed Dublin boy, Michael McConkey to play Beau Geste as a child. The two major locations used were the house and grounds of Adare Manor in Co Limerick and, once again, Kilmainham Jail for the prison scenes.

1978 proved to be an eventful year with several diverse styles of film going into production. The most prestigious of these was *The First Great Train Robbery*, based at the National Film Studio and filmed at various locations throughout the country. Michael Crichton directed from his own novel and screenplay this $7 million production for Dino de Laurentis Productions. The film starred Sean Connery as the brains behind the robbery, Lesley Ann Down as his mistress and Donald Sutherland as a pickpocket. The story told of a train robbery of gold bullion bound for the Crimea.

Producer John Foreman, who had such successes as *Butch Cassidy and the Sundance Kid* and *The Man who would be King* to his credit chose Dublin because it possessed some of the best preserved Georgian and period buildings in the world. They were ideal to recreate nineteenth-century London. Several coaches were constructed for the Victorian train laid on the wheels of CIÉ rolling stock and pulled by the famous 184 steam engine from the Transport Museum at a cost of $250,000.

Stunts were an important feature of the film, ranging from a rooftop escape from Glencree Recreation Centre to scaling the exterior wall of Heuston Station. The most spectacular stunts were performed by Connery for the hair-raising climax on top of the moving train. The star used no stuntmen for this sequence that was filmed along the line at Moate, Co Westmeath. The train reportedly had a maximum speed of 35 mph but the pilot of the helicopter from which the scene was being filmed stated that it was travelling at 55 mph. Connery and Crichton went to the engine and discovered that there was no speedometer. They asked the driver how he judged the speed and he replied 'we just count the poles'.

A disillusioned Vietnam veteran of Irish descent who comes to Belfast to join the Provisional IRA of the 1970s is the subject of *The Outsider*. The film was produced by a Dutch company and based on the book, *The Heritage*, by Colin Leinster. Unable to film in Northern Ireland, the producers reached an agreement with a residents' association to take over an area of Ringsend in Dublin and transform it into a working class district of Belfast. Peace lines, political slogans, a red post box and bombed buildings were erected as large crowds flocked to see director Tony Luraschi at work. Interiors were filmed in Ardmore. The film stars Craig Wasson, Patricia Quinn, Niall Toibin and J. G. Devlin, with the American actor, Sterling Hayden in a cameo role.

Producer Gene Corman, who had filmed *The Red Baron* in Ireland some years previously, returned with a cast headed by Lee Marvin, Mark Hamill, Kelly Ward and Robert Carradine to make *The Big Red One*. The film was written and directed by Hollywood veteran, Samuel Fuller, based on his own World War II experiences. The plot tells of a sergeant who leads a group of raw recruits in the First Infantry Division (nicknamed The Big Red One) into Sicily and destroys a huge German gun. The film demonstrates the ultimate futility of war. The principal location for this gripping war drama was Israel with a two-week stint in a variety of Irish castles and stately homes including Trim Castle and Carton House.

It was only a matter of time before the movie-makers realised the enormous box office possibilities of North Sea oil. Screenwriter, Jack Davies wrote an inventive story involving a gang of terrorists who hijack an oil rig and hold the British government to ransom for £25 million

The film was *North Sea Hijack*, directed by Andrew McLaglen, son of the great character actor, Victor. Andrew had last worked in Ireland some twenty years previously when he was John Ford's assistant on *The Quiet Man*. He assembled a strong cast headed by Roger Moore, James Mason and Anthony Perkins and spent five weeks filming in the Burren and Galway Bay area.

McLaglen explained his reason for coming to Ireland:
We needed to simulate a port so we came to Galway, which was just big enough for what we wanted. We put up Norwegian signs on the dock and local warehouses, while other scenes were shot on the deck of ships being loaded up. We filmed right up to the Aran Islands on the way to the actual oilrigs in the North Sea. The weather was appalling and we experienced some incredible gales. For five weeks we filmed in the hills and dales of Galway (which also stood in for Scotland) without losing the spirit of the story. Everything we wanted was right there within a few miles, from the sea to castles.

Filming simultaneously in Co Clare was *Tristan and Isolde* with Richard Burton and Kate Mulgrew, as the ill-fated pair, under the direction of Tom Donovan. Cyril Cusack and Niall Toibin took other leading roles. The producer had high hopes for the films and there were tentative plans to follow it with a production based on the life of Countess Markievicz. Unfortunately on its initial screening at the Cork Film Festival it received harsh reviews from the critics. As a result it experienced distribution difficulties and did not receive a commercial screening.

During the seventies the National Film Studios were utilised for other purposes besides film production. Commercials provided the main source of income. Other projects included John Boorman's post production of *Heretic, Exorcist 11*, Blake Edward's second unit material for *The Pink Panther Strikes Again* and the editing of *Teardrops*, which was shot in Turkey, and the dubbing of it into English using Irish actors exclusively for the English language version. The music for the film was arranged and performed by traditional musician, Donal Lunny.

The late seventies saw the emergence of a new Irish film company, Tara Films, the brainchild of radio and television personality, Morgan O'Sullivan. He approached best-selling author, Frederick Forsyth, then living in Enniskerry, to write a film treatment which he in due course presented to NBC television in New York. With dogged perseverance O'Sullivan assembled the pieces of his package. The American-based Irish director, Michael O'Herlihy, agreed to direct. Rod Taylor, Joanna Pettit and Cyril Cusack were cast. Finally O'Sullivan signed a deal with NBC and the $1 million *Cry of the Innocent* went into production. The locations were counties Dublin, Wicklow and Kerry. Although there was a small crew, 80% of the people working on it were Irish. O'Sullivan had instigated a system, in conjunction with ANCO (the industrial training authority) whereby a number of newcomers were trained in techniques of film-making. This authority is now defunct and has been replaced by FAS.

O'Herlihy worked fast and completed the film in twenty-three days. It was a thriller in which Rod Taylor is bent on tracking down the killers who planted a bomb in a plane which crashed into his house, killing his family. The film enjoyed both a cinema and television release and in America filled the prestigious Film of the Week spot. It attracted good reviews from the American media, a typical comment designating it several points above the average telemovie.

O'Herlihy returned to Ireland within a year to direct a screen version of one of Barbara Cartland's phenomenally successful novels, *The Flame is Love*. The love story is set in France but O'Herlihy persuaded NBC and producer Ed Friendly to shoot it in Ireland. Dublin's Georgian buildings and Bray's period style railway station were perfect backdrops for the costume drama. The stars are Linda Purl and Timothy Dalton.

The same station, a mere two miles from Ardmore, also features prominently in *The Hard Way*. Young film-makers, Richard F. Tombleson and Kevin Grogan, approached John Boorman with their initial script and he allowed them the

*Above*: A location scene in Ringsend for *The Outsider*.

*Left*: Richard Burton and Kate Mulgrew, as the ill-fated pair, *Tristan and Isolde*.

facilities of the studio to shape it into a working scenario. Tombleson was assigned to direct and Michael Dryhurst to produce this thriller with an Irish setting. Boorman acted as executive producer. The casting teamed the slit-eyes gunman of so many westerns, Lee Van Cleff, with the rugged Patrick McGoohan. The most surprising casting was of the novelist, Edna O'Brien, as McGoohan's wife. The film experienced a number of problems, not least the fact that the director was replaced by Dryhurst after one week's shooting. The final result was a routine body-strewn thriller.

# 21

# EXCALIBUR AND AFTER

John Boorman had a life-long ambition to make a film based on the legend of King Arthur and Camelot. From time to time he had presented characters and symbols from the Arthurian period in other guises in his films, such as *Deliverance*, *Zardoz* and *Point Blank*. One of the most noticeable of these was the hand emerging from the lake in *Deliverance*. In 1975 he wrote a draft script which ran close to four hours and then handed the text over to Rospo Pallenburg who helped him shape it into the final draft. The project, which went through several name changes, including *Merlin* and *Knights*, eventually became *Excalibur* after its completion. The huge success of *Star Wars* led indirectly to *Excalibur* going into production in 1980: the studios that had previously rejected the idea now regarded fantasy as good box office.

The National Film Studio received a major boost when Boorman decided to shoot the entire $11.5 million production there (even though several other countries had made tempting offers to him). Directly and indirectly the film ploughed a considerable amount of revenue into the Irish economy. Of the 280 technicians, over 200 were Irish and an average of 260 Irish extras were employed each week. Boorman insisted that Irish film apprentices were employed in all departments. He accorded the young Irish writer, Neil Jordan, facilities to shoot a documentary on the making of the film.

Boorman's belief was that the NFSI should be involved in producing films themselves but was wary of the government providing cash as this would have left them open to interference. His hope was for greater participation by Irish business interests and he sought to realise this through *Excalibur*. Through the Allied Irish

Nigel Terry in a dramatic scene from *Excalibur*.

Investment Bank, Boorman put forward a proposal to a consortium of Irish companies to put up $3 million towards the making of the film. In short they would own the negative for one year, share in the profits and hopefully would gain some tax advantages. He received commitments from all the interested parties that the scheme would be allowed to operate, but the Allied Irish Investment Bank demanded written confirmation from the Revenue Commissioners. This was not forthcoming and following a year's negotiation the deal fell through and a frustrated Boorman went to Hollywood to finance the project. One of the largest Hollywood film companies, Orion, then fully financed the film.

*Excalibur*, the biggest undertaking ever mounted at Ardmore, was based on a mixture of historical fact and romantic fiction which was most vividly recounted in Thomas Malory's *Morte d'Arthur*. Boorman did not take a fee as a producer, director or writer but settled for a percentage of the profits. He had an immense number of problems to contend with on the production – budget, schedule, weather and technical hitches. During the shooting schedule Ireland experienced one of its worse ever summers, with rain practically every day. This inevitably caused the film to run over schedule and therefore over budget. The working day was not the conventional 8 a.m. to 5 p.m. but varied between all-night shooting and a 1 p.m. to 9 p.m. schedule.

Boorman set the film in the landscapes he knew so well, the bleak bogs of Sallygap, Childers Wood in Roundwood, the Sugarloaf, the Norman Cahir Castle in Co Tipperary and the rich forests and mist-capped mountains of Co Wicklow. The splendour of Camelot was erected on the back lot of Ardmore. The studio stages had to be extended to facilitate some of the major interior scenes.

The story begins as idyllic young Arthur releases the enchanted sword Excalibur from the stone and goes on to build the empire of Camelot, marry Guinevere and establish the Knights of the Round Table. Merlin, the mysterious magician and King Arthur's counsellor, observes and influences developments. Their solitude and contentment begin to crumble when Arthur's knight, Lancelot, becomes Guinevere's lover and Arthur's evil half-sister, Morgana, tricks both Merlin and the king – posing as Guinevere she conceives a son by Arthur. Their son, Mordred, is raised with one purpose: to kill his father and claim the throne. As Camelot disintegrates the Knights of the Round Table are sent in search of the Holy Grail and Arthur goes into battle with his son.

Whereas for the demanding role of Merlin he cast internationally famous actor, Nicol Williamson, the remainder of the cast consisted mainly of performers from the London stage. Helen Mirren as the evil temptress Morgana; Cherie

Lunghi as Queen Guinevere; Nicholas Clay as Lancelot and Nigel Terry playing Arthur from young man to elderly king. Many Irish actors featured prominently in the cast including Liam Neeson, Gabriel Byrne, Niall O'Brien and Eamonn Kelly.

Boorman used light and shade for atmospheric effect. Music and colour changed dramatically with the rise and fall of Camelot. The director centres the film on the character that has most fascinated him – that of Merlin, the sorcerer. In its opening weekend in America *Excalibur* grossed over $35 million. The final income was estimated to be in excess of $200 million. On those figures the Irish companies would have had a substantial return for their investment. *Excalibur* was one of the high points at the Cannes Film Festival and was awarded a prize for its artistic contribution. It received an Oscar nomination for director of photography, Alex Thomson.

That same year three other contrasting films were produced in Ireland. The first was a German/Irish production with an English soundtrack, entitled *Fire and Sword*, directed by Veith Von Fuerstenberg and starring Peter Firth and Leigh Lawson. This version of the Tristan and Isolde legend was filmed in a variety of locations from the Cliffs of Moher, Co Clare and Achill Island, Co Mayo to Glendalough, where an entire medieval village was re-created.

The highly talented Swiss director, Alain Tanner, moved his small unit into the isolation of Letterfrack in Connemara to film *L'Annees Lumieres* (English title, *Light Years Away*), a mystical fable set in the year 2000. It was a Swiss/French production starring Trevor Howard and Mick Ford. The hero is Jonah (Ford), presumably the same figure of Tanner's earlier film, *Jonah Who will be 25 in the Year 2000*, who becomes an apprentice to an eccentric recluse, Yoshka (Howard). Gradually Jonah discovers the ultimate aim of Yoshka's obsessive study – to discover the secret of flight. A number of Irish actors appeared in small roles. The film won the Jury Special Award at the Cannes Film Festival.

A section of one of the most expensive film flops (to that time) was filmed in Ardmore. The film was the $48 million *Inchon*, funded by the Moonies and starring Laurence Olivier, Jacqueline Bisset and Ben Gazzara. When Reverend Sun Myung Moon decided to enter the film business he chose the most heroic episodes of the Korean War and General Douglas MacArthur's surprise landing at Inchon as the subject matter. One of his leading disciples, Japanese newspaper publisher Mitsuharu Ishii, took charge of the project. The original budget was set at $18 million with Andrew McLaglen as director but there followed a succession of problems as a result of which McLaglen resigned and was replaced by Terence Young.

Production commenced in Korea in January 1979 with Olivier as MacArthur. From the onset the production was plagued by problems, from typhoons and an earthquake, which demolished the sets, to the government's reluctance to grant permits. There was also a major blunder in which 300 ships turned right instead of left, out of camera range.

The film's final sequence featured a victory parade through Seoul following MacArthur's successful campaign. The general waved from his limousine, then stepped into Government House, where a cheering crowd greeted him. This triumphal conclusion – lasting only three minutes on screen – had to be shot over the course of four months in three different countries, and then edited at great expense. Moon himself created most of the difficulties. He felt that there were not enough people in the original scene and asked Ishii to try again. This involved bringing the entire crew back to Korea at a total cost of nearly $1 million. The resulting footage pleased Moon, but the large number of people in the sequence failed to match the previously filmed view of MacArthur in his limousine. As Olivier had already returned to England and declined to make another trip to Korea for this single shot, the Moonies had to satisfy themselves with transporting him to Ireland. Renting Ardmore they placed Olivier in a stationary car, then filmed him again against a back projection of the cheering throngs. The proprietor of the upmarket Mirabeau Restaurant, Sean Kinsella, was hired as Olivier's private chef. He liquidised the star's meals that had to be consumed through a straw to avoid disturbing his make-up.

The film gained some of the most vicious reviews ever penned. Included in the chorus of condemnation were judgements such as: 'The worst movie ever made... A turkey the size of *Godzilla*' (*Newsweek*). 'A near total loss as well as a laugh...' (*Playboy*). 'As military spectacles go, one of the sorriest in movie history' (*Time*). It surpassed even *Cleopatra* and *Heaven's Gate* as one of the most expensive flops in movie history.

The Motion Picture Company of Ireland was set up by John Boorman and Sheamus Smith to produce low budget films in Ireland. In 1981 their production, *Angel* was the first film to receive a grant of £100,000 from the Irish Film Board. The balance of the budget, £400,000, was provided by the new British independent television service, Channel Four. The day-to-day filming operations were in the hands of two relatively unknowns, Barry Blackmore as producer and author Neil Jordan as director and screenwriter. The film, shot in six weeks on location in the Bray and Dublin areas, was set in Northern Ireland and centres on a disillusioned saxophonist who witnesses the murder of his manager and a young girl and sets out on a trail of revenge.

Stephen Rea in Neil Jordan's *Angel*, the first movie to receive a grant from the Irish Film Board.

Stephen Rea headed the all-Irish cast of Honor Heffernan, Ray McAnally, Marie Keane and Donal McCann. The film was retitled *Danny Boy* in America to avoid confusion with a soft-porn film of the same name.

The film caused a degree of controversy when the Association of Independent Producers, who were not represented on the Film Board, were suspicious of its intention. They voiced their anger that the film had received the first grant from the Film Board, which only had three members appointed – including Boorman – and four places left vacant. In reality, when the project came up for consideration Boorman declared his involvement and withdrew.

*Angel* seemed the ideal vehicle to pioneer the intentions of the Irish Film Board with only four of the forty-seven people credited not based in Ireland. The film received considerable interest when it was screened at the Cannes Film Festival and was the critical hit of the year in Britain with Chris Menges' photography and Honor Heffernan's performance receiving particular praise.

Jordan's next two films were shot in England. *The Company of Wolves* with Stephen Rea, David Warner and Angela Lansbury, was an intelligent and visually sumptuous horror film. This retelling of the Little Red Riding Hood fairy tale proved Jordan's ability as a director and a master of visual style. The film was described by a Los Angeles critic as 'the most exciting British film of 1984.'

Jordan next wrote and directed *Mona Lisa* with Bob Hoskins, Cathy Tyson and Michael Caine. This gritty thriller was highly praised and consolidated the praise of Jordan's two earlier films. Hoskins received an Oscar nomination for his portrayal of George, the ex-con who is obsessed with a high-class black call girl.

# 22

# THE IRISH FILM BOARD

In 1974 when the National Film Studio was established the board was given the studio but no finance to operate it. This lack of capital injection by the government led to serious losses at Ardmore as the re-equipping and modernisation had to come from bank loans. Even studio chairman, John Boorman, did not accept his annual remuneration of £1,000. In the late seventies there was a dramatic fall-off in the number of days given over to the shooting of commercials, the main source of income for the studio. Sheamus Smith attributed this to the recession, which led to Irish companies using old television and cinema commercials.

The coalition government had planned to reconstruct and refinance the studio. Originally when the NFSI was set up the then minister, Justin Keating, had instructed that some of the surplus land around the studio should be sold off and the revenue ploughed back to improve its financial position. The order was later rescinded after pressure came from the board. As a result of further suggestion by a later minister, Des O'Malley, tentative plans were drawn up to develop part of the land. Boorman had architect Jeremy Williams design draft plans to develop the surplus land in a crescent-shaped scheme of eighteenth century town houses, which would preserve the studio as a unique and highly specialised employment industry. Bray Urban District Council refused planning permission for the scheme on the grounds that the area involved was zoned residential.

Despite being used in the production of the enormously successful *Excalibur*, Ardmore again had substantial losses – the studio had no stake in that film's box office success. Minister for Industry and Commerce, Michael O'Leary, expressed concern at the financial state of the company and undertook to keep it in operation. The expected increase in business following the success of *Excalibur* did not materialise. A big budget television series based on Sir Walter Scott's *Ivanhoe*, transferred to England after Ardmore had been considered.

Frequently, NFSI board member, Vincent Corcoran, voiced criticism concerning the activities of the Board:

> *Excalibur* tied up the studio for nine months and only yielded rental payment of £65,000. They had a Cecil B. de Mille complex, concentrating on attracting big foreign productions, where they should have put more effort into getting independent finance for Irish films.
>
> The government should sell the studio if they are unable to ensure that it would continue to be used for film production.

At the end of 1981 a number of official and unofficial approaches were made to purchase the studio and proposals were put to the Department of Industry and Commerce. A consortium, headed by a prominent businessman, Vincent Donoghue, made a bid to purchase the studio for £1.5 million and gave guarantees of additional employment. A Hollywood film consortium, headed by Jack Conrad, proposed a £20 million film investment package and envisaged two thousand film industry workers being employed. The department accepted none of the offers.

On 2 April 1982, John Boorman resigned as chairman of the National Film Studio of Ireland and as a board member of the Irish Film Board. The following day the Minister for Industry and Commerce, Albert Reynolds, in a surprise move announced that the studio was to close. He convened a special board meeting of the operating company and stated that a liquidator would be appointed. He was confident that people from a related industry – video manufacturing or small budget film-makers – would purchase the studio. The government decision to close the studio was based on the fact that since it was set up by statute its average annual loss was £500,000. The minister declared that they were no longer a viable proposition and would be auctioned off in two lots – the studio and five acres of surrounding land in one parcel, and the remaining twenty-five acres for development.

Boorman was not notified in advance of the minister's decision nor was managing director, Sheamus Smith, or any members of the board. Smith claimed that the studio had difficulty offering competitive rates to foreign film producers and its closure would seriously damage Ireland's chances of attracting big budget feature films in the future.

Even before Michael McNulty was appointed liquidator, the forty-six strong studio work force organised an effective action group and lobbied the government and opposition parties. Their spokesman, Eamonn O'Higgins said:

> The workers want Ardmore retained by the state for three reasons – firstly the guarantee of our jobs, secondly as a service to the Irish film industry and thirdly as an important section of the Irish economy. No one would see the government closing RTÉ or the Abbey, and Ardmore Studios are in a similar position.

Ironically the studio was closed at the time that the Film Board was finally being established. The bill, which had been recommended by the Huston Report in the early seventies, was not introduced by the government until December 1979. Then followed the slow parliamentary process of debating the provisions of the bill. The proposed legislation provided for the setting up of the Film Board which would disburse a fund of £4.1 million over a four-year period by way of investment, grant or loan to cover all or part of the costs of production wholly or partly made in the state. The bill caused considerable concern among independent film producers and Irish film workers. As a result the Association of Independent Producers of Ireland (AIPI) was formed to offer a united front in opposition to the bill.

In 1980 the minister, Des O'Malley, introduced the Film Bill in the Dáil. It provided for an Irish Film Board to promote and develop an Irish film industry. The only film to receive a grant the first year was the controversial *Angel*. The remaining fund was returned to the exchequer. The funding of *Angel* by the Film Board angered the AIPI because Boorman was both a Film Board member and the film's executive producer.

Head of Television Features at RTÉ, Muiris MacConghail, was appointed chairman of the Irish Film Board and Michael Algar, chairman of the Irish Film and Television Guild, was appointed chief executive. AIPI ended their boycott of the board when their chairman, Tiernan McBride, was appointed a member. The board stated that their objective was to assist in the making of totally Irish films, i.e. films that used Irish writers, Irish directors, Irish production companies, Irish technicians, Irish post-production facilities and Irish distribution. In 1982 the board considered eighty proposals, from which they selected twenty-two to receive aid.

Following the closure of Ardmore, several multi-million pound films were lost to the country. One was the Michael Caine/Laurence Olivier thriller, *The Jigsaw Man*, under director Terence Young that had to transfer to England. A disillusioned John Boorman cancelled plans to direct a film, *Little Nemo*, at the studio. The biggest loss was the James Bond film, *Never Say Never Again*, which was to have utilised Ardmore for studio work.

The film version of Willy Russell's successful play, *Educating Rita*, again starring Caine, was to be made in Ardmore but had to transfer to Paris for studio work. Location shooting for the film, which re-united Caine and his *Alfie* director, Lewis Gilbert, did go ahead in Dublin, principally at Trinity College. Julie Walters plays Rita, a working class hairdresser who signs on for adult education classes with Caine as her tutor. Soon Rita is torn between her expanding intellectual horizon, her boring home life and the alcoholic tutor. Irish actors Malcolm Douglas, Jeananne Crowley, Godfrey Quigley and Pat Daly feature in supporting roles. Caine, Walters and Russell were all nominated for Academy Awards for their work.

Five months after its closure by the government, Ardmore Studios was purchased for £1.1 million by Ardmore Completion Communications, headed by Vincent Donoghue, who had made two earlier unsuccessful bids for the property. Donohoe's partners in the new company included Peter Sprague, chairman of the billion dollar National Semiconductor Corporation, Rex Pyke, a London-based film producer whose credits included *Akenfield*, and American director, Doug Trumbutt who was responsible for the special effects on Kubrick's *2001: A Space Odyssey*. The new company intended to continue operating Ardmore as a film production centre as well as a film-processing laboratory and to manufacture the special photographic equipment for Showscan. Donohoe was forced to withdraw from the deal when he was unable to secure financial backing.

Several other potential purchasers opened discussions with the liquidator but no deal went ahead. In 1983, after paying over £2 million to meet Ardmore's debts, the then Minister for Industry and Commerce, John Bruton, set up a review body to examine the viability of the studio on the assumption that it should not cost the exchequer anything. The group consisted of representatives of the Irish Film Board and the Departments of Industry and Commerce, Finance, and the Arts. They submitted their report to the minister three months later. Under a government covenant the lands surrounding Ardmore were exclusively zoned for film-making purposes until October 1987.

While the future of the studio was being decided, a small feature film was being shot, not in Bray but in Cloghane, on the Dingle Peninsula. The Kerry village was chosen as the location for *Sense of Wonder*, a £400,000 film by Argentine director Martin Donovan. Of 150 local people employed on the film, 28 had speaking parts and three of the Kerry voices had to be dubbed for the

Michael Caine and Julie Walters in *Educating Rita*, much of which was shot around Trinity College, Dublin.

international market. The film starred Anne Chaplin, the youngest daughter of Charlie, in her film debut. During the twenty-one days filming, the sixty strong crew took up every available bed in the village.

This was the first feature film by Donovan who also wrote the screenplay based on the death of his seventeen-year-old brother in a car crash. Frequently he changed the script, moving the action outdoors to avail himself of the magnificent scenery. The film had its first public screening in Dingle's Phoenix Cinema.

In July 1984, following months of negotiations, Ardmore was sold to a Pakistan-born, American based film-maker and businessman, Mahmond Sipra, for £994,000, under an Irish registered company, Bondly Limited. Sipra agreed to the clause that the studio was to be retained as a film-making centre. He had only entered the film business two years previously when he came to the rescue of the Terence Young film, *The Jigsaw Man*, which ran out of money at a crucial stage with only ten day's shooting remaining. On seeing footage, Sipra stepped in with $8 million needed to clear all debts and guarantee completion.

Sipra injected £100,000 into Ardmore to enable it to commence operation. Within months the company announced several major companies were to use the studio. There was an adventure film, *Khyber Horseman*, and *Gun Bus*, to be followed by *Buried Alive* starring Peter O'Toole. Fears were again expressed when all the films were deferred. By October news had broken that Sipra's companies were facing financial problems and there were doubts about the studio's future. Soon the electricity supply was cut off owing to non-payment and the security staff were made redundant. In January 1985 worse was to come when Justice Barrington appointed Robert Stewart as provisional liquidator. Again the studio was back on the market.

Over the following months many inquiries and inspections were made by potential purchasers. Towards the end of the year Mary Tyler Moore Enterprises made an agreement to acquire Ardmore if the American television network NBC agreed to 'pick up' a new series they were planning. MTM Enterprises, the producers of such highly successful series as *Hill Street Blues*, *Lou Grant* and *Remington Steele* had filmed a pilot programme, *92 Grosvenor Square*, and if it succeeded, the thirteen-part series, at $1 million per episode, would be filmed at Ardmore. The pilot, with David McCallum and Hal Holbrook, dealing with intelligence work during World War II, was screened on both sides of the Atlantic in December and a final decision expected in January was postponed. In March 1986 when a definite decision was not forthcoming on the proposed series MTM Enterprises requested a further extension from the liquidator but this was refused and the deal collapsed. The studio was once more put on the market.

Following months of uncertainty and additional bidders, in September 1986 Justice Lardner in the High Court made a judgement approving the sale of Ardmore Studios to a consortium, comprising Mary Tyler Moore Enterprises, Morgan O'Sullivan's Tara Productions and the National Development Corporation for £975,000, a 25% deposit having already been paid. Morgan O'Sullivan became managing director and within two months, three episodes of MTM's series *Remington Steele* with Pierce Brosnan, were filmed at the studio. There followed enquiries from many leading directors and producers including Neil Jordan, Robert Altman and Michael Cimino for his proposed film on the life of Michael Collins. O'Sullivan attended the Cannes Film Festival, promoting the studio while £1 million was spent refurbishing the property and building a large new stage.

23

# IRISH FILM-MAKERS

From the beginning of film-making history international producers have always enlisted the best of Irish acting talent but largely ignored Irish directing talent. Despite the fact that directors of Irish ancestry have reached the pinnacle of success in Hollywood, until the mid 1980s there were only two outstanding native directors – Rex Ingram and Michael O'Herlihy. Ingram, a Dubliner, gained his reputation in Hollywood during the silent era and will be best remembered for the masterly *Four Horsemen of the Apocalypse* and his discovery of Rudolph Valentino.

O'Herlihy, born in Dún Laoghaire, Co Dublin, served his apprenticeship with Hilton Edwards and Micheál MacLiammóir and worked with them as a designer at the Gate Theatre in the early fifties. Running parallel with his love for the theatre was his love for the sea. He sailed from Ireland in a yacht across the Atlantic, with the ambition of finding a job in the American film industry. Following a difficult period, he finally got a job with Warner Brothers where he learned the craft of film-making. While serving as a technical advisor on *Darby O'Gill and the Little People*, he established a friendship with Walt Disney that led to him making several films for Disney, including *The Fighting Prince of Donegal*. He combined his film work with television and soon established himself as one of the foremost television directors in Hollywood, directing such shows as *Hawaii Five-O*, *The Man from U.N.C.L.E.* and *The A-Team*. When he returned to Ireland in the late seventies to shoot Frederick Forsyth's *Cry of the Innocent* and Barbara Cartland's *The Flame is Love*, he expressed a desire to produce more films here and to assist in the formation of a native film industry.

From as far back as 1896 the only form of film-making to run at a consistently high level in Ireland was the documentary. From shaky views of trains and fire engines this medium began to capture the historical events at the beginning of the century and slowly evolved into a unique art form. Norman Whitten of Central Film Supply compiled a large library of film stock covering a variety of scenic and topical issues during the twenties. Some of these were incorporated into other films, thus providing a forerunner to the services of a second-unit.

Also during the twenties Norris Davidson made a series of short films on various aspects of life in Ireland at the time. This form of film-making was not officially termed documentary until the 1930s. This decade also produced the unique *Man of Aran* from Robert Flaherty. The thirties saw many fine documentaries from Richard Hayward, including *Lough Corrib* and *In West Kerry*. Hayward alternated his documentary work with feature films.

The greatest successes in documentary have been Gael Linn's two epic historical reconstructions *Mise Eire* and *Saoirse?* assembled by George Morrison with an impressive music score by Seán Ó Riada. They each ran for approximately ninety minutes and were exceptionally well received by the public. Morrison also directed over twenty short films covering a range of Irish life and culture. In the early sixties Gael Linn produced a weekly newsreel in Irish for cinemas. This series was produced by Jim Mulkerns and Colm O'Laoghaire and ran for 267 editions until it fell victim to television.

The survival of the documentary is due in no small way to the work of a dedicated group of directors including Patrick Carey, Bob Quinn, Louis Marcus, George Morrison, Vincent Corcoran and Eamonn de Buitléar. For many years this small band struggled to find finance for each new production. These short films were sponsored in the main by commercial companies but occasionally a government department would commission a film on a particular subject, such as road safety or hygiene. Only in these circumstances was finance forthcoming directly from an official source. Few documentaries are a commercial proposition and in the past were shown in support of feature films. Since the early 1980s this practice was dispensed with.

These film-makers produced films of a remarkably high quality, which have won many international awards. Amongst those of outstanding merit have been Patrick Carey's *Yeats's Country*, *Waves* and *Errigal*; Colm O'Laoghaire's *Water Wisdom* and *Irish Gossamer*; Louis Marcus' *Peil* and *Rhapsody of a River*; Vincent Corcoran's *Ireland*; Kieran Hickey's *The Light of Other Days* and *Faithful Departed*, based on the Lawrence Collection of the late nineteenth and early twentieth century photographs in the National Gallery of Ireland; Eamonn de

Director George Morrison who was responsible for *Mise Éire* and *Saoirse?*

Film director and writer Kieran Hickey whose first short was *A Child's Voice*.

Cinematographer and director Thaddeus O'Sullivan who directed *On a Paving Stone Mounted*.

Vincent Corcoran, whose work *Ireland* was widely praised.

Buitléar's many wildlife studies and George Morrison's *The Easter Rising* and *Look to the Sea*.

In 1976 the Arts Council launched an inventive scheme in the form of a Film Script Award which was to be presented annually. It took the form of an open competition in which film-makers born or resident in Ireland could submit original scripts for consideration.

The first award went to *Poitín*, which was co-written by Colm Bairead and Bob Quinn, who also directed. The production received a further £5,000 from the Department of the Gaeltacht and additional assistance from other sources. *Poitín* was made with the involvement of local people in Connemara and traces the antics of a poitín maker (Cyril Cusack) and his accomplices (Donal McCann and Niall Toibin). The film with Irish dialogue and English sub-titles was premiered in Carraroe. Some years previous Quinn had made another important film, *Caoineadh Airt Uí Laoire*, that looked at a modern theatrical presentation of the eighteenth-century poem about the death of a Gaelic aristocrat and combined scenes of the rehearsal with cinematic account. The film with Seán Bán Breathnach and Caithlín Ní Donnchú also had Irish dialogue and English subtitles.

RTÉ producer, Tom McArdle, made his feature directorial debut with *The Kinkisha*, written by his twin brother John, who also starred. The film, which they financed privately, deals with the effects of superstition on a Galway marriage. *It's Handy When People Don't Die*, set in Wexford during the 1798 Rising, was the second feature directed by Tom McArdle in 1980. The events are seen through the eyes of Art, a simple village youth who listens to stories and myths as events unravel around him. The film was superbly shot on location with a reliable cast headed by Garrett Keogh, Brendan Cauldwell and Bob Carlile.

Kieran Hickey, whose first venture as a short feature director was a ghost story, *A Child's Voice*, written by David Thompson and starring T. P. McKenna. Hickey's next film, *Exposure*, was the recipient of the second Arts Council Film Script Award that had increased to £12,000. Set in a rural hotel, the film describes an encounter between three surveyors and a French female photographer and features Catherine Schell, T. P. McKenna, Bosco Hogan and Niall O'Brien. The film was shot on 16mm and achieved on a small budget. He followed this with *Criminal Conversations*, another short feature.

Hickey's most ambitious undertaking was the screen version of William Trevor's short story, *Attracta*, which was adapted for the screen by the author. The film received a grant of £104,000 from the Film Board. The veteran stage and screen actress, Wendy Hiller, who won an Oscar for her performance in *Separate Tables*, was signed to play the role of the spinster teacher whose visit to the grave

*Right*: A poster for the 1925 film, *Irish Destiny*, directed by I. G. Eppel. This love story was set against the background of the Troubles and featured the burning of the Customs House.

*Below*: Maureen O'Hara and John Wayne in John Ford's 1952 classic, *The Quiet Man*.

Gregory Peck in a visually stunning scene from *Moby Dick*, directed by John Houston in Youghal, Co Cork. Huston won the New York Critics Best Director Award for the film.

David Lean with Sarah Miles and Robert Mitchum on the set of *Ryan's Daughter*.

The £500,000 Walt Disney production, *Guns in the Heather*, about two boys, one American, one Irish, who become involved in mystery and intrigue. Kurt Russell and Patrick Dawson play the boys.

John Boorman's futuristic film *Zardoz*, which is set in 2293. The title is derived from *The Wizard of Oz*.

Helen Mirren as Morgana in *Excalibur*.

A scene from Neil Jordan's *Company of Wolves*.

Young Russian mouse, Fievel Mousekewitz, in *An American Tail*, which grossed over $50 at the US box office.

Jaye Davidson as Dil in *The Crying Game*. Stanley Kubrick had at one point warned Neil Jordan that the role was probably uncastable. Davidson received an Oscar nomination for Best Supporting Actor.

Richard Harris as Bull McCabe in *The Field*.

Ruaidhrí Conroy and Ciaran Fitzgerald in the magical *Into the West*.

Aidan Quinn and Moya Farrelly in *This is My Father*.

John Boorman

John Huston

Jim Sheridan

Neil Jordan

Colin Farrell

of a Belfast victim of violence evokes memories of her own experience. The strong supporting cast included Kate Thompson, John Kavanagh and Deirdre Donnelly. *Attracta*, which was photographed on a three weeks' schedule by Sean Corcoran, won a Drama Award at the Celtic Film and Television Festival in Glasgow.

The late seventies brought a number of significant short features and documentaries from Irish directors. Another Arts Council Script Award winner, Neville Presho, directed *Desecration* that depicts the clash of cultures when a valuable find is discovered under an archaeological site, which is deemed a national monument. In the cast are Tom Hickey, John Murphy and Eamon Keane. Tiernan MacBride directed a notable short, *Christmas Morning*, in 1978, a visualisation of the old ballad Arthur McBride, played and sung by Paul Brady. The film starring Godfrey Quigley and Paul Bennett, was Ireland's entry in the short film competition at the Cannes Film Festival. Tim Booth, made an ambitious animated short, *The Prisoner*, based on W. B. Yeats' poem with music supplied by Gary Moore and Phil Lynott.

Another young film-maker to produce an important short feature was Joe Comerford with a 16mm film, *Down the Corner*, which was based on Noel McFarlene's book of the same name. Set and filmed in Ballyfermot, a working class district of Dublin, the film features local youths in the main roles. The modest budget of £20,000 included £7,000 from the British Film Institute. Comerford was to follow this with *Travellers* from a script by Neil Jordan, about the life of two young itinerants. The films were in the main by Irish writers and directors, dealing with Irish themes.

The first large investment by the Film Board was a grant for *Angel*. The next notable Irish feature film of the eighties was based on Robert Wynne Simmons' Art Council award-winning script, *The Outcasts*. The film, set in rural Ireland before the Famine, was directed by Wynne Simmons with financial assistance from the Film Board of £47,000 and Channel Four. *The Outcasts* stars Cyril Cusack, Mick Lally and Mary Ryan. The story looks at a time of poverty and superstition when the power of magic is accepted everywhere. Scarf Michael is a wedding fiddler, but he has become a social outcast because his magic is said to bring unhappiness and even death. An introverted girl, Maura, is regarded as backward by the community until she comes under the influence of Michael. The Film Board made an additional grant of £25,000 in order to blow-up the print from 16mm to 35mm and for promotional costs. The film won an award at the Brussels Fantasy Film Festival.

Twenty years after directing Edna O'Brien's *Girl with Green Eyes*, Desmond Davis returned to counties Wicklow and Dublin to film the earlier adventurers of Babs and Kate with *The Country Girls*. The Mr Gentleman role was filled by Sam Neill and the two girls rebelling against a convent education were sensitively played by Maeve Germaine and Jill Doyle. Others in the cast include John Kavanagh, Niall Toibin, Sheila Flitton and Agnes Bernelle. The Film Board made a £75,000 investment in the film, ten per cent of the total budget, which was also financed by Channel Four. The film attracted excellent business in Irish cinemas and at the date of screening had the second highest viewing rate of any film shown on Channel Four.

In 1982 two films by emerging young Irish directors went into production simultaneously. Shooting on location in Strokestown, Co Roscommon and Kilmainham Jail was *Anne Devlin*, directed by Pat Murphy and produced by Tom Hayes. Bríd Brennan, who played a key role in *Maeve*, was cast as Robert Emmet's devoted servant with Bosco Hogan as Emmet. A native of Dublin, Pat Murphy moved to Belfast with her family in 1966. While studying art at Hornsby in London, she made a short feature, *Rituals of Memory*. At film school she met John Davies and Robert Smith with whom she made her feature debut, *Maeve*, for the British Film Institute. The budget for *Anne Devlin* was £600,000 with the Film Board providing £200,000.

The award-winning film-maker of *Wheels* and *Our Boys*, Cathal Black, directed *Pigs*, a feature film on location in Dublin. The film refers to the lifestyle of a group of people in a squat in the inner city Dublin. James Brennan, who wrote the screenplay, stars as the central character, dropout Jimmy. The squat attracts a sad assortment of characters; George (George Shane) a broken middle-aged man, Tom (Maurice O'Donoghue) a gibbering unfortunate, Ronnie (Liam Halligan) a pusher, Orwell (Kwesi Kay) a Jamaican, and Mary (Mary Harper) a prostitute. The dirge-like score by Roger Doyle was most effective in capturing the despairing atmosphere. The film was produced by David Collins and received a grant of £90,500 from the Film Board. One of the most outstanding aspects of both films was the excellent photography of Thaddeus O'Sullivan. These films made a vital breakthrough when their producers managed to attract significant private investment in Ireland. *Anne Devlin* received a private investment of £250,000. Unfortunately both only received a limited release and failed to register with critics and audiences.

*Cal* was the first feature film by ex-RTÉ director, Pat O'Connor, who in 1984 won the prestigious BAFTA for his direction of the RTÉ/BBC co-production, *The Ballroom of Romance*, which was named Best Television Drama in Britain. O'Connor's experience in television drama and current affairs served him well in making *Cal*, a sensitive moving story set against the troubles in

Northern Ireland. The film, produced by David Puttnam, the Oscar-winning producer of *Chariots of Fire* for Goldcrest Films, was based on a screenplay by Bernard McLaverty from his novel. The film, with substantial American backing, was filmed entirely on location in counties Wicklow and Kildare.

It is a story of a nineteen–year old Catholic, Cal McCluskey, who lives with his father in a working class housing estate near Belfast. He is on the fringe of the IRA and wants out. When their home is burned by the Protestant UVF, Cal takes refuge in a cottage on a farm where he works. He is attracted to Marcella, the Catholic widow of an RUC man murdered by the IRA. Cal was the driver for the assassination squad. Their love affair drifts to an inevitable tragic conclusion. *Cal* was widely acclaimed at the Cannes Film Festival, with Helen Mirren winning the Best Actress Award. Others in the cast include a young unknown, John Lynch, as Cal, Ray McAnally, Donal McCann, Tom Hickey and John Kavanagh.

Despite the fact that not a single feature was produced in Ireland in 1984 there existed a strong core of eager young film-makers with no shortage of experience and projects. With Film Board assistance they were striving to produce films identifiable with the cultural heritage of the country and the social and moral climate of the present. An indication of their number is evident from the list of eighty projects initially submitted to the Film Board for consideration. With this amount of activity it would appear that the long-awaited Irish film industry was finally taking off.

One of the earliest producers to attempt to attract private companies to invest in a film was John Boorman with *Excalibur*, but his elaborate plan collapsed owing to complications with the bank. *Pigs* and *Anne Devlin*, despite their artistic achievements, failed to receive widespread cinema release at home or abroad and deterred further investors. However, the efforts of Channel Four encouraged film-makers to make low-budget films and had formulated a policy of investing in worthy projects. Several Irish-made productions, already mentioned, received generous funding from them.

Considerable interest was shown in Thaddeus O'Sullivan's first short feature, *On a Paving Stone Mounted*, which concerns emigration and stars Maureen Toal and Paul Bennett. O'Sullivan, who was highly praised for his cinematography on *Pigs* and *Anne Devlin*, chose a short story by Sean O'Faolain, *The Woman who Married Clark Cable*, as the basis for his next production. The short black and white film shot on a tight schedule in Dublin, features Bob Hoskins and Brenda Fricker. The film received good critical reviews, winning the *Sunday Independent* Film Award and was nominated for a BAFTA as the Best Short Film.

Stephen Brennan and Eamon Morrissey from *Eat the Peach*.

Helen Mirren and John Lynch in *Cal*, adapted from the novel by Bernard MacLaverty.

In 1985 a new company, Strongbow Film and Television Productions, was launched, headed by Oliver Maloney, John Kelleher and David Collins. They intended to avail of the Business Development Scheme introduced in the Finance Act 1984 whereby investors could gain tax relief for investments of between £500 and £25,000. Their ambitious package of Irish feature films and television series began with a feature film, *Eat the Peach*, directed by Peter Ormond. The company raised £1 million from individual and group investors, and further finance was received from the Irish Film Board and Channel Four.

*Eat the Peach* deals with the realisation of one man's dream – to build a motorcycle 'wall of death' in his own backyard. The unusual extension to his house provokes the hostility of his friends and neighbours. The idea for the film had come to director Ormond from a real life incident where a Co Longford man had built his own 'wall of death'. Shooting of the £1.7 million film took place at Allenwood, Wicklow, Meath and Dublin. Stephen Brennan and Eamonn Morrissey play the central characters with Niall Toibin, Catherine Byrne and Joe Lynch in supporting roles. The British actress, Sarah Miles, shot a cameo role for the film but it was edited from the final production. The film title, *Eat the Peach*, is taken from 'The Love-Song of J. Alfred Prufrock' by T. S. Eliot, in which the anti-hero asks himself, 'Do I Dare to Eat the Peach.' The film was distributed widely and was a box office hit in Ireland.

Strongbow Productions followed its success with a £2 million four-part television series, *When Reason Sleeps*.

In the mid 1980s radio and television personality, Mike Murphy, established New Irish Film Productions, for which he raised most of the £1.8 million budget for their first film, *The Fantasist*. His main role was to inspire confidence in projects and raise development capital. *The Fantasist* is a modern day thriller, based on the novel *Goosestep* by Patrick McGinley, under the direction of Robin Hardy. The film with Timothy Bottoms, Moira Harris, John Kavanagh and Liam O'Callaghan went into production in Dublin. There was ill feeling when the popular actor from the *Glenroe* television series, Mick Lally, replaced Cyril Cusack. The film did not live up to expectations and was roasted by the critics.

Another Irish film, *The End of the World Man*, directed by Bill Miskelly and produced by Marie Jackson, won two of the three awards in the children's section of the 1986 International Berlin Film Festival – the UNICEF Award and the Berlin Children's Jury Award. The citation for the first award stated that the film 'shows children in an accessible way that they can take action and influence social circumstances.'

The first film to go before the cameras in 1986 was *Rawhead X*, an Anglo-

Irish co-production by Paradise and Alpine Pictures. The £1 million horror film, directed by George Pavlow was co-produced by David Collins, Kevin Attew and Don Hawkins. Two Americans, David Dukes and Kelly Piper, took the leading roles with the strong supporting cast headed by Niall Toibin, Ronan Wilmot, Sheila Flitton and Derry Power. The film was shot on various locations in Co Wicklow. The story concerns a man who digs up a huge stone, which lay in a field for hundreds of years and releases a monster.

Bob Quinn's next production, *Budawanny*, was adapted from the novel *Súil le Breith*, by Connemara priest, Pádraic Standún. This low budget feature film concerns a priest who impregnates his housekeeper and the ramifications of the situation. Independent film-maker Quinn shot the film on Clare Island, off the Mayo coast, with Donal McCann and Margaret Fegan in the leading roles. Quinn did not invite any of the Irish critics to its first screening in Galway because he felt that film-making should be an art form, rather than a hype steeped business.

The communications course in the College of Commerce, Rathmines was responsible for turning out a number of young graduates who made impressive first films, including Siobhan Twomey and Fergus Tighe. Dubliner Twomey wrote and directed *Boom Babies* on a budget of £18,000 with assistance from the Irish Film Board, RTÉ and a private investor. The film, set in contemporary Dublin, parallels the lives of two young people from opposite sides of the city, Aisling Toibin and Andrew Connolly. They meet when Connolly and his mates steal her Humber on Dollymount Strand.

*Clash of the Ash*, Fergus Tighe's directorial debut, was filmed in his native Fermoy, Co Cork. The film, produced by Jane Grogan, charts the conflict of a Leaving Cert student and promising hurler, Liam Heffernan, 'as his search for identity in the confines of a small town leads to his disillusionment and ultimate departure'.

Other notable productions from young film-makers during the mid-eighties included Yellow Asylum's film of Samuel Beckett's, *Eh Joe*, directed by Alan Gilsenan and stars Tom Hickey, with the voice of Siobhan McKenna. Another Dublin-based company, City Vision, made an impressive short, *Sometime City*, directed by Joe Lee and Frank Deasy and produced by Hilary McLoughlin. It was well received by audiences and critics at festivals in London, Edinburgh, Cork and Dublin. City Vision made the breakthrough into feature films with *The Courier*, a thriller set against the drug scene in Dublin. The film stars Gabriel Byrne as the villain and two newcomers, Pádraig Ó Loinsigh and Cáit O'Riordan.

# 24

# FILM BOARD AXED

The first feature film to fully utilise the facilities of MTM Studio was an Irish thriller, *Taffin*, with Pierce Brosnan in the title role. He plays a professional debt collector who is recruited by a local community to prevent corrupt businessmen from building a chemical plant in the town. Francis Megahy directed the $5 million production in a variety of Wicklow and Dublin locations with a large Irish cast headed by Ray McAnally, Alison Doody, Jim Bartley, Alan Stanford and Jonathan Ryan. The film was co-produced with MGM and received substantial Irish investment.

By late 1987 Ireland was experiencing one of its busiest periods in over a decade of major film and television series in production or post-production. In Galway Joe Comerford was completing *Reefer and the Model*, his West Coast thriller. The film, produced by Lelia Doolin, was initiated with an Arts Council Script Award. Ian McElhinney plays a trawler captain who teams up with Carole Scanlan, Ray McBride and Sean Lawlor to rob a mobile bank. A critic at the Berlin Film Festival termed it an Irish western with undertones of Bonnie and Clyde. The film won the Europa Prize of £150,000 at the Barcelona Film Festival.

Many familiar Dublin landmarks feature in Jack Clayton's production of *The Lonely Passion of Judith Hearne*, based on the novel by Brian Moore and starring Bob Hoskins and Maggie Smith. Supporting roles were filled by Wendy Hiller, Marie Kean, Alan Devlin and Aine Ní Mhuirí. The setting of the original novel was transferred from Belfast to Dublin of the 1950s. Smith plays a lonely, Irish spinster who has taken to drinking and moves from boarding house to boarding house. In one she meets the single, middle-aged Hoskins and is attracted by his

*Above left*: Pierce Brosnan in *Taffin* from 1987.

*Above right*: Prunella Scales in *The Lonely Passion of Judith Hearne*.

*Right*: Doreen Hepburn and Barnard Hughes in Hugh Leonard's *Da*.

sophisticated manner. Her dependence on him proves to have tragic consequences.

In September five important productions began shooting: – *Da, Now I Know, Troubles, Echoes* and *The Dawning*. Dalkey, Co Dublin was the setting for a feature film based on Hugh Leonard's award-winning play, *Da*, and his autobiographical book *Home Before Night*. The film directed by Matt Clark had Martin Sheen and Barnard Hughes adopting 'Irish' accents to play father and son respectively. Three actors play Charlie the son: as a young boy by Hugh O'Connor, in his late teens by Karl Hayden and by Sheen as an adult. Following four weeks in Atlanta, Georgia, Strongbow Productions began location work in Dublin on *Now I Know* with Mathew Modine and Maeve Germaine. This humorous love story was written and directed by Robert Pappas.

James Mitchell's much publicised, *Troubles*, adapted from the novel by J. G. Farrell, began a shoot in Greystones, Co Wicklow and Killala, Co Mayo by the Irish company Little Bird. Following an initial delay and re-casting Ian Charleston, Ian Richardson and Emer Gillespie played the leading roles. Dunmore East, Co Waterford, was the principal location for a mini-series based on Maeve Binchy's best-selling novel, *Echoes*, with Geraldine James, Alison Doody and John Kavanagh. Jennifer Johnston's novel, *The Old Jest*, adapted for the screen by Moira Williams and re-titled *The Dawning* set in Co Wicklow in 1920 was filmed in counties Cork and Wicklow. The film stars Anthony Hopkins, Jean Simmons and Trevor Howard.

Following the phenomenal success of his first three films Neil Jordan went into production on *High Spirits* in late 1987. He filmed exteriors for this $12 million black comedy, based on his own screenplay, at Dromore Castle in Co Limerick. Interiors were filmed on an elaborate set of Castle Plunkett at Shepperton Studio. His international cast was headed by Peter O'Toole, Daryl Hannah, Beverly D'Angelo and Steve Guttenburg and from Ireland, Donal McCann, Liam Neeson, Ray McAnally and Tom Hickey. Singer Mary Coughlan made her acting debut. Derek Meddings who made Superman fly and created many of the effects in the James Bond films was in charge of the special effects. The film is set in Castle Plunkett, whose owner attracts American tourists by advertising ghosts and banshees but they get a rude awakening as they encounter many real ghosts. Jordan found the same reluctance as did John Boorman of encouraging Irish companies to invest in the film and had to raise finance in the United States.

For *We're No Angels* Jordan cast Robert de Niro, Sean Penn and Demi Moore in the leading roles. This was the first occasion in which Jordan did not initiate the project but directed a script by David Mamet. He filmed the remake of the Humphrey Bogart classic in Canada but it was badly received by the critics.

In June 1987 two government decisions were to have serious implications for the future of film-making in Ireland. The first move was an amendment to the 1987 Finance Bill by finance minister, Ray MacSharry, making provision for companies to obtain a tax write-off against profits for annual investments of up to £100,000 in Irish film production companies. These companies who had to be incorporated in Ireland and be tax residents here provided up to sixty per cent of the cost of a film by means of this incentive. The Taoiseach, Charles Haughey, announced that the Irish Film Board was being wound up and the Arts Council, who already had a statutory function to promote the arts, 'including the cinema,' would be responsible for future funding. There was widespread condemnation by native and foreign film-makers of the Board's abolition. Despite this setback a new breed of Irish film-makers continued to achieve international acclaim with an impressive list of high quality films.

1988 saw the directorial debut of two more Irish directors, Aisling Walsh and Jim Sheridan. Walsh, from Navan, studied at the National Film and Television School in London and from the time she first developed the original story for *Joyriders*, she hustled until she raised the finance from Granada Film Productions. The contemporary theme tells of a young battered wife, who deserts her children and runs away with a joyrider on a voyage of mutual self-discovery in Co Clare. Patricia Kerrigan and Andrew Connolly play the young couple and English actress, Billie Whitelaw plays a cameo role as a country and western singer working in a run-down hotel. Veteran character actor, David Kelly, steals the film as a farmer.

A project that obsessed producer Noel Pearson for many years was to bring the life of the disabled Dublin writer, Christy Brown, who could write and paint with his left foot, to the screen. While Jim Sheridan and Shane Connaughton were working on the script based on Christy's book, *My Left Foot*, Sheridan became desperate to direct it. He had never directed a film before, but Pearson had enough confidence in him to put him in charge of the £1.7 million film.

The central role is played by Daniel Day-Lewis who spent months in preparation and remained in character throughout the entire production, impressing everybody by his absorption in the part. Hugh O'Connor plays Christy as a boy, with Ray McAnally and Brenda Fricker as the parents. Other members of the cast include Ruth McCabe, Fiona Shaw, Éanna MacLiam and Cyril Cusack as Lord Castlewelland. The film intercuts flashbacks of his formative years with scenes at a stately home. *My Left Foot* was shot in seven

*Above*: Daniel Day-Lewis and Fiona Shaw in a scene from *My Left Foot*.

*Left*: Oscar-winner, Brenda Fricker, who played Christy Brown's mother in the film.

weeks in Ardmore Studios and the Bray area. Following its opening the film broke box office records and received rave reviews.

A coup for MTM was attracting *Three of a Kind*, the first major American network show to be filmed outside the United States. The series was made by the same team behind the successful *Hill Street Blues* and *Lou Grant*, starring Beau Bridges and Ian Ogilvy. It centres on the exploits of a trio of spies working from a high-class restaurant in the south of France. An entire French street was built in the studio for the proposed thirteen-part series. The first episode was to serve as a prototype that would be used to test how a full series would fare in the United States. Unfortunately the results were not encouraging and plans to make the series were scrapped.

Despite a take-over of MTM Enterprises by the British Television South Company, Ardmore was constantly in demand. The studio became the base for *The Real Charlotte*, a four-part mini-series, based on the novel by Sommerville and Ross. The series, with a three months shooting schedule, was produced by Gandon Productions with Tony Barry as director and Niall McCarthy as producer. Heading the strong Irish cast were Jeananne Crowley, Patrick Bergin, Sorcha Cusack and Aiden Grennell. Like *The Irish R. M.* the setting was the Irish countryside at the end of the nineteenth century. The studio was also used by Ronan O'Leary to shoot a television version of the successful stage play, *Fragments of Isabella*, with Gabrielle Reidy.

A form of film-making new to Ireland was animation and the American Company, Sullivan-Bluth was to introduce this industry to Dublin. In 1986, feeling dissatisfied with Hollywood, animated producer, Don Bluth, who had served his apprenticeship with Walt Disney, joined with financier Morris F. Sullivan and explored various options before settling in Dublin with IDA backing. They brought in Canadian and American animators and recruited 260 Irish, mostly graduates from the arts colleges, and ultimately hoped to increase this figure to 600. Steven Spielberg contacted Bluth to discuss working together and with Spielberg's support the company made *An American Tail* that was completed in the Dublin studio. The $9.3 million film tells of a mouse, who emigrates to America, became a smash hit at the American box office where it grossed over $50 million.

Their second feature was the $14 million, *The Land Before Time Began*, a Spielberg/Lucas presentation of a Don Blush film, produced entirely at the Dublin studio. The film secured a complete American distribution and made the number one spot at the US box office. The story, in marked contrast to the action-packed *An American Tail* set at the turn of the century, is set in prehistoric times and recounts the adventures of five young dinosaurs that embark on the adventure of a lifetime to find a hidden valley.

Soon Sullivan-Blush Ireland had tripled in size to become the largest animation studio in Europe. In 1988 the company secured a joint financing agreement of £40 million for three animated films with Goldcrest Films and Television. The studio completed their third feature, *All Dogs Go to Heaven*, featuring the voices of Burt Reynolds, Dom Deluise, Loni Anderson and singing to the music of Charles Strouse.

Work then got underway at MTM Studio on *Rock A Doodle* which combines live action and animation and was released in 1990. Voices include Glen Campbell, Phil Harris and Sandy Duncan. The constantly expanding company also planned to establish an entirely new division for television and commercial animation. The studio's principal aim − to make Ireland the world centre of classical animation − seemed well on target, but due to a combination of factors Sullivan-Blush was forced to close.

# 25

# OSCARS FOR IRELAND

From the beginning of 1989 a number of major films with top-line stars were announced to go into production in Ireland, but for a variety of reasons, chiefly financial, none came to fruition. Despite this set back a number of smaller productions, mainly indigenous, did go before the cameras.

Director Pat O'Connor returned from success abroad with *A Month in the Country* and *January Man* to direct the film version of William Trevor's novel, *Fools of Fortune*. Academy Award winning actress, Julie Christie, took the leading role with Mary Elizabeth Mastrantonio, Iain Glen, John Kavanagh and Rosaleen Linehan in support. Filming for the £2.5 million production was undertaken in Dublin, Mullingar, Aran Islands and Robertstown with interiors on sets at MTM Ardmore. This co-production between the international Polygram and the successful London-based Working Title, opens in the Black and Tan era of the 1920s and relates how the Troubles affect the Quinton family. Their tranquil life style is shattered with an outbreak of violence, the burning of their big house and the cold-blooded killing of some of the family.

Ronan O'Leary used MTM Studio for the entire six-day shoot of *Fragments of Isabelle* that he completed on a budget of £150,000. Gabrielle Reidy recreated her stage role of Isabelle Leitner, a survivor of Auschwitz. The one-woman monologue based on the best-selling Pulitzer nominated book was interspersed with documentary clips from the harrowing days of the Holocaust in Germany and Hungary. The story, which tells of Isabelle and her family's arrest and imprisonment in Auschwitz, was well received by both critics and the public. Within six months of its release it was in profit.

The Derry Film and Video Workshop was initially set up to counteract how life in the city was portrayed in the media. They produced an impressive feature film, *Hush-A-Bye Baby*, directed by Margo Harkin. In the film, a young Derry girl (Emer McCourt) discovers she is pregnant and the dilemma she faces. Her boyfriend is arrested and her letter to him is censored because it is written in Irish. The singer, Sinead O'Connor, appears in a cameo role.

The highly respected lighting cameraman, Thaddeus O'Sullivan, made his debut as a feature director with *December Bride*, from a screenplay by David Rudkin, based on the novel by Sam Hanna Bell, set in Co Down at the turn of the century. Principal locations for the film were Strangford Lough and Dublin with interiors again being filmed in Ardmore. The cast is headed by Donal McCann and Ciaran Hinds as Presbyterian farmer brothers who both fall in love with Saskia Reeves, a servant girl they employ. When she has a baby she refuses to disclose to the local rector which of the brothers is the father.

Within a week of collecting yet another award for *My Left Foot*, director Jim Sheridan and producer Noel Pearson went into production on their second film, a screen adaptation of John B. Keane's successful stage play, *The Field*. Ray McAnally was cast in the central role of Bull McCabe but sadly died only months before filming commenced. He was replaced by Richard Harris, making a welcome return to the screen, who went into character by growing a bushy white beard and having his teeth blackened. Other roles were played by John Hurt as the Bird, Tom Berenger as the American and Sean Bean as the Bull's son, Tadhg. They were supported by a strong team of Irish players headed by Frances Tomelty, Brenda Fricker, John Cowley, Sean McGinley and Eamon Keane.

The central theme in the film is the confrontation between the Bull and the American for possession of a field. Sheridan's screenplay greatly opened out the original plot, adding new characters and taking advantage of the misty beauty of Leenane in Co Galway, the location for the bulk of the winter shoot.

In the latter part of 1989, Ken Loach filmed *Hidden Agenda*, a political thriller set in Northern Ireland, under a cloak of secrecy in Dublin, Belfast and London. The film based on a screenplay by Jim Allen, deals with the murder of an American civil rights investigator in Belfast and the subsequent investigation that uncovers a web of conspiracy. The leading roles are played by Brad Dourif as the American, Frances McDormand as his colleague and Brian Cox as a detective.

Early in 1990 there was more good news for Sheridan when *My Left Foot* was nominated for five Academy Awards. They were Day-Lewis as Best Actor, Brenda Fricker for Best-Supporting Actress, Jim Sheridan for Best Director, Jim

*Above*: John Hurt, Richard Harris and Sean Bean in a scene from *The Field*.

*Right*: Nicole Kidman and Tom Cruise in *Far and Away*.

Sheridan and Shane Connaughton for the best adapted screenplay and, most significantly, it secured a place on the important short list of five for Best Picture of the Year. At the British Academy Film and Television Awards (BAFTA), a week before the Oscar ceremony Day-Lewis received the Best Actor Award and Ray McAnally won a posthumous award as Best Supporting Actor for his portrayal as Christy's father.

On 26 March at the 62nd Academy Awards in the Dorothy Chandler Pavilion, Los Angeles, Kevin Kline announced the nominees for Best Supporting Actress: Angelica Huston, Lena Olin, Julia Roberts, Dianne Wiest and Brenda Fricker. He opened the envelope to announce… Brenda Fricker. There was even better news for *My Left Foot* when Daniel Day-Lewis beat such formidable competition as Tom Cruise, Morgan Freeman, Robin Williams and Kenneth Branagh to win the Best Actor Award. In his acceptance speech he thanked Hugh O'Connor who plays the young Christy and Christy Brown himself. This was a remarkable achievement for the £1.7 million budget film, which was to receive an enormous box office boost with worldwide receipts estimated at £20 million. The two Oscar winners were given a civic reception on their return to Dublin.

Following the amazing success of their first film, Sheridan and Pearson were approached by all the major companies to sign contracts. They finally agreed a major contract with Universal under which they would produce a minimum of two films over the next three years for the studio, with an option to make five films in that period. Part of the agreement would be a fund to develop 'an Irish craft industry to train directors, writers and cinematographers in a series of seminars.'

Due to the success of *My Left Foot*, postproduction on *The Field* was delayed and the world premiere in Dublin was moved back to September. *The Field* opened to rave reviews and broke box office records at Irish cinemas with Richard Harris receiving an Oscar nomination for his performance. Pearson and Sheridan were onto another winner.

Neil Jordan returned to his hometown of Bray to film his sixth film, *The Miracle*. The film, with a budget of £2.5 million, was based on another of his screenplays and starred Beverly D'Angelo and introduced two newcomers, Niall Byrne and Lorraine Pilkington. The drama set in summertime Bray tells the story of two teenagers, Jimmy and Rose. Jimmy becomes obsessed with Renée, a blonde American, who is appearing in a musical. It later transpires that she is his mother whom he thought was dead. The film-makers transformed Bray's seafront with pink railings along the prom, fairy lights and new facades for cafes, hotels and amusement arcades. The tourist season commenced early with a protracted stay by Fossetts Circus and a carnival. Sightseers were treated to the sight of a lion in the sea and elephants on the prom. Hundreds of locals were hired as extras and children were paid for attending the circus. Director of photography, Philippe Rousselot, magnificently captured the atmosphere of the seaside town.

While the final 'cut' was being called on *The Miracle*, a major film was going before the cameras in Dublin. It was by the first of a new breed of young Irish writers, Roddy Doyle, to have their work adapted for the screen. British director, Alan Parker, whose hit films include *Midnight Express, Bugsy Malone* and *Mississippi Burning*, was chosen to direct *The Commitments* based on Doyle's novel, set in the fictional north Dublin suburb of Barrytown. The film chronicles the efforts of a group of young working class Dubliners to form a soul band. Parker conducted an open audition in Dublin's Mansion House and invited people between 18 to 25 who could sing and play instruments to attend. Over 3,000 people were auditioned in exhaustive sessions before Parker finally chose his mainly unknown cast as members of the Irish soul band. They were Andrew Strong, Johnny Murphy, Michael Aherne, Dave Finnegan, Dick Massey, Felim Gormley, Robert Arkins, Bronagh Gallagher, Ken McCusker, Maria Doyle Kennedy, Angeline Ball and Glen Hansard. Colm Meaney plays the father of the Rabbitte family.

As with his earlier film, *Fame*, Parker attempted to capture the infectious energy of a group of unknowns in their efforts to achieve success. Manager Jimmy Rabbitte assembles the band called The Commitments but as they begin to taste success tensions flare amongst the motley group. Roddy Doyle collaborated on the witty screenplay with Dick Clement and Ian La Frenais. The film, shot in a variety of unglamorous locations throughout the city, captured perfectly their working class environment. *The Commitments* won four BAFTA Awards including Best Film, Best Director and Best Adapted Screenplay. Gerry Hambling won a Best Film Editing nomination at the Oscars. The film was widely acclaimed and broke records at the Irish box office.

*The Snapper* was the second of Roddy Doyle's books based on the life of the Rabbittes in Barrytown, to be brought to the screen. In contrast to *The Commitments'* big budget and high profile, *The Snapper* was filmed for Channel 4's series of new films for a television screening. Due to the amazing critical reception the film received it was given a cinema release and won many plaudits for Colm Meaney as the father and Tina Kelleher as his pregnant daughter.

Director Stephen Frears shot interior scenes for the production on stages at

Ardmore Studios, with location work in Darndale and Kilbarrack in north Dublin. Meaney was again in form as the father whose daughter Sharon announces her pregnancy but will not reveal the identity of the father. Ruth McCabe and Patrick Laffin play other leading roles with a group of young unknowns playing the younger members of the Rabbitte family.

The last in the Barrytown trilogy to be filmed was *The Van*. In 1991 the book was short-listed for the prestigious Booker Prize. Colm Meaney again plays the leading role as Bimbo who is made redundant. He goes into partnership with his pal Larry and buys a chipper van, hoping to make a killing during the World Cup. Comedian Brendan O'Carroll, Ger Ryan and Donal O'Kelly co-starred. Stephen Frears again directed the film in the north Dublin estate of Kilbarrack.

By the end of the year technical crews were stretched to the limit with three other feature films going into production in Dublin. *Hear My Song*, directed by Peter Chelsom, based on the life of the larger-than-life singer, Joseph Locke, was a Limelight/Windmill Lane Production with a £2 million budget. American character actor, Ned Beatty, plays the elder Locke, with Terry Mulligan as the younger man. Others in the cast include David McCallum, Adrian Dunbar and Shirley Anne Field.

*Fatal Inheritance* tells of an American heir-hunter who arrives in Ireland to trace the sole heir to a $3 million fortune of a deceased relative in America. The suspense love story, set in Northern Ireland, was shot around Skerries, Rush and Laytown, Co Meath. The film stars Kevin Davies, who also wrote the script, Emma Samms, David McCallum and Irish actors, Darragh Kelly, Anna Manahan and Jim Bartley.

Craftsmen constructed another entire village above Dunquin on the Dingle Peninsula in Co Kerry for the $40 million production *Far and Away*. Oscar winning director, Ron Howard directed the film, which starred Tom Cruise and Nicole Kidman and featured many Irish actors including Colm Meaney, Cyril Cusack and Niall Toibin. For the first time since *Ryan's Daughter* local people were recruited for parts as villagers. There was much amusement amongst the locals on hearing Cruise's Irish accent. Strict rules applied to extras and others involved in the production and they were forbidden to approach or speak to Tom Cruise, who was surrounded by minders. Anybody infringing the rules would be instantly dismissed.

Once again the film-makers took over Killruddery House in Bray, Co Wicklow and transformed it into the stately home of the Kidman character. The other main Irish locations were Shrewsbury Road, Fitzwilliam Square and the Temple Bar area of Dublin where an elaborate Boston street set was constructed.

Roddy Doyle's Barrytown trilogy on the big screen: *The Commitments*, *The Snapper* and *The Van*.

800 extras were employed to portray Irish emigrants arriving in New York on a large set constructed beside the Guinness Brewery. The American sequence of the film was shot in Montana where the newcomers race to stake their claim. Cruise plays Joseph Donnell, a young Connemara man who sets out in 1893 to avenge the death of his father, a tenant farmer, who has fallen victim to a landlord and is forced to immigrate to America. Kidman played the daughter of the big house who falls in love with Cruise.

Redhills, Co Cavan, was the setting for *The Playboys,* an entertaining drama set in 1950s' rural Ireland, about the impact of the arrival of a travelling theatre group on a small community. The middle-aged sergeant becomes infuriated when a strolling player falls in love with an unmarried mother. The film, from a screenplay by Shane Connaughton, was directed by Gillies MacKinnon. Albert Finney plays the sergeant, Aidan Quinn the young actor, Robin Wright the unmarried mother and Milo O'Shea the owner of the travelling theatre.

With mediocre reviews for *High Spirits, We're No Angels* and *The Miracle,* Neil Jordan turned to a low budget film based on his original screenplay. In Ireland Jordan found great difficulty in raising the budget for *The Crying Game,* originally titled *The Soldier's Wife.* Despite a short stint of location work in Ireland, with a carnival sequence in Bettystown, Co Meath, the bulk of the production was shot in England. He again teamed up with Stephen Rea who plays Fergus, an IRA man involved in kidnapping Jody, a British soldier and holding him hostage. An understanding develops between the two men and when Jody is killed, Fergus goes to London to console his wife, Dil. Fergus falls in love with her only to discover that Dil is a man. Adrian Dunbar, Miranda Richardson, Jaye Davidson and Forest Whittaker co-star. Excellent marketing and the surprise shock revelation were the drawing factors of the film in America where it grossed over $63 million at the box office. The film was nominated for six Academy Awards and Jordan won an Oscar for Best Original Screenplay.

Donald Sutherland and Julie Christie were reunited for starring roles in *The Railway Station Man,* based on the novel by Jennifer Johnston. The quirky love story filmed in Donegal, also stars John Lynch and was directed by Michael Whyte.

*Into the West,* from a screenplay by Jim Sheridan, tells the tale of two boys Ossie and Tito, who steal a white horse, Tír na nÓg, after it has been acquired by a rich, unscrupulous horse stud owner. With his traveller friends Kathleen and Barreller, the children's father, Papa Riley, sets off after the boys as they head into the west. The film directed by Mike Newell, on a £5 million budget, stars Gabriel Byrne as Papa Riley and Ellen Barkin as Kathleen. Following a nationwide search, two young boys were cast in the main roles. Ossie is played by six-year-old Ciaran Fitzgerald and Tito by eleven-year-old, Ruaidhrí Conroy. Other leading roles are played by David Kelly, Brendan Gleeson and Colm Meaney. The film was shot on location over a ten-week period in Wicklow, Dublin, Portarlington and Dog's Bay, near Roundstone in Co Galway. Some tricks of the trade were employed during filming, with six identical white horses, three Irish and three French, being used as Tír na nÓg. For the riding sequences a jockey frequently replaced the boys with a beanbag strapped to his back. The film was an instant success in Ireland where it took over £1 million at the box office.

*High Boot Benny* saw a return of writer/director Joe Comerford with his first production since *Reefer and the Model*. The cast is headed by Marc O'Shea, Frances Tomelty as the school's Protestant matron and Alan Devlin the ex-priest. The film centres on Benny, a seventeen-year-old delinquent, who finds refuge in a radical school run by an ex-priest and matron on the southern side of the Irish border. When the body of a police informer is discovered in the school, suspicion falls on all three. The film is a gripping, political and psychological drama.

# 26

# FILM-MAKING BOOM

I n 1993 there was a marked improvement with ten feature films going into production in Ireland. Several positive factors contributed to this upsurge in the industry.

Neil Jordan winning an Oscar for Best Original Screenplay for *The Crying Game*, again focused attention on Ireland's small but talented band of film-makers. An equally significant factor was the appointment of the Labour TD, Michael D. Higgins, as the first Minister for Arts, Culture and the Gaeltacht. The minister immediately realised that given the correct infrastructure there was potential for growth in this sector. He re-established the Irish Film Board with headquarters in Galway. Lelia Doolan was appointed chairman and Rod Stoneman its chief executive. The board was allocated a budget of £10 million for development and production over a five-year period. The department had a two-pronged strategy of building the skills and resources of the industry through attracting large budget foreign films, which encouraged the indigenous industry through development grants from the Film Board. The Film Board did not itself produce films, but provided loans and equity investments to independent Irish film-makers to assist them in the development of production of between six and eight Irish films per year. It could also co-produce with other agencies to improve the marketing, sales and distribution of Irish films, and to promote training and development in all areas of film-making. Another function of the board was to raise public awareness of the cultural, social and economic benefits of a vibrant film-making industry in Ireland, making full use of Irish talents, creative and technical.

With the high profile and good financial return from film production, Section 35 of the Finance Act introduced in 1983, became an attractive proposition for investors. A private investor could invest up to £25,000 annually in an approved film project with tax relief available at the top rate of the investment, provided a substantial part of the work involved in the making of the production must be undertaken in Ireland. The minister must also certify the film company as qualifying for the purposes of tax relief. The investment must be for a minimum of three years, except in the case of low budget productions or larger corporate investors. Investors in productions with a budget of less than £1 million could withdraw after a year without any clawback of tax relief, as can corporate investors who have invested more than £1 million into a qualifying film.

Jim Sheridan's next film to go into production in 1993, *In the Name of the Father*, was based on Gerry Conlon's book, *Proved Innocent*. The film centres on the experience of a young Belfast man, Gerry Conlon, who along with friends and family members, was wrongly convicted by British courts in 1975 for the terrorist bombing of two pubs in Guilford. The film recalls the relationship between Gerry and his father Guiseppe, played by Daniel Day-Lewis and Pete Postlethwaite respectively. Emma Thompson co-stars as lawyer, Gareth Pierce, and singer Don Baker makes his screen debut as an IRA man. Others in the cast include John Lynch, Corin Redgrave, Gerard McSorley and Joanna Irvine.

The bulk of the filming took place in Kilmainham Jail with Ringsend and Sheriff Street in Dublin doubling as working class Belfast. Jim Sheridan co-wrote the screenplay with New York-based Irish writer Terry George. Daniel Day-Lewis approached the role of Conlon with an intense level of preparation, including spending two days and nights in a cell, submitting himself to twelve hours of interrogation by a team of real detectives, to help perfect his Belfast accent.

On its release, *In the Name of the Father* became embroiled in a controversy over questions of accuracy. The film was a massive box office hit in Ireland, taking over £2.5 million. An even greater achievement was receiving seven Oscar nominations for Best Picture, Best Director, Best Actor, Best Supporting Actress, Best Adapted Screenplay and Best Editing, but the film lost out to *Schlindler's List*, which swept the boards.

Another indigenous film, *Broken Harvest*, was the first venture of director, writer and executive producer, Maurice O'Callaghan. It took him ten years to raise the £1.25 million budget to bring his bitter-sweet story about the effects of the War of Independence, the Civil War, emigration and politics on a small Cork community, to the scene. The film shown in flashbacks records the memories of

Pete Postlethwaite and Daniel Day-Lewis in Jim Sheridan's *In the Name of the Father*.

Julia Brendler and Ruaidhrí Conroy in *Moondance*.

Hugh Grant in *An Awfully Big Adventure*.

Jimmy O'Leary's 1950s' rural childhood, darkened by the discovery that his father, a hero of the War of Independence, is locked into a thirty year feud with another man dating back to the Civil War. The story also shifts to present day New York. The screenplay was written by solicitor and part-time actor, Maurice O'Callaghan and his sister Kate and was produced by their brother, Gerry. The film was shot over a six-week period in West Cork. The leading roles are played by Marian Quinn as Catherine, Colin Lane, Darren McHugh and Niall O'Brien. The film was completely financed by Irish money with O'Callaghan sinking a good deal of his own capital into the production and raised finance under Section 35. *Broken Harvest* had its first screening during the Dublin Film Festival and received generally encouraging reviews.

Shooting simultaneously in West Cork was *War of the Buttons*. This film, adapted by Colin Welland from a Louis Pergaud novel and filmed by Yves Robert in 1962 in a French setting, was transferred to a rural Irish setting. Producer David Puttnam, who has a house in West Cork, chose locations within a short radius of his base including Skibbereen, Union Hall and Castletownsend. Casting directors, Ros and John Hubbard, conducted a wide search for child actors before recruiting their troop of unknown youngsters led by Gregg Fitzgerald and John Coffey, with Eveanna Ryan as the tomboy caught in the middle. The adult stars are Colm Meaney as Geronimo's father, Johnny Murphy the local postman and Liam Cunningham as the teacher. *War of the Buttons* is an engaging yarn directed by John Roberts, who won an Oscar for his student film, *This Boy's Story*. The plot of *War of the Buttons* tells of children from two small towns located on either side of an inlet in West Cork who form small armies and battle against each other for supremacy. Their token of victory: the removal of an opponent's buttons and shoe laces; hence the title. The showdown with the children marching into battle in cardboard armour with dustbin lids is set in a Gothic ruin overlooking Rosscarbery Bay. Release of the film was delayed following a court injunction by parents of one of the children extras, who objected to him appearing briefly with his bottom bare in one of the skirmishes between the groups. The film took £500,000 at the Irish box office.

Also in production that summer was *Widow's Peak*, directed by John Irvin. Originally Hugh Leonard had written the screenplay of the film as a vehicle for actress Maureen O'Sullivan and her daughter, Mia Farrow, but it took a decade to get the project into production with Joan Plowright playing the part intended for O'Sullivan. This comedy whodunnit is set in rural Ireland of the 1920s, known as Widow's Peak because it is ruled by women, almost all of them widows. Mia Farrow plays a spinster, Miss O'Hare, who feels that her position within the community is threatened by the arrival of a beautiful rich American, Edwina. Soon the ladies of Widow's Peak have murder on their mind. Adrian Dunbar and James Broadbent take the main male leads. The £14.5 million budget film was mainly shot around the Blessington Lakes in Co Wicklow and picturesque Inishtioge, Co Kilkenny. Locals in both venues were employed as extras.

Realising the potential of film, Wicklow Film Commission was established to promote the county as a film base and to find suitable locations, arrange street closures and generally to facilitate the requirements of film-makers. The county was chosen as one of the locations for *Moondance*, a rite-of-passage drama based on *The White Hare* by Francis Stuart. The film directed by Dagmar Hirtz for Little Bird Productions under co-producers James Mitchell and Jonathan Cavendish also used locations in West Cork and Dublin. The plot relates how two brothers, 21-year Patrick and 14-year-old Dominic live an idyllic lifestyle in a dilapidated country house in West Cork. They spend their time fishing and catching rabbits. Their only regular visitor is their Aunt Dorothy, but with the arrival of a pretty German girl, Anya, they both develop a romantic attachment to her and their emotional lives descend into confusion and turmoil. Ian Shaw and Ruaidhrí Conroy play the brothers, with Julia Brendler as Anya. Other roles are taken by Marianne Faithful as the mother, and comedian Brendan Grace as the publican. Van Morrison provides the music.

Controversial American director, John Sayles, adapted *The Secret of Roan Inish*, from the book *The Secret of Ron Mor Skerry* by Rosalie K. Fry, a favourite Celtic children's story for the screen. He filmed with Oscar-winning cinematographer, Haskell Wexler, entirely on location in Donegal over the summer months, building a cottage beside the beach. The film set in the late 1940s Ireland has an unemployed widower sending his young daughter, Fiona, to live with her grandparents in a small fishing village in Donegal. Her grandfather tells Fiona the story of how, years earlier, her baby brother, Jamie, was swept out to sea in his cradle, and Fiona becomes obsessed with finding the boy. Her search begins on the nearby island of Roan Inish (seal-island), where she finds herself on the trail of a mysterious half-human sea creature called the Selkie.

Mick Lally and Eileen Colgan play the grandparents and Jeni Courtney, the young girl. Others in the cast include Richard Sheridan, John Lynch, Cillian Byrne and Susan Lynch. Lally summed up his experience of working on the film. 'It was a children's film made by adults.' He felt it a most enjoyable experience, as Sayles was a pleasant character and his temperament perpetrated down through everybody working on the crew. The beautifully conceived family film came in under-budget and the surplus was divided between cast and crew.

In November that year, Bray-born director, Paddy Breathnach, who served his apprenticeship with the award-winning short, *A Stone of the Heart*, went into production with *Ailsa*, his first feature film. The film, adapted by Joseph O'Connor, from his own short story, was produced by Ed Guiney on a budget of £200,000. Newcomer Brendan Coyle plays the main role of Myles, a Dublin man, who lives an uneventful life with his girlfriend until he discovers the body of his landlord in the house. The tragedy makes a deep impression on him. A beautiful American woman who moves into the flat beneath his, arouses his curiosity. The atmospheric psychodrama charts his dark journey into the heart of obsession. The photography of Cian de Buitléar captures the starkness of the decaying Georgian house. Other roles are played by Andrea Irvine, Gary Lydon, O. Z. Whitehead and Juliette Gruber. The film was critically acclaimed and won the prestigious first prize of £250,000, towards their next project, at the San Sebastian Film Festival.

The incentives of filming in Ireland were to attract *An Awfully Big Adventure* to be shot entirely in Dublin, although the story line is set in Liverpool of the 1950s. The main locations were the Olympia Theatre, Henrietta Street, the docks and a football pitch in Bray. The film is based on the Beryl Bainbridge novel, which was nominated for the Booker Prize in 1990. Despite its £3 million budget, the production was able to gather a formidable cast headed by Alan Rickman, Hugh Grant, Peter Firth and Prunella Scales. Grant and director Mike Newell, who had previously directed *Into the West*, were at the time enjoying a major box office success in America with the comedy, *Four Weddings and a Funeral*. The central character in *An Awfully Big Adventure* is Stella, a rebellious seventeen-year-old who gets a job as an assistant stage manager on *Peter Pan* at a Liverpool repertory theatre, where she becomes infatuated with the gay actor-manager and falls in love with the actor playing Captain Hook. Georgina Coates made her film debut as Stella.

# 27

# BRAVEHEART

In 1994, following a meeting with Morgan O'Sullivan and Minister for the Arts, Michael D. Higgins, actor Mel Gibson announced that production on his $53 million film, *Braveheart*, scheduled to be filmed entirely on location in Scotland would be, for the most part, made in Ireland instead. Six weeks of filming had already taken place in Glen Nevis, near Fort William, when Gibson switched the entire production to Ireland. One of the attractions for Gibson was that 1,500 members of the defence forces would be made available to him for the large-scale battle scenes. There was outrage in Scotland, particularly as the subject matter of the film, William Wallace, was a thirteenth-century Scottish rebel, who defied King Edward Longshanks. The minister also secured specific staffing requirements including the creation of twelve traineeships to work on different aspects of the production.

Ten million pounds was raised from Irish investors under Section 35 of the Finance Act towards the budget. Mel Gibson had the multiple roles of director, co-producer and starring as Wallace. Originally Gibson had offered the directorial job to Terry Gilliam. FCA members from around the country gathered at the Curragh Camp where they were based. They were broken into groups of fifty men in thirty platoons under the command of officers. Each morning in military fashion the troops moved from marquee to marquee, from costumes to make-up to hair as they dressed as members of the Scottish or English armies. The soldiers underwent strenuous training in hand-to-hand combat, archery and marching. For most of the shoot they worked with the second unit. The battle scenes were an opportunity for local rivalries between FCA units to be settled.

Gibson, his face coated in woad, urged the troops on through a megaphone. The resulting combat scenes are brutal and magnificently choreographed and edited.

Gibson transformed castles and landscapes into Scottish locations. Trim Castle became Stirling Castle and the bloody battles were re-enacted at the Curragh and the Sally Gap/Manor Kilbride area. Interior castle sets were constructed on enormous stages in Ardmore Studios. The production team worked from July to October and along with the soldiers, hundreds of extras were employed. Other leading roles are played by Patrick McGoohan as King Edward I, Sophie Marceau as Princess Isabelle and Catherine McCormack as Murron. A strong force of Irish actors have leading roles including Brendan Gleeson, Sean McGinley, David O'Hara, Peter Hanly, John Kavanagh, Gerard McSorley and Niall O'Brien. The critics were overwhelming in their praise for the film and the battle scenes were regarded as being some of the most realistic ever filmed. *Braveheart* was nominated for ten Academy Awards and ended up winning five including Best Film and Best Director Award for Gibson.

*Frankie Starlight* was producer Noel Pearson's first production since *The Field*. The £4 million film was based on Chet Raymo's novel, *The Dork from Cork*, with a screenplay written by Raymo, Ronan O'Leary and Michael Lindsay-Hogg. Director Lindsay-Hogg filmed the drama in Dublin, Cork, Kildare and Kingsville, Texas.

Henrietta Street in Dublin again features as one of the main locations. The story, stretching from the end of World War II to the mid-1980s is told by Frankie, a dwarf who recounts his mother, Bernadette's flight from France during the war. She stows away on an American troopship but is discovered and put ashore at Cork where she gives birth to Frankie. She has an affair with a customs officer that is to play an important part in both her and Frankie's life. Anne Parillaud plays the young woman, with Matt Dillon and Gabriel Byrne as her lovers. Dublin artist Corbin Walker makes his debut as Frankie and Alan Pentony as the boy.

*Words Upon the Window Pane* was an ambitious undertaking for first-time director, Mary McGuckian. She had written the screenplay but it was at Pat O'Connor's suggestion that she became director. It took her three years to get the film into production and raise the $3 million budget. Funding came from a number of sources in Europe, which meant the production had to utilise facilities in numerous locations. A complicated shooting schedule was arranged with exteriors filmed in Dublin at some popular venues including Trinity College, Dublin Castle and Henrietta Street and interiors at a studio in Luxembourg. Post-production was completed in Germany and England. The film was an

*Left*: Mel Gibson and FCA troops prepare to do battle in *Braveheart*. The film was originally to have been made in Scotland.

*Below left*: Victoria Smurfit in her screen debut in *The Run of the Country* from 1995.

*Below right*: Albert Finney as Alfie Byrne in *A Man of No Importance* from 1994.

adaptation of W. B. Yeats' short play of the same name. It recounted the passionate lives of Jonathan Swift and his two lovers, Stella and Vanessa, which evolves at a séance in a drawing room in Dublin in which Swift's secret wife, Stella lived and died 200 years previously. A quest begins to uncover the identity of the disturbed spirits in order to put them to rest. Mary McGuckian gathered an impressive cast of international stars including Geraldine Chaplin, Geraldine James, Ian Richardson, Gemma Craven, John Lynch, Bríd Brennan, Donal Donnelly, and Jim Sheridan as Swift. Niall Byrne's music provided the appropriate dramatic balance.

*A Man of No Importance* is an enjoyable film set in Dublin of the early 1960s and directed by Suri Krishnama. Albert Finney plays Alfie Byrne, a Dublin bus conductor, an amateur theatre producer and a raconteur of the works of Oscar Wilde. Alfie lives with his sister Lily and enchants his passengers by reciting poetry to them. His passengers appear as cast members in his production of *Salome* as Alfie learns about life and himself. Barry Devlin's witty script quotes liberally from Wilde. A strong cast headed by Brenda Fricker, Michael Gambon, Tara Fitzgerald and Rufus Sewell, supports Finney. The film was shot over a five-week period on a £2 million budget by Little Bird Productions.

Within months, Albert Finney was back in Ireland filming *The Run of the Country*. On this occasion it was back to Co Cavan for his second role as a sergeant in a rural drama by Shane Connaughton, based on his novel, *A Border Station*. Victoria Smurfit makes her screen debut as Annagh, a Protestant girl, and Matt Keeslar plays Finney's son. The story centres on eighteen-year-old Danny, whose mother has recently died. Danny rebels against his father, the local sergeant, but falls in love with a Protestant girl. The film touches on many issues from politics and religion to drink and emigration. In conjunction with the film, Connaughton kept a diary on the progress of the film which was published in book form as *A Border Diary*.

Maeve Binchy is one of Ireland's most successful and popular writers. Her best-selling book, *Circle of Friends*, a coming-of-age story, was adapted for the screen by Andrew Davies and directed by Pat O'Connor. This was O'Connor's first film in Ireland since directing William Trevor's *Fools of Fortune*. The Binchy novel is set in Ireland in 1957 and follows the romantic entanglements of three girls removed from the confines of village life when they go to university in Dublin. A trio of newcomers Minnie Driver, Saffron Burrowes and Geraldine O'Rawe play the girls. Hollywood heart-throb, Chris O'Donnell, and Colin Firth provide the romantic interest. Many prominent Irish actors including Mick Lally, Tony Doyle, John Kavanagh and Tom Hickey play character parts. The film was shot in Kilkenny with the attractive village of Inistioge undergoing a transformation and Kilkenny city doubling as Dublin. The $9 million budget film did exceptionally well at the American box office and remained in the top ten charts for many weeks.

Another indigenous film to go before the cameras was *Korea*, which saw the return of Cathal Black to feature films after an absence of ten years following his highly acclaimed *Pigs* and *Our Boys*. The film, based on a John McGahern short story, was filmed in Leitrim and Dublin, on a low budget, raised from a range of sources in Europe. The main roles are played by Donal Donnelly, Vass Anderson and two newcomers, Andrew Scott and Fiona Molony. The story, set in a Co Cavan village in 1952, tells of Eamon Doyle spending his last summer with his father, John, fishing in the lake. Luke Moran, son of Ben, is killed in Korea, and his body is returned to the village for burial in a lakeside cemetery. When Eamon falls in love with Una Moran, his father feels betrayed, as he has been an archenemy of Ben Moran since the Civil War. The film won many awards including Special Jury Prize for Best Film at the Amiens Film Festival in France.

*Undercurrent*, shot on a shoestring budget, over a two-year period, was the first feature film for Brian O'Flaherty. The film, a thriller set in contemporary Dublin, features a diverse group of characters. When the daughter of a prominent politician disappears, two cynical detectives are assigned to the case. The cast includes Owen Roe, Stanley Townsend, Tina Kelleher, Orla Charlton, Ali White and Liam Cunningham.

# MICHAEL COLLINS

The first production to be filmed in 1995 was *Nothing Personal* originally called *All Our Fault*. The film for Little Bird in association with Film Four and British Screen was scripted by Daniel Mornin from his novel *All Our Fault* and directed by Thaddeus O'Sullivan. The leading roles were taken by Ian Hart, John Lynch, Michael Gambon, Gerard McSorley, Maria Doyle Kennedy and James Frain. The film-makers returned to Ringsend to once more transform its red-bricked terraced streets into the Belfast of 1972 during a ceasefire as loyalists and IRA gangs attempt to provoke each other into breaking the truce. The film follows a squad of loyalist paramilitaries led by war-weary Kenny and his psychopathic accomplice, Ginger. Tommy, a young teenager, impressed by the power and violence is invited by Kenny to go on patrol. This becomes a baptism of fire as the gang torture an innocent Catholic, who Kenny discovers was a childhood friend. Locals in Ringsend watched as pro-British and anti-Republican slogans were sprayed on gable-ends and steps and lamp posts were painted red, white and blue. Nightly buses and cars were burnt out during mock riots.

Film-makers constructed a wooden flyover in the suburb of Fettercairn in Tallaght, Co Dublin for *The Disappearance of Finbar*. On completion of the Irish segment the cast and crew moved to Lapland and Stockholm for further location work. The film, a co-production between City First Productions, Samson Films and Victoria Films, was adapted by Dermot Bolger and Sue Clayton from the novel by Carl Lombard, originally titled *The Disappearance of Rory Brophy*. The film tells of eighteen-year-old Finbar who jumps off a flyover bridge in Dublin and disappears. No body is found and his best friend, Danny, reluctantly embarks

Michael Gambon, Ian Hart and Gary Lydon in *Nothing Personal*. The film was shot in Ringsend, Dublin which was transformed into Belfast in 1972.

Luke Griffin in *The Disappearance of Finbar*, which involved a mythical journey across Europe.

Jared Leto in the bigscreen version of Ferdia Mac Anna's novel, *The Last of the High Kings*, which was filmed in the north Dublin village of Howth.

on a journey to try and discover the truth behind Finbar's disappearance that brings him on a mythical journey across Europe to Scandinavia. In a tango hall at the end of the world, Danny learns about what holds people together and what tears them apart. Jonathan Rhys-Myers, Luke Griffin, Fanny Risberg and Sean McGinley star in the film, which was directed by Sue Clayton.

For his fifth film, *Driftwood*, director Ronan O'Leary assembled his cast of James Spader, Anne Brochet and Barry McGovern, for a week's rehearsal before shooting commenced. O'Leary co-wrote the screenplay with Richard Wearing and described the film as 'an unnerving love story of obsessive and possessive love, and a Polanski-esque adaptation of the female psyche'. The psychological thriller with a $5 million budget, was shot on the Aran Islands in March with interiors at Ardmore Studios. Rob Lowe was originally mentioned as the male lead, then William Defoe, but finally James Spader was cast as a mysterious stranger who arrives on an island and encounters a lonely French woman.

Writer-director, Gerry Stembridge made his film debut with *Guiltrip*, set in a midlands garrison town and shot on location in Maynooth, Co Kildare. Stembridge and producer Ed Guiney made the film on a modest budget of £850,000, which they experienced difficulty in raising due to its subject matter. The Irish-French-Italian co-production told of 'a fatal day in the life of a young Irish couple, with an army corporal applying army life discipline to his quiet wife'. Through a series of flashbacks we witness how each of the main characters has spent the previous 24 hours. Along with Stembridge, lighting cameraman Eugene O'Conn and film editor Mary Finlay, also made their feature film debuts on *Guiltrip*. In the gritty, topical drama Stembridge draws brilliant performances from Andrew Connolly as the corporal and Jasmine Russell as his long-suffering wife. They are superbly supported by Michelle Houlden, Pauline McLynn and Peter Hanly. The film won awards at the International Film Festival at Amiens in France for Best Film, Best Actor (Connolly) and Best Actress (Russell) and at Thessalonika in Greece for Best Screenplay (Stembridge). The film won widespread critical acclaim and Stembridge was acknowledged as a major force in Irish film.

The population of Ballycotton, Co Cork was overjoyed with the news that *Divine Rapture*, a big budget film, starring Marlon Brando, Johnny Depp and Debra Winger was to be shot in their area over the summer months. Before filming commenced the production was involved in controversy when the Bishop of Cloyne, Dr John Magee, refused permission for any scenes to be shot in the local Catholic church. Undeterred, the film crew, under director Thom Eberhardt, moved into Ballycotton and filming commenced. When financial backing from the United States was not forthcoming the producers were forced to halt filming. Following a period of confusion the production was finally wound up and the film was never completed.

Another beneficiary of the enormous increase in film-making was Ardmore Studios in Bray. Chief executive, Kevin Moriarity, was particularly pleased with the development as many major television series were based at the studio including *The Family*, *The Old Curiosity Shop*, *Scarlett*, *Kidnapped* and *Jake's Progress*. Elaborate interior and exterior sets were constructed to accommodate the individual productions.

An adaptation of Daniel Defoe's romantic novel, *Moll Flanders*, was based at Ardmore, with location shooting at Dublin Castle, Foster Place, Old Conna, Powerscourt and Bantry House, Co Cork. An original tall ship was anchored off the Wicklow coast at Brittas Bay and at Wicklow Harbour. A brothel sequence was filmed in Iveagh House in Dublin. The $14.5 million production, written and directed by Pen Denshan, starred Robin Wright, Morgan Freeman, Stockard Channing, Geraldine James, John Lynch, Brenda Fricker and Jim Sheridan. *Moll Flanders*, set in the eighteenth century, tells the tale of Moll, daughter of an unknown father and a prostitute, who was hanged for thievery.

Shooting simultaneously in Dublin on a modest budget was *Snakes and Ladders*, written and directed by Trish McAdam. The comedy centres on Jean and Kate, partners in a comic street performance, who share a room and an attraction for a musician. The film stars Pam Boyd, Gina Moxley, Sean Hughes, Rosaleen Linehan and Paudge Behan. Following the Dublin shoot the unit spend a week in Berlin.

*My Friend Joe*, based on a screenplay by David Howard and Declan Hughes, was also shot on location in south Dublin. The family film directed by Chris Bould, tells of two children each of whom dreams of belonging to the other's world. Chris is bored with his family and dreams of the adventure of a travelling circus. In contrast the mysterious Joe wants to be part of a normal family. The story depicts the cruel reality of the adult world in which Joe lives and the pleasant life style of Chris. The film ends with an exciting chase sequence. Starring in *My Friend Joe* are John Cleere, Joel Grey, Schuyler Fisk, Stanley Townsend and Pauline McLynn. The film won the Crystal Bear Award for Best Children's Film at the Berlin Film Festival.

Another feature film aimed at young audiences was *The Boy from Mercury*, making the feature film writing and directorial debut of film editor, Martin Duffy. The production, the first Irish-made science fiction feature film tells of eight-year-old Harry Cronin, growing up in a Dublin working class suburb in

1960. Harry's father is dead, his mother is worn out and his brothers and sisters have little time for him. He lives in a world of fantasy and believes that he comes from the planet Mercury. He is really only happy when he can escape into the world of Flash Gordon at the local cinema or can signal the flashing lights of the Mercurian spaceship in the sky. When his friend is bullied, Harry seeks the help of the Mercurians. The film produced by Marina Hughes for Mercurian Productions, features in the title role nine-year-old unknown, James Hickey from Saggart in west Dublin, and a predominantly Irish crew. Hugh O'Connor plays his older brother, veteran British actress Rita Tushingham is cast as his aunt and Tom Courtenay as his uncle.

Following his Oscar success with *The Crying Game*, Neil Jordan was assigned to direct the big-budget *Interview with the Vampire*, starring Tom Cruise, Brad Pitt, Christian Slater, Antonio Banderas and Stephen Rea. The film, based on Anne Rice's bestseller, chronicled the life of the 'undead' Louis and his interaction with other vampires. The Irish director proved himself and drew credible performances from his top cast in this lavish, dark tale, which remains faithful to Rice's novel.

With the overwhelming success of *Interview*, Warner Brothers and Geffen Pictures were to support a long-held project of Jordan's, a biography of Michael Collins. This was the culmination of a twelve-year quest by the writer/director to bring the life of the Irish hero to the screen, despite attempts by Michael Cimino and Kevin Costner amongst others, to film the Collins story. The film follows events from the Easter Rising of 1916 to 1922, culminating in Collins' death. Jordan assembled an impressive cast headed by Liam Neeson as Collins, Julia Roberts as Kitty Kiernan, Alan Rickman as Eamon de Valera, Stephen Rea as Ned Broy and Aidan Quinn as Harry Boland.

The film was shot over a fourteen weeks schedule in eighty locations throughout counties Dublin and Wicklow with the film-makers transforming City Hall, Dublin Castle, Henrietta Street and Gardiner Row into the 1916-22 period. At Grangegorman a replica of the GPO and O'Connell Street were constructed in what was the largest set ever built in Ireland. To recruit extras for the large crowd scenes the film-makers made an appeal for people who would receive no payment. Posters went up throughout Wicklow and Dublin seeking volunteers. Thousands turned up for the Collins' address at Rathdrum, Co Wicklow, the Dev speech at Grangegorman and for the dramatic Bloody Sunday re-enactment in the Carlisle Grounds in Bray. Along with the high calibre cast, Jordan surrounded himself with an award-winning team headed by Oscar-winning cinematographer, Chris Menges, production designer Anthony Pratt and costumes expert Sandy Powell.

Alan Rickman, Liam Neeson and Aidan Quinn in a scene from *Michael Collins*.

Liam Neeson in a passionate speech from *Michael Collins*.

The film fared extremely well at the Irish box office but was criticised for some of its historical accuracy. It was nominated for two Oscars: Best Cinematographer, Menges, and Best Original Dramatic Score, Elliot Goldenthal.

Shooting on a £2.25 million budget and much lower profile around the north Dublin fishing village of Howth was *The Last of the High Kings*. The film based on the novel of the same name by Ferdia Mac Anna, was directed by David Keating, making his directorial debut and co-writing the screenplay with actor Gabriel Byrne. The latter headed the cast with Colm Meaney, Stephen Rea, Catherine O'Hara and the younger team was headed by Jared Leto, Jason Barry and Christine Ricci. The film tells of an amusing coming-of-age in the summer of 1977, when some young people experience changing relationships with parents and friends. Frankie, who believes he will fail his exams, is obsessed with two girls, Jayne and Romy. His mother who is the most powerful person in his life tells her children that they are descended from the high kings of Ireland.

The majority of films shot in Ireland over the previous decade had been indigenous low budget productions by Irish directors. However, a number of large budget Hollywood financed productions moved into Ireland for tax breaks and to avail of the scenery.

While many of the small budget films were shot entirely on location, *Space Truckers*, with a budget of $23 million, moved onto extensive sets at Ardmore Studios. The production ran into financial difficulties and almost collapsed but a rescue deal was arranged. The only location scenes were shot at Dollymount Strand in Dublin, doubling for the Mojave Desert, and the civic offices at Wood Quay. American star, Dennis Hopper, played John Canyon, an interplanetary long distance haulier who agrees to take a black-market shipment of mysterious sealed containers to earth.

Stephen Dorff, Debi Mazar and Charles Dance play other leading roles. Stuart Gordon directed the production. A special effects warehouse was constructed where miniature sets were assembled for the space flight sequences. When the main shooting was completed the visual effects team continued for another five months.

While these multi-dollar films were in production the veteran Hollywood producer/director Roger Corman set up a permanent film studio in Connemara. He was anxious to establish a European base and to avail of Section 35 tax concessions and chose Tully in Co Galway as the venue to be called Concorde Anois. Corman had made his reputation producing a series of horror films, including *The Pit and the Pendulum* and *The Raven*. Even before the studio was constructed, two low budget films went into production in quick succession –

*Bloodfist VIII: Trained for Action* and *Spectre*.

*The Fifth Province* marked an impressive feature film directorial debut by Frank Stapleton. Stapleton also co-wrote the quirky script with Nina Fitzpatrick, which was described as a 'surreal comic fable set in contemporary Ireland'. Brian F. O'Byrne stars as a would-be writer struggling against the dank weather and his own psychosexual problems. The film that was shot over six weeks in Cavan, Wicklow and Dublin also co-starred Lia Williams, Anthony Higgins and Ian Richardson. *The Fifth Province* won the Best First Feature Award at the Galway Film Festival.

With Noel Pearson as producer and Liz Gill making her directorial debut, *Gold in the Streets* told of a group of young Irish people seeking their dreams in America. James Belushi plays New York bartender, Mario, who is not surprised when Liam, another young Irish man, enters his premises. Liam quickly adapts to this little Ireland in the Big Apple where his new friends work illegally and dodge immigration officers. They fall in and out of love as they struggle to realise their dreams.

Exteriors were filmed in New York and the interiors of the bar in Ireland. Ian Hart, Jared Harris, Aidan Gillen, Louise Lombard and Lorraine Pilkington head the strong cast.

*November Afternoon* is a low budget film from the successful writing/directing duo of John Carney and Tom Hall. The film deals with two couples whose relationships begin to crumble over an eventful weekend. Karen and her husband return from London to Dublin to visit Karen's brother Robert and his partner. Vague tensions arise between the brothers-in-law as the realisation that Karen and Robert are conducting a clandestine incestuous affair, simmers below the surface. The four players are Michael McElhatton, Jayne Snow, Tristan Gribbin and Mark Doherty. It is photographed in an intimate, claustrophobic atmosphere by Mark Waldron.

# 29

# I WENT DOWN

From 1996 there was encouraging news from the Irish sector as indigenous directors moved away from the Troubles and dark dramas set in the 1950s to original scripts based on contemporary topics.

Director Paddy Breathnach teamed with playwright, Conor McPherson, on a black road movie comedy, *I Went Down*. McPherson wrote the richly detailed screenplay in which two ill-matched criminals are despatched to Cork by a Dublin criminal to track down a criminal associate. Brendan Gleeson plays the oil-slick-coifed Bunny Kelly – who reads cowboy novels – and his young sidekick, Peter McDonald, aptly named Git Hynes. They spark off each other with the sharp, witty dialogue, which shifted the characters away from the usual stereotypes. Tony Doyle plays the tough Dublin crime boss, Peter Caffrey, the kidnap victim and Antoine Byrne as Git's ex-girlfriend. The film proved an assured second feature for director Breathnach and became a huge hit at the Irish box office. *I Went Down* won the New Director's Prize at the San Sebastian Film Festival.

*Separation Anxiety* is the feature film debut of Mark Staunton who directed the impressive short *The End*. The script is by Canadian writer, Shelagh Harcourt, who features in the cast alongside Susan Collins, Kevin Gildea, Conor Lambert and Brendan Dempsey. The film is a contemporary comedy of manners set against the background of the first divorce case in Ireland. Kevin is a waster, Sally is his upwardly mobile wife and both try to come to terms with the fact that their relationship is over. The location is Dublin's Temple Bar where the bawdy and irreverent twenty-something friends become involved in commitment, betrayal, lust and love.

Following from his success with the James Bond films, Pierce Brosnan set up his own production company, Irish Dreamtime, with Beau St Clair. The first film from the new company was based on an original screenplay by Eugene Brady, who made his directorial debut with the film. *The Nephew* details the resurfacing of a bitter feud between two men on a small island off the Irish coast with the arrival of a young nephew who acts as a catalyst to open old wounds – not least because he is black. The film was shot around the Roundwood area of Wicklow. Brosnan plays the leading role as the publican. Supporting him are Donal McCann and Sinead Cusack, with newcomers Hill Harper and Aisling McGuckin as the young lovers.

*This is My Father* was a family affair and long time ambition for the Quinn family. Aidan Quinn plays the leading role, sister Marian appears in the film, Paul is the writer and director, and Declan the director of photography. The screenplay is based on a story their mother had told them and follows an Irish-American teacher who returns to Ireland to uncover his father's identity. Much of the film is told in flashbacks to 1930s' Ireland as a young couple attempt to maintain their love affair in the face of strong opposition from the community and local clergy. A strong cast was assembled and along with Aidan Quinn, James Cann, John Cusack, Colm Meaney, Brendan Gleeson, Pat Shortt and Stephen Rea starred. Newcomer Moya Farrelly made a striking film debut.

Pat O'Connor returned to Ireland to direct *Dancing at Lughnasa*, based on Brian Friel's 1991 Tony Award-winning play. Rather than filming in Donegal, the original setting of the play, O'Connor chose Lacken and west Wicklow as his wind-swept location. A fine cast headed by Meryl Streep, Catherine McCormack, Kathy Burke, Bríd Brennan, Sophie Thompson and Michael Gambon was assembled to bring the Mundy family to life. O'Connor extracted a remarkable ensemble piece from the five women, with Streep capturing precisely the Donegal accent.

The story is set in rural Ireland in the summer of 1936 with Europe on the edge of war. In Ballybeg, the Mundy family shelter in their small home – five sisters, one brother and Michael, the love child of Christina, the youngest sister. The film is seen through the eyes of the boy as he feels the joy and security of his close-knit clan. At Lughnasa, a Celtic harvest festival, a wildness bursts forth in the Mundy cottage in the form of a spirited dance. This is a rare display of happiness in the sisters' poignant journey into heartbreak.

Following the scale of Michael Collins, Neil Jordan returned to Ireland for a low budget film, *The Butcher Boy*, as his next project. He co-wrote the screenplay of the award-winning novel with its author, Pat McCabe. The story revolves

Brendan Gleeson in *I Went Down*.

Eamonn Owens in *The Butcher Boy*.

A joyous scene from *Dancing at Lughnasa* featuring Catherine McCormack, Bríd Brennan, Meryl Streep, Kathy Burke and Sophie Thompson.

around young Francie Brady and his descent into madness. His father is an alcoholic and his mother suffers from mental illness before committing suicide. The film is seen through the eyes and mind of Francie.

Jordan lined up an all-Irish cast headed by Stephen Rea, Fiona Shaw, Niall Buggy, Brendan Gleeson, Ian Hart and Sinead O'Connor as the Blessed Virgin. Eamonn Owens gives a remarkable performance as the disturbed Francie. The lush photography of Adrian Biddle captured the atmosphere of rural Ireland in the early 1960s on locations in Monaghan, Dublin, Kildare and Wicklow. The lively musical score of Elliot Goldenthal added immensely to the tone of the film.

Critics and audiences alike were enthralled with Jordan's ingenuity in transferring such a difficult novel so successfully to the screen.

Jordan's next two films were shot outside Ireland. *In Dreams* was a psychological thriller about a serial killer and his obsession with the mother of one of his victims. Annette Benning and Robert Downey, Jr play the leading roles.

Jordan followed this with *End of the Affair*, adapted from Graham Greene's novel, set against a background of London during World War II. Julianne Moore and Ralph Fiennes play the lovers of the title with Stephen Rea and Ian Hart in support.

*A Love Divided* is based on a real life incident in the Co Wexford village of Fethard-on-Sea in 1957. The story explores the shattering impact of one woman's decision to stand up for her principles, and follows the marriage of Seán, a Catholic, and Sheila, a Protestant, in the small village. They live happily with their two daughters until the time comes for the eldest girl to go to school. Tradition dictates a Catholic schooling, but Sheila wants the choice. The local priest, Fr Stafford, insists that the young girl goes to a Catholic school and Seán reluctantly goes along with him. Faced with opposition from all quarters, Sheila flees with her daughters.

Director Syd Macartney and screenwriter Stuart Hepburn brought an honest, unsentimental appraisal to the recreation. Liam Cunningham and Orla Brady play the couple with conviction and Tony Doyle was ideally cast as the pompous priest who insists on God's law, regardless of the consequences. The production was filmed in Rathdrum, Co Wicklow and in Co Antrim.

Johnny Gogan is writer and director of *The Last Bus Home*, which was set during the Pope's visit to Ireland in 1979. The story revolves around a punk band 'The Dead Patriots' and the self-discovery of the band members. While the neighbourhood embarks to the Phoenix Park, punk Reena ducks out with the help of her grandmother. In the deserted streets she tracks down Jessop, a punk guitarist. Their attraction is immediate and when her parents return, Reena and Jessop have sealed their alliance in other ways.

Grogan successfully captures the emotions of the individuals and the character of Dublin city through a variety of unusual locations. The strong cast includes Brian F. O'Byrne, Annie Ryan, Gemma Craven, Garret Keogh and Donal O'Kelly. The film won the Best Film award at Cherbourg Film Festival and has enjoyed worldwide distribution.

Dublin is also the setting for *Pete's Meteor*, the feature film debut for writer/director Joe O'Byrne, who in the past had worked extensively in the theatre. The magical tale centres on twelve-year-old Micky who lives in the inner city with his brother and sister in their grandmother's house. He has an unwanted guardian angel, Pete. The area is ravaged by drug dealers and is patrolled by the gardaí. The children's parents have died from AIDS contracted from heroin abuse. One night a meteorite crashes into their backgarden and changes Micky's life. He charges 20 pence to see the meteor that he believes is a sign from his parents.

The script is witty and O'Byrne seems a natural to extract the best from the children. O'Byrne marshalled his cast headed by Brenda Fricker, Mike Myers, Dervla Kirwan and Alfred Molina against a backdrop of an unglamorous Dublin.

*Night Train* is an original screenplay by playwright Aodhán Madden and makes the feature film directorial debut of television producer/director, John Lynch. John Hurt plays Poole, a seedy small time crook, just out of prison and being pressurised by crime boss (Lorcan Cranitch) for money he owes. When the gang closes in, Poole flees his flat and finds accommodation in a terraced house with dour Mrs Mooney (Pauline Flanagan) and her frustrated daughter, Alice (Brenda Blethyn). Poole has a passion for model trains and sets up his train in his room. Love develops between Hurt and Blethyn and he sweeps her off on the real Orient Express where he has stashed the money.

John Lynch directs this romantic thriller in an assuring fashion and draws believable performances from the principals particularly Hurt, Blethyn and Flanagan. Others in the cast are Peter Caffrey, Lorcan Cranitch and Rynagh O'Grady. Lynch and cinematographer Seamus Deasy shot on location in Venice and Dún Laoghaire and Ranelagh in Dublin.

# 30

# FILMS AND THE NORTHERN CONFLICT

Over the past sixty years the conflict in Northern Ireland has provided film-makers with raw material for scores of films. The majority of these films have been from an IRA and republican point of view.

Most film-goers are familiar with the classic *Odd Man Out*, directed by Carol Reed in 1946. Neil Jordan's debut film *Angel* and his Oscar-winning *The Crying Game* also have strong Northern dimensions. Jim Sheridan's *In the Name of the Father* and *The Boxer* are also set against a backdrop of the troubles. Alan J. Pakula's *The Devil's Own* establishes an IRA man as the central character. Pat O'Connor's *Cal* features a young disillusioned IRA man who falls in love with his victim's widow. Robert Mitchum played an unlikely IRA man in *A Terrible Beauty*, as has James Cagney in *Shake Hands with the Devil*. With the exception of *Odd Man Out* none of the above were actually filmed in Northern Ireland, but in counties Wicklow, Louth and Dublin. The Sherrif Street and Ringsend areas of Dublin regularly stood in for working class Belfast.

Daniel Day-Lewis was able to revive his Belfast accent, perfected in *In the Name of the Father*, for his role in *The Boxer*. Sheridan and Day-Lewis reunited for this production set against the Northern Ireland troubles. Day-Lewis plays former IRA member, Danny Flynn, who has just been released from prison after a fourteen-year sentence. Back in Belfast he cannot escape his past and attempts to revive his boxing career. His lifetime love, Maggie, has survived by marrying his best friend and raising a son. In the midst of turmoil they fall in love again.

The Belfast street scenes were shot on Sheriff Street, Dublin, while one elaborate set of a London hotel ballroom was constructed in Ardmore. 450 extras were employed for a week as the audience for the final boxing match. Barry McGuigan was advisor for the boxing scenes. The supporting cast was headed by Emily Watson, Brian Cox, Ken Stott and Gerard McSorley.

Another blockbuster film to be partly shot in Ireland was *The Devil's Own*. The $100 million action film starred Brad Pitt and Harrison Ford and was directed by veteran American director, Alan J. Pakula. In the film, which was set in Northern Ireland in 1992, Pitt plays a Provisional IRA man who becomes involved in a shoot-out with the SAS. He escapes from Ireland and travels to Newark where he gets a room in the home of Ford, an Irish-American cop. Ford unwittingly gives him refuge in his home and treats him like the son he never had. From here Pitt plans to ship arms back to the IRA.

The opening sequence of the film was shot in Blessington, the coastline of north Dublin and Inchicore. An exciting gun battle was staged over a period of a few days in the small Dublin suburb. Many fans gathered to catch a glimpse of Pitt, but crew members kept the star concealed behind black sheeting.

In the main, films with a Northern Ireland setting have been indigenous low budget productions, with the Troubles as an integral part of the screenplay. In more recent time, with the cessation of violence and the ceasefire there has been a substantial increase in film production north of the border.

A number of these films have been based on the successful books of Northern Ireland writer, Colin Bateman. His *Cycle of Violence* concerns a young journalist who arrives in the small town of Crossmaheart to work on a local newspaper. The man he is replacing is missing, presumed dead. When the young journalist attempts to discover what happened he is drawn into a web of intrigue. Henry Herbert directed the film, which stars Gerald Rooney and Mari Lennon.

Next Colin Bateman adapted his own novel, *Divorcing Jack*, for the screen. This comedy thriller, starring David Thewlis and Laura Fraser, made the directorial debut of David Caffrey. Thewlis is an abrasive journalist working in Belfast whose problems begin when he picks up a young art student (Fraser) in the Botanic Park. The next morning he finds her dead in bed. Soon he has the IRA, RUC, UVF and British army on his trail in this fast-moving irreverent comedy. The film marks a notable feature debut for Caffrey.

*This is the Sea*, borrowing its title from the Waterboys' song, was the second feature film for writer-director Mary McGuckian, who signed up Gabriel Byrne, Richard Harris, Samantha Morton and John Lynch. Although filmed primarily in counties Dublin and Wicklow, with a location stint in Belfast and Co Antrim, the story is set in contemporary Northern Ireland. Despite the ceasefire few people are left untouched by the continuing tension that grips the city. Twenty-year-old Hazel, from a Protestant Plymouth Brethren background, falls in love with Malachy, a Catholic. Their relationship becomes entangled in a web of prejudice and interference. Her mother's attempts at ending the relationship end in tragedy.

Another film shot in the North around this period was *Titanic City*. The setting of the screenplay was Belfast in 1972, with Julie Walters as a housewife who initiates a peace movement. This action has unforeseen consequences for her family and community. Roger Mitchell directed the film from a screenplay by Ann Devlin.

In *Bogwoman*, writer/director Tom Collins spans two decades in the life of a Donegal woman, Maureen, a young unmarried mother from an island off Donegal. In the late 1950s she moves to Derry to marry her boyfriend, Barry. The film revolves around the woman and her relationship with her past − her parents on her island home, her future with her family and neighbours on the Bogside in Derry and taking her place behind the barricades as the Civil Rights movement explodes during the late 1960s. Rachel Dowling gives a gritty performance as the young woman. Others in the cast include Peter Mullan, Sean McGinley and Maria Macdermottroe. Cameraman Peter Robertson skilfully captures the sense of Maureen's emotions over the contrasting landscapes of counties Donegal and Derry.

A much more graphic film set against the worst period of mid-1970s' Belfast is *Resurrection Man*. The film was based on Eoin McNamee's book concerning the psychopathic blood lust of a knife-wielding loyalist terrorist gang known as the Shankill Butchers. Marc Evan extracted a strong performance from Stuart Townsend in the leading role. He receives solid support from James Nesbitt and Brenda Fricker. The film combines elements of a documentary and gripping thriller. *Resurrection Man* and 1995's *Nothing Personal* were practically unique as they depict the conflict from a loyalist perspective.

*Sunset Heights* is another gritty thriller set in a futuristic Derry of 2007. The £1.3 million film was written and directed by Colm Villa and is located in a city where law and order is maintained by rival punishment squads. Toby Stephens is a young man who has managed to remain uninvolved − until his son is murdered during a wave of child killings in the city. The gripping film, which stars Toby Stephens, Jim Norton, James Cosmo and Patrick O'Kane, was filmed in Donegal and Derry.

*An Everlasting Piece* is an Irish comedy set in Belfast and features Barry McEvoy who also wrote the screenplay. McEvoy co-stars with Brian F. O'Byrne as barbers who secure a hair piece franchise in 1980s' Belfast. Anna Friel and Billy

Daniel Day-Lewis in *The Boxer*.

James Nesbitt in *Resurrection Man*.

Brad Pitt as an IRA man in *The Devil's Own*.

Richard Harris in *This is the Sea*.

Connolly co-star in the film, which was directed by Barry Levinson. Steven Spielberg was an executive producer on the film and when the subject matter was regarded as being embarrassing to Britain, it only received a limited release in the UK. Shortly afterwards Spielberg was awarded a knighthood by the Queen.

Another off-beat comedy is *The Most Fertile Man in Ireland*, which takes a hilarious and irreverent look at sexual politics in Northern Ireland. Eamonn is a 24-year old Belfast man whose life changes dramatically when it is discovered that he has the highest sperm count in the country.

All the other men of the province have become impotent and Eamonn is soon in demand by women of all ages, as he becomes 'the most fertile man in Ireland'. A feud develops between republicans and loyalists for his services. Kris Marshall plays the eager Eamonn, with a strong supporting cast headed by James Nesbitt, Bronagh Gallagher, Kathy Kiera Clarke and Kenneth Cranham. Dudi Appleton directs at a frantic pace in Dublin and Belfast.

# 31

# SPIELBERG IN COUNTY WEXFORD

In 1997 the Irish film industry received a major boost when it was confirmed that Steven Speilberg was to shoot a portion of his new film *Saving Private Ryan* on location here. Mel Gibson had spoken to Spielberg about the tremendous co-operation he had received in Ireland during the shooting of *Braveheart* and encouraged him to make his film there. Another incentive for the American director was the offer from the Department of Defence of the availability of hundreds of trained soldiers for the battle scenes.

For his $70 million anti-war film, based on the true story of the Niland brothers, Spielberg chose Curracloe Beach in Co Wexford. He regarded this long stretch of beach, framed by dunes, as the most suitable location resembling Omaha Beach in Normandy where hundreds of American GIs landed. The D-Day landing in 1944 was decisive and a turning point in World War II.

The film stars Tom Hanks as Captain Miller leading his men on a mission to find a soldier whose three brothers have been killed in combat. They want to save the one remaining member of the family. The other leading actors are Matt Damon, playing Private Ryan, Edward Burns, Tom Sizemore, Barry Pepper and Jeremy Davies.

The battle scenes feature hundreds of soldiers, mostly from the Irish army. Brigades of FCA men were used as extras and dressed as American troops. For weeks before filming commenced they trained in Wexford with Vietnam veterans and stuntmen. Although the landing was portrayed as utter chaos each move was thoroughly rehearsed in advance. Amputees were recruited and fitted with false arms and legs, which were bloodily blown off during the battle.

The dramatic beach-landing scene from *Saving Private Ryan* which was filmed at Curracloe Beach in Co Wexford.

Curracloe Beach was totally transformed into a stunning replica of the Normandy Beach by the film set designers and tradesmen from the locality. Hardened war veterans, on set as technical advisors, could hardly accept it was only make-believe. There was a great buzz of excitement in the Wexford area as locals enjoyed the international spotlight and hoped to catch a glimpse of Hanks and Spielberg. Many halls and hotels in Wexford were used as holding bases for the cast and crew. At Curracloe security was extremely tight on the set and only accredited people were allowed through security checks. At the time it was reported that a psychopathic stalker had threatened to kill Spielberg.

The film's opening 25-minute D-Day landing sequence is one of the most realistic and brutal images of battle ever conveyed on film. The platoons of American troops being ferried onto the beach were subject to tank, cannon and machine gun fire from the German lines. Some of the teenage GIs were vomiting with fear as they witness the bodies of their young colleagues being blasted apart. Blood spurts from their wounds and the sea runs red. The misty, hand-held frenzied photography of Janusz Kaminski and the souring score of John Williams added greatly to the harrowing images of the slaughter.

*Saving Private Ryan* became one of the most critically acclaimed films of the year and was nominated for eleven Academy Awards – winning five – including an Oscar for Spielberg's direction and Kaminski's cinematography. The other awards were for best sound, best film editing and best sound effects editing. The film was a worldwide hit and took over $250 million at the American box office.

Following the positive publicity of Gibson and Spielberg shooting non-Irish films there, the Irish film industry became the envy of Europe with its lucrative tax concessions. The Irish Film Board and other interested bodies had to remain in a strong position to fight off competition from the United Kingdom, North America, Canada and cities in Europe such as Prague to gain future big budget productions for their countries. The market place has since become much more competitive with other countries introducing even more enticing tax breaks for the escalating costs of film production. In recent years the Isle of Man has become an attractive location and many productions with Irish settings including *The Brylcreem Boys* and *Waking Ned* have been shot there.

While Spielberg was filming in Wexford, an Irish director Cathal Black was shooting his low budget production, *Love and Rage* on Achill Island, Co Mayo. Black was directing a period screenplay by Brian Lynch set in the nineteenth century on the windswept island where a tough English woman, Agnes MacDonnell, meets her match in the mysterious James Lynchehaun whom she employs as her land agent. Despite their class and age difference, a passionate affair ensues.

Black assembled a strong cast headed by Greta Scacchi, Daniel Craig, Stephen Dillane, Valerie Edmond and Donal Donnelly. The production attracted by the tax breaks of the Isle of Man moved there for part of the shoot.

That year, Greta Scacchi was a familiar face in Ireland in period costume because she also played a leading role in *Serpent's Kiss* alongside Ewan McGregor, Richard E. Grant and Pete Postletwaite. First time director and former lighting cameraman, Philippe Rousselot chose Sixmilebridge, Co Clare as the principal location for his lavish production set in Gloucestershire in 1699. The film deals with a young craftsman who is commissioned by a wealthy landowner's wife to create a spectacular garden. McGregor, playing the gardener, soon becomes involved with her and her daughter.

George Orwell's classic novel, *Animal Farm,* was filmed in a specially built studio on the Luggala Estate. The film directed by John Stephenson features over a hundred live animals and some created electronically. Each of the principal animals had a double and for months before filming commenced the animals went through a rigorous training procedure.

Pete Postlethwaite plays Jones, the abusive drunken farmer who sparks a revolt led by the pigs at the head of an army of neglected animals. Soon the pigs become as brutal as the humans. The story is a satire on Stalinist Russia. Among the voices are Julia Ormond as Jessie the Dog, Ian Holm as Squealer and Patrick Stewart as Napolean.

# 32

# ANGELA'S ASHES

It was inevitable that *Angela's Ashes*, the Pulitzer Prize winning book by Frank McCourt, of his impoverished childhood in Limerick, would be brought to the big screen. Since his highly successful production of *The Commitments*, director Alan Parker had been looking for another opportunity to work in Ireland. When producers Scott Rudin and David Brown offered him the job of directing *Angela's Ashes* he readily accepted.

Parker wanted to remain true to the novel as he had done recreating Roddy Doyle's gritty northside Dublin in *The Committments*. Parker was meticulous when it came to casting the McCourt children. He auditioned 15,000 young hopefuls from all over Ireland before selecting the three boys who would depict young Frank at different ages. He finally chose Joe Breen, Ciaran Owens and Michael Legge as the older Frank. They are amazingly convincing as the children. The adults in the cast are Emily Watson as Angela and Robert Carlyle as Malachy, her alcoholic husband, Pauline McLynn as the quirky aunt, Ronnie Masterson as the grandmother and Brendan Cauldwell as the principal. From all of them, particularly the younger actors, Parker draws outstanding performances. Throughout the film, actor Andrew Bennett speaks Frank McCourt's words in a voice-over.

*Angela's Ashes* is the harrowing story of a family of young children thrown out on the streets of Limerick in the 1930s when their alcoholic father is unable to find work. Parker was uncompromising in his depiction of the appalling poverty and degree of survival endured by the family

Limerick has changed so radically from the 1930s that Parker was unable to find many locations which resembled the city of McCourt's book. The slums of Roden Street no longer exist and had to be recreated on a disused site off Benburb Street in Dublin and in Ardmore Studios. With the controversy over McCourt's depiction of his native city the film-makers were refused permission to shoot in Limerick churches. Other scenes were shot in Dublin, Cork and Wicklow.

The opening fifteen minutes of the film draw quite an impact with the death of several of the young McCourt children. *Angela's Ashes* proved a huge hit in Ireland but the main criticism was of the constant rain throughout the film.

1998 was one of the more productive years for film-making in Ireland for some time and several crews were shooting simultaneously in the Dublin/Wicklow area. In Ringsend Anjelica Huston was directing and starring in *The Mammy*, later renamed *Agnes Browne*. Rosie O'Donnell was cast in the leading role but when she withdrew Huston stepped in herself. The screenplay was based on the best-selling book by Brendan O'Carroll and set in 1960s' Dublin.

Agnes Browne is a Moore Street trader trying to raise seven children following the untimely death of her husband. Despite her straitened circumstances, Agnes has a natural optimism and a fierce determination to keep the family strong and united. Romance enters her life in the guise of Pierre, a local French baker.

The supporting cast includes Marion O'Dwyer, Ray Winstone, Arno Chevrier and Brendan O'Carroll. The singer, Tom Jones, makes a cameo appearance as himself.

The French actor, Gerard Depardieu was to have played the baker but he had an accident shortly before filming commenced.

The residents of Ringsend once again enjoyed their invasion by the film-makers and many of them were recruited as extras in the film. The community centre served as the film base and the set designer transformed Thorncastle Street into an authentic replica of Moore Street, complete with stalls and traders.

A very contrasting film shooting in Dowth and Slane, Co Meath was *The Last September* based on a script by John Banville from Elizabeth Bowen's novel. The story is set against a background of the Anglo-Irish aristocracy in 1920s' Ireland. Sir Richard Naylor and his wife, Lady Myra, live in their country mansion, Danielstown.

Their niece, Lois, who is seeing a captain in the British army, is lured by a menacingly young man hiding in their grounds. What unfolds is the young woman's coming of age in a period of Irish struggle.

Joe Breen as the young Frank McCourt in *Anglea's Ashes*.

Marion O'Dwyer and Anjelica Huston in *Agnes Browne* which was directed by Huston.

The highly acclaimed theatre director, Deborah Warner, made her screen directorial debut with this film which starred Fiona Shaw, Maggie Smith, Lambert Wilson, Keeley Hawes and Michael Gambon.

The distinguished Canadian director, Atom Egoyan came to Ireland for a short stint of location work in Glanworth, Co Cork on *Felicia's Journey*, based on the haunting novel by William Trevor. The story concerns Felicia, from a small Irish town who discovers after her boyfriend, Johnny, has gone to Birmingham, that she is pregnant. She travels to England in search of him. She meets the solitary Joseph Hilditch who pretends to help her but he is a sinister figure and in a series of flashbacks his dark past emerges. He is a serial killer of young women he has picked up, mainly prostitutes and runaways. He makes secret videos of his victims before killing them. Having selected Felicia as his next victim the truth behind her journey complicates his plans.

The film stars a flawless Bob Hoskins as Hilditch and the young Irish actress, Elaine Cassidy, who creates an aura of innocence as Felicia. Others in the cast are Peter McDonald as the boyfriend and Gerard McSorley as Felicia's father.

Balbriggan, Co Dublin is an unlikely setting for a film, but it was where writer/director Stephen Bradley chose as the principal location for *Sweeney Barrett*. The prolific Brendan Gleeson plays against type as the simple-minded Sweeney. When he loses his job in a travelling circus he arrives in the port of Dockery, looking for work. His simple nature makes him easy prey in the corrupt town of smugglers dominated by the vicious detective, Mannix Bone. Sweeney strikes up a friendship with a young boy, Conor, whose father resumes a vendetta with Bone. When it appears that Bone is getting away with murder, Sweeney extracts revenge transforming himself into a hero for the town. Liam Cunningham plays Bone and others in the cast are Lynda Steadman, Tony Rohr and Dylan Murphy. Bradley packs a powerful punch with his first film and creates a gritty realism in a mythical world

*Flick* is a thought-provoking film directed by Fintan Connolly with David Murray, David Wilmot, Mannix Flynn and Catherine Punch. This drama centres on twenty-something, middle class Jack Flinter who is drifting through life much to the annoyance of his girl friend, Alice. When Jack meets up with a German woman, Isabelle, he is forced to confront his dilemma.

# 33

# THE MANY FACES OF THE GENERAL

Following the assassination of the notorious Dublin criminal Martin Cahill, known as the General, in August 1994 and the killing of the journalist, Veronica Guerin, film-makers showed a remarkable interest in their stories.

First into production was a film written, produced and directed by John Boorman, based on Paul Williams' book, *The General*. Boorman decided to shoot this gritty thriller in black and white for Warner Brothers. He cast Brendan Gleeson as the enigmatic Dublin criminal and supporting him in the large cast are Adrian Dunbar, Sean McGinley, Maria Doyle Kennedy and Angeline Ball. The only non-Irish actor in the cast is the American Jon Voight as Cahill's adversary, Inspector Ned Kelly.

The film illustrates Cahill's brutality as the ruthless leader of his gang and his cunning in skilfully executing the Russborough House art theft. Cahill also had a devilish sense of humour while frequently giving the gardaí the slip and a flagrant disregard for the authorities, other criminals and the paramilitaries, which led to his ultimate demise.

Cinematographer Seamus Deasy's richly textured black and white photography and the atmospheric jazz score of Ritchie Buckley added greatly to the mood of the film. At the 1998 Cannes Film Festival John Boorman won the Best Director award. In Ireland the film received some criticism for glamorising the central character and lampooning the gardaí.

The $12 million production for Little Bird, *Ordinary Decent Criminal*, was the second version of the life of Martin Cahill to go before the cameras. In this fictional account Cahill is named Michael Lynch and the other characters also have fictional names.

Gerry Stembridge wrote the original screenplay, which Thaddeus O'Sullivan directed on location in Dublin and Wicklow. This version took a more light-hearted approach to Lynch/Cahill and his exploits. While the Hollyfield flats in Rathmines are being demolished Lynch stages a sit-in. In an amusing sequence the gang steal Caravaggio's 'Taking of Christ'. The plot also explores his tangled love life and his involvement with two sisters. This version gives a quirky, comical touch to the storyline.

O'Sullivan lined up an impressive cast headed by Kevin Spacey, Linda Florentino, Peter Mullan, Colin Farrell and Stephen Dillane. Spacey and the other non-Irish players made feeble attempts at their Dublin accents.

The third production based on the life and death of Martin Cahill is *Vicious Circle*, mainly shot in the dockland area of Dublin. In this BBC produced, made for television version, director David Blair employs a grittier, more menacing edge to the story. He follows the same subject matter – the dysfunctional childhood, the jewellery heist, the IRA dimension and his complicated love life. Starring in this production are Ken Stott, giving an unsympathetic portrayal as the master criminal, Andrew Connolly as his main garda adversary and John Kavanagh as the IRA chief.

The life and death of the Dublin journalist Veronica Guerin is the subject of another thriller set in Dublin, entitled *When the Sky Falls*. John McKenzie directed from the screenplay by Colum McCann, Michael Sheridan and Ronan Gallagher. Like the Thaddeus O'Sullivan approach, McKenzie used fictious names for the real life characters. The story relates how the female journalist, Sinead Hamilton/Veronica Guerin, finds herself propelled into a world of crime where the judiciary is powerless to respond. She exposes the world of the criminals but pays the ultimate price.

American actress, Joan Allen, stars as Guerin-alias Hamilton in the film who was shot dead on 26 June 1996. Patrick Bergin plays the detective and others in the cast include Pete Poselthwaite, Liam Cunningham, Jimmy Smallhorne, Jason Barry and Kevin McNally.

Another biographical Irish film, *Nora*, was directed by Pat Murphy from a script by Gerry Stembridge and Murphy. It took Murphy a number of years to get this film into production. The story tells of the early relationship of a spirited young Galway woman, Nora Barnacle, and the writer, James Joyce. Spanning eight years from 1904 the film explores the early stages of their often volatile relationship. She persuades him to start a future together away from Dublin and

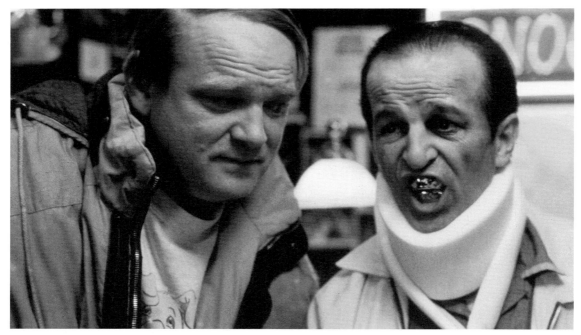

Brendan Gleeson and Sean McGinley in John Boorman's film, *The General*.

Kevin Spacey as Martin Cahill, this time in *Ordinary Decent Criminal*, here with Linda Fiorentino.

they move to Trieste, Italy where their passionate and tempestuous life together continues. Joyce is haunted by the fear that his work will never be published but Nora anchors his instabilities and the couple's relationship is bonded by a deep, sexual love.

The versatile actress, Susan Lynch, plays Nora with a fiery passion and Ewan McGregor is suitably tormented as the young Joyce. Others members of the cast include Peter McDonald, Andrew Scott and Kate O'Toole. Director of photography Jean-Francois Robin exquisitely captures the shifting landscapes of Dublin, Italy and Germany.

The classic autobiographical play, *Borstal Boy*, by Brendan Behan, took Peter Sheridan ten years to bring to the screen. Eventually the production came on stream and Sheridan directed and adapted the screenplay, which remains true to Behan's dialogue but the storyline is opened out considerably. *Borstal Boy* tells of a defiant, idealistic teenage Irish boy who goes to English and is arrested as an IRA bomber. He is sent to Borstal where the governor has an enlightened approached to his young prisoners. Here Behan experiences homosexual tendencies and is drawn to writing for the first time.

The cast features American actor, Shawn Hatosy, as the young Behan, alongside Danny Dyer, Joe Taylor and Michael York as the understanding governor. The film was shot chiefly in a disused barracks in Co Kildare.

The loss of freedom against the Northern Ireland troubles provided the ingredients for two films, *H3* and *Silent Grace*. *H3* – one of the bleakest H-Blocks of the Maze prison – sets the scene for a fictional account of events during the 1981 hunger strike. The screenplay was co-written by Laurence McKeown, who took part in the original protest. The film charts the hunger strikers' struggle and their sense of dignity and camaraderie. Director Les Blair was able to extract believable performances from his principals, Brendan Mackey, Aidan Campbell, Kevin Elliot and Tony Devlin. Belfast and Co Wicklow served as the main locations.

Kilmainham Jail provided a ready made set for *Silent Grace*. Writer/director Maeve Murphy tackled the controversial real life event of an unshakeable bond between two very different women. An unlikely friendship emerges when a young joyrider is placed in the same cell as the highest-ranking Republican prisoner. At first they are in conflict but the IRA woman saves the younger inmate's sanity and in return she helps to save the political prisoner's life. The main roles are played by Orla Brady, Cathleen Bradley, Cara Seymour, Dawn Bradfield and Conor Mullen.

# 34

# DISCO PIGS

The trend of Irish directors shifting away from adaptations, gloomy sagas set in the 1960s and brooding melodramas continued as they tackled original romantic comedies of life in contemporary Dublin.

The prolific screenwriter, actor and director, Gerry Stembridge who had written screenplays for *Ordinary Decent Criminal* and co-scripted *Nora* went into production on his own production *About Adam*. This snappy romantic comedy is set in present day Dublin. The film begins with Lucy, who has finally met someone she can love for more than three weeks, the handsome and charming Adam. He is a devious individual who beds Lucy and her two sisters.

Stuart Townsend is the loveable Adam who is as primal as his name suggests. Frances O'Connor, Charlotte Bradley and Kate Hudson play the sisters and Rosaleen Linehan is the roguish mother. The film is inventively written and directed by Stembridge in a modern Dublin of coffee bars, galleries and pent house apartments.

It is obvious with *About Adam* and Stembridge's earlier production, *Guiltrip*, and numerous screenplays, that of the new breed of Irish directors he is the one most comfortable with the genre of cinema.

*When Brendan Met Trudy* is another romantic comedy, scripted (and co-produced) by Roddy Doyle and starring Peter McDonald and Flora Montgomery. Another director, Kieron J. Walsh, makes his feature debut with this quirky comedy.

When straight-laced Brendan, a teacher, choir singer and movie buff meets the scatty Trudy in a Dublin pub he discovers fun for the first time in his adult life. The relationship brings him to new highs particularly in the field of sex. Brendan is stunned when he learns that Trudy is not a pre-school teacher but a burglar and so begins a new facet in his life. Peter McDonald and Flora Montgomery capture beautifully the contrasting personalities of the two main characters. Maynard Eziashi, Eileen Walsh, Pauline McLynn, Barry Cassin, Pat Kinevane and Terry Byrne give admirable support..

Both *About Adam* and *When Brendan Met Trudy* did exceptional business at the Irish box office.

Jim Sheridan's daughter, Kirsten, made her feature film directorial debut with *Disco Pigs*. The film is based on the successful stage play of the same name by Enda Walsh. The obscure plot has Pig as King and Runt the Queen of the magical Pork City, speaking their own unique language. They were born on the same day, live next to each other and are the best of friends. On the eve of their seventeenth birthdays, their love experiences a crisis, threatening to destroy their private world and puts their very lives at risk.

Newcomers Cillian Murphy and Elaine Cassidy play the young lovers. Others in the cast include Sarah Gallagher, Charles Bark, Eleanor Methven, Brian F. O'Byrne and Geraldine O'Rawe. The film was shot in Dublin, Cork and Bray, Co Wicklow. The film won the main prize at the Rassenga International Youth Festival in Switzerland.

*On the Edge*, known as *The Smiling Suicide Club* during production, is an offbeat love story set in a medical centre dealing with young people at risk of suicide. Heading the cast are the busy Cillian Murphy and Stephen Rea, supported by Tricia Vessey, Gerard McSorley, Paul Hickey, Anna Manahan and Jonathan Jackson. The versatile John Carney directed the film, mainly on location in Grangegorman. From the opening sequence of a car sailing over a cliff the director and cinematographer Dermot Diskin display their combined visual style.

Carney and his collaborator, Tom Hall, also co-wrote and co-directed two other productions, *November Afternoon in 1995* and *Park*. Their tightly knit ensemble screenplays concentrate on exploring relationships in turmoil. In *Park* Catherine leaves her house with plans to meet a school friend in a park. The park-keeper spends the morning telling her stories about his past as they wander around the park searching for her friend. Six years later, Catherine is found hanging from her bedroom window. The leading players are Claudia Terry, Des Nealon, Jayne Snow and Patrick Laffin. Carney and Hall were later to work in similar capacities on the highly successful television series, *Bachelors Walk*.

*Accelerator* is a fast-moving road movie developed by a young team headed by director and co-screenwriter Vinny Murphy and cinematographer Seamus Deasy.

Cillian Murphy and Elaine Cassidy in Kirsten Sheridan's *Disco Pigs*.

Stuart Townsend and Kate Hudson in a scene from *About Adam*.

Peter McDonald in exhuberant mood in *When Brendan Met Trudy*.

The film centres on Johnny T. who is on the run from paramilitaries in Belfast. When he flirts with Louise, girlfriend of his old adversary, Whacker, a fight ensues. They and their associates decide that there is only one way to sort out their differences – a car race from Belfast to Dublin. They break into a carpark, overpower the security guard and steal six cars. The fierce, no holds barred race is on. The performances of the actors who include Stuart Sinclair, Gavin Kelty and Aisling O'Neill all ring true. Most of the filming involved night-time shooting of the high powered car chase in north Dublin. *Accelerator* won the Best Director Award at the UIP Awards.

*Saltwater* is another film shot along the north Dublin coastline, the screenplay based on Conor McPherson's award winning play, *This Lime Tree Bower*. Originally the play was written as a series of monologues but McPherson opened it out into a comedy-drama about the life of an Irish-Italian run fish shop in an off-season seaside resort. Widowed father, George Beneventi, grieving for the loss of his wife, is in debt to a local loan shark. His oldest son, Frank, hatches a plan to rob the bookies and solve their financial problems, while his other two sons have female problems. McPherson assembled a dependable team of actors headed by Brian Cox, Peter McDonald, Brendan Gleeson, Conor Mullen and Eva Birthistle and filmed in Bettystown and Skerries. McPherson, on the crest of a wave as one of Ireland's promising new playwrights was also making his directorial debut with this film. He displays an acute ear for dialogue and developing three-dimensional characters.

John Boorman returned to Ardmore Studios to shoot interiors for his glossy production of John Le Carre's classic spy novel, *The Tailor of Panama*. The film features a strong cast headed by Pierce Brosnan, Geoffrey Rush, Jamie Lee Curtis and an almost unrecognisable Brendan Gleeson. Brosnan is disgraced British secret agent, Andy Osnard, a venal deceitful man, exiled to Panama for conduct unbecoming. Never one to resist a challenge, Osnard sets about finding a way of regaining his reputation. He connects up with a Walter Mitty-type, ex-Saville Row tailor, named Prendal, played by Rush who provides Osnard with information that has the potential to topple the government. There are shades of Graham Greene's *Our Man in Havana* in the storyline and dry witted script based on the screenplay by Boorman, Le Carre and Andrew Davies. The film was lavishly shot in Panama.

Writer/director Kevin Liddy set his feature, *Country*, on a much smaller canvas. The film centres on the lives of three men, Frank Murphy and his sons, Con and Jack. When Frank's sister-in-law returns from London she brings emotional warmth that Frank and his sons had forgotten existed. Their evolving relationships take place against the background of tension between the locals and a group of travellers. The cast features Dean Pritchard, Des Cave, Lisa Harrow, Pat Laffan, Marcella Plunkett and Gary Lydon.

*On the Nose* is an Irish/Canadian co-production directed in Dublin by David Caffrey. He lined up an impressive cast of Dan Aykroyd, Robbie Coltrane, Brenda Blethyn, Éanna MacLiam and Zara Turner. The screenplay by Tony Philpott is a whimsical tale in which the luck of ex-gambler, Brendan, who works as a porter in a medical college, changes when he makes an amazing discovery. The preserved head in a jar has an uncanny knack of picking the winning horse in a race. As Brendan's daughter's future depends on the necessary cash to attend university, he is forced to break a promise to his wife. There follows a series of amusing incidents as Brendan and his colleagues attempt to conceal their find. It is a slim plot on which to hitch a ninety-minute film and wastes the talents of Aykroyd, Coltrane and Blethyn.

Morgan O'Sullivan was the co-producer on the off-beat drama, *Not Afraid, Not Afraid* which was filmed on location in counties Wicklow and Dublin. The veteran actress, Dianne Wiest, plays Paula who believes she is dying of cancer and is deserted by her husband of 25 years. She sets out on an obsessive quest to poison her wayward husband and then kill herself. She hadn't reckoned on being joined by her Down's Syndrome grandson, Thomas, who decides to accompany her. The film charts their growing friendship with caustic humour and unsentimental insights as they take off on an eventful journey. The film is co-written and directed by Annette Carducci and also stars Jack Davenport and Miriam Margoyles.

Director Gilles Mackinnon, who made *The Playboys* in Ireland, returned to shoot *The Escapist*, an action thriller over an eight-week period in Dublin. Johnny Lee Miller plays a man pushed beyond the limits when his pregnant wife is murdered during a vicious break-in. He reinvents himself as a hardened criminal and infiltrates the prison to pursue his obsession with the man who murdered his wife. Actors and extras had a gruelling experience in the prison sequences, which were shot in Wheatfield Prison and a disused coal yard. Also in the cast are Jodhi May, Gary Lewis, Andy Serkis and Philip Barrantini.

# 35

# THE COUNT OF MONTE CRISTO

In 2000 the landscapes of Co Wicklow provided the setting for several diverse films. First before the cameras was the umpteenth re-make of Alexander Dumas's classic novel, *The Count of Monte Cristo*. The bulk of the film was shot in Ireland at Powerscourt House and gardens, Killruddery House, the Silver Strand, Brittas Bay and Duncannon Fort in Co Wexford, standing in for the French locations of the story. The production then moved to Malta for five weeks for concluding scenes on the waterfront. There was a spectacular garden party scene, complete with fireworks, filmed over three nights in Powerscourt, when the count makes his appearance in a hot air balloon. The 200 extras, clad as regal party guests, were digitally transformed into 2,000 people.

In charge of the €40 million production was the American director, Kevin Reynolds, who had previously directed *Robin Hood: Prince of Thieves* and the monumental flop *Waterworld*. In true American style, Reynolds did not address the extras directly, only the actors. This was in contrast to Irish directors who speak to everybody. Jim Caviezel plays the famous prisoner, Guy Pearce the devious Modego, Richard Harris the prisoner and Dagmara Dominczyk provides the love interest.

The story tells of the trials of Edmund Dantes, the earnest young sailor who is living a charmed life. When his friend, Fernando Modego, betrays him, the deception quickly leads to his downfall. Following years of imprisonment on an island fortress Dantes finally escapes. He returns to search for the treasure of the island of Monte Cristo, to find his lost love and to plot revenge on his enemies.

The central location for *How Harry Became a Tree* is close to the Sally Gap

Cillian Murphy and Kerry Condon in *How Harry Became a Tree* from 2001.

Matthew Rhys in *Peaches*, part of which was shot in a house in Sandymount.

Jim Caviezel and Dagmara Dominczyk in *The Count of Monte Cristo*.

where the film-makers built a small church and a traditional Irish cottage with a cabbage patch beside it in the windswept mountainous area. Cast and crew had to work here for four weeks experiencing some of the most extreme weather conditions typical of the Wicklow Mountains. Despite the hardship, the adverse weather added visually striking images of the Sally Gap area.

The film is directed by the Serbian film-maker, Goran Paskaljevic, making his first English language feature film. He describes the film as a parable about hate and the clash between traditional culture and modernisation. The screenplay was adapted from a Chinese fable, which Paskaljevic transformed to post-Civil War Ireland with the film serving as a metaphor for the Bosnian conflict. The Civil War is over but matters are far from settled with Harry. He has compiled a list of grievances that are distinctive to him. Harry's figure of hate is O'Flaherty, the richest man in the town.

Colm Meaney, playing against type, is Harry Maloney and Cillian Murphy his simple son, with Adrian Dunbar as his archenemy O'Flaherty. Kerry Condon and Pat Laffan fill other leading roles. Colm Meaney gives a masterly performance as the man obsessed by hatred. *How Harry Became a Tree* won many international awards including Best Screenplay at the Ghent Film Festival.

Counties Wicklow and Dublin provided the background for a nine-week shoot on writer-director Stefan Schwartz's film, *The Abduction Club*. Leading the cast in this swashbuckling bodice-ripping romp is Matthew Rhys, Daniel Lapaine, Sophie Myles and Liam Cunningham. The film is a romantic drama set in Ireland in 1780 where two Irish bachelors find themselves hampered in their search for wives by their lowly status as younger sons. With no inheritance to offer, they are forced to kidnap eligible girls and propose to them at a safe distance from disapproving parents.

Matthew Rhys also stars in the low budget *Peaches* which is set in the Camden Town area of London, but filmed primarily in Dublin by writer-director Nick Grosso. *Peaches* is a slang word for women and the film observes a group of young Londoners over one eventful summer. Frank is resolved not to make any hasty decisions that could jeopardise the last lazy summer of youth. When one of his friends moves on he has to face up to the real world. The exteriors were shot in London but interiors were filmed in a house in Sandymount. The spirited performances of Rhys and the rest of the cast, Kelly Reilly, Justin Salinger, Matthew Dunster and Sophie Okonedo make this a gem of a film.

Director/screenwriter Johnny Grogan chose counties Leitrim, Sligo and Fermanagh as the bleak landscapes for *The Mapmaker*. The production was threatened with the outbreak of foot and mouth as backers sought to withdraw the €1.4 million budget unless they got an assurance that production would not be halted. An agreement was reached with the Department of Agriculture and filming commenced. For *The Mapmaker* Grogan reunited with Brian F. O'Byrne who on this occasion plays a cartographer commissioned to draw a tourist map of a parish on the border. He becomes aware of tensions in the area, with conflict between the locals and forestry manager. When the mapmaker uncovers a body buried years earlier he revives the mystery of the man's disappearance. Supporting O'Byrne in the cast are Susan Lynch and Brendan Coyle. The film won the Special Jury Prize at the Amiens International Film Festival.

# 36

# BLOODY SUNDAY

A Granada film production, *Bloody Sunday*, about the deaths of thirteen unarmed civilians when British soldiers opened fire on a civil rights march in Derry's Bogside on 30 January 1972, commenced shooting in Derry. The film was adapted from Don Mullan's book, *Eyewitness Bloody Sunday*, based on eyewitness accounts of the tragic day. The film concentrates on the stories of four men on the day: civil rights activist Ivan Cooper; teenager Gerry Donaghy who is reluctantly drawn into the conflict; a young soldier who is ordered into the Bogside; and Brigadier Patrick MacLellan, commander of the British army in Derry. Starring in the production is James Nesbitt as Ivan Cooper, a Protestant civil rights campaigner from Strabane who was a founding member of the SDLP. Tim Piggot Smith plays General Ford and Gerard McSorley is the RUC chief. Others in the cast are Kathy Kiera Clarke, Barbara Adair, John Carlin and Allan Gildea.

Director and screenwriter Paul Greengrass begins his reconstruction of the events by staging a parade in Derry following the same route as the original. Locals were invited to participate and they turned out in their hundreds. Greengrass shot the film in a documentary style and cinematographer Ivan Strasburg constantly used shaky hand-held cameras to emphasise the sense of reality. On completion of the Derry segment the production moved to the Ballymun area of Dublin with its tower blocks which was transformed into a replica of the Bogside. Many locals were recruited as extras and dressed in the mini-skirts and bell-bottoms of the period. Conditions were difficult during the Ballymun shoot with cold, damp weather. Some local youths poured urine into the tea urn and replaced the rubber rocks used during the riot with real ones and hurled them at the troops. There was further friction when it was alleged that locals were being paid less than other extras. Other locations were Grangegorman and the Bray Head Hotel.

The budget was so tight on the production that it was only towards the end of the schedule that it was decided that a helicopter could be used for one day. The U2 song 'Bloody Sunday' was played over the closing credits. The film opened to excellent reviews in the United States but as it was transmitted on television before receiving a cinema release it was not eligible for consideration for the Academy Awards. *Bloody Sunday* received many accolades at film festivals including the Golden Bear for Best Film at Berlin and major awards at the Rio and British film festivals.

Shooting simultaneously in the Wicklow Mountains was *Reign of Fire*, the most expensive at $100 million, and technically ambitious film ever made in Ireland. Co-producing the film for Spyglass Pictures was Morgan O'Sullivan. The production was directed by Rob Bowman who had directed the *X-Files* for television and cinema and starred Matthew McConaughey, Christian Bale and Izabella Scorupco. Irish actors in the cast include Gerry O'Brien and Ned Dennehy. Having checked out Irish castles by air, Bowman found them unsuitable and built a charred castle and workings in the Wicklow Gap. The production had the double problem of bad weather and the outbreak of foot and mouth disease. These set backs delayed construction and shooting in the Wicklow Gap to April and May when the grass was green. In post-production the green had to be digitally removed and the land appears as charred. This process cost an additional $250,000. Another impressive set, of a segment of London, was constructed beside the old Pidgeon House in Ringsend.

The film opens in present day London, when a young boy, Quinn, discovers the egg of a dragon. Twenty years later deadly dragons have overrun the world and have wiped out most of the earth's population. Wicklow Gap stands in for rural Northumberland where a group of survivors and their families, led by an adult Quinn, played by Christian Bale, shelter in the bowels of an old castle. From there they attempt to fight back against the dragons. Brash American GI McConaughey zooms in with a tank and helicopter to assist them. A core of fifty extras was chosen as survivors for the duration of the shoot. They had to endure long days and severe conditions on the Wicklow Gap. With fires and fireballs in constant use there were some dangerous times on set. Only one dragon, a 'dead' one actually appeared on set during filming as the remainder were added later by computer. Before developing their dragons the design team turned to sources

James Nesbitt in *Bloody Sunday*, which was based on Don Mullan's research and book.

Izabella Scorupco in a scene from *Reign of Fire*.

from nature based on National Geographic footage.

While new directors were emerging in Ireland, Neil Jordan was on location in France for his thirteenth film, *The Good Thief*, a remake of the 1955 French film, *Bob le Flambeur*. The film, shot in Nice and Monte Carlo, centres on an ageing gambler who plans to pull a final heist on a casino. The stars are Nick Nolte, Nutsa Kukhianicze and Ralph Fiennes. Despite his international reputation and track record Jordan's next production on the Borgias collapsed due to funding.

Some of Dublin's most scenic attractions were chosen as locations in a five-week shoot for the action-comedy, *Highbinders*, with the Hong Kong action star, Jackie Chan. The bulk of the $35 million film was shot in the vicinity of Dublin Castle and on the quays.

The film deals with an international slavery smuggling racket in Hong Kong that is traced to Ireland. Chan is Eddie Yang, the detective investigating the case. He teams up with two Interpol agents and travels to Dublin in search of a talisman. The highbinder of the title is a person who is killed and returns to life with a special magic as happens to the Chan character. The English comedian, Lee Evans, co-stars in the film along with Claire Forlani and Julian Sands as the villain.

Directing the film is the veteran Hong Kong director, Gordon Chan, with Jackie Chan and Sammo Hung in charge of the action scenes. A complex chase scene through the grounds, walls and gateways of Dublin Castle took three weekends to shoot. In another dangerous stunt, Chan, attached to a wire, climbs up the outside of an eight-storey building. He is a strong advocate of performing all his own stunts, despite experiencing some minor bangs and falls. The production later moved to Hong Kong and Thailand to complete shooting.

Originally the Irish section of the film was set in Australia but the producers moved to Ireland after a fruitful meeting with people involved in the Irish film industry. At the end of shooting it was rumoured that Chan would return to Ireland to shoot a sequel to *Shanghai Noon* but this production was in fact switched to Prague. On its release two years later *Highbinders* was retitled *The Medallion* and fared badly at the US and Irish box office.

Four years after *The Boxer* Jim Sheridan began shooting his next production a comedy-drama, *In America* (known as *East of Harlem* during production), in Dublin and New York. The screenplay, written by Sheridan and his daughters, Kirsten and Naomi, originated as an autobiographical picture of his experiences in New York in the 1980s with his wife and two daughters. The film covers an eventful year as the couple, Johnny and Sarah Sullivan and their two young daughters survive a series of hard knocks. The couple have lost a child and the film explains the traumatic effect this has on the family.

In the leading roles of the $10 million film, Sheridan cast two non-Irish actors. British actor, Paddy Considine plays a character loosely based on Sheridan himself and Samantha Morton is his wife. The scene-stealers in the film are young Dublin sisters, Sarah and Emma Bolger as their children. Djimon Hounson plays the important role of the enigmatic Mateo. Others in the cast include Michael Sean Tighe and Juan Hernandez, with Jim Sheridan himself playing a cameo role along with other members of the crew. Sheridan's plan was to shoot with cinematographer, Declan Quinn, all the interiors in Dublin and on sets of the junkie-riddled tenement in Manhattan in Ardmore Studio and the exteriors in New York. Unfortunately the horror of September 11 occurred during shooting and the schedule had to be altered with production designer Mark Geraghty camouflaging areas of Dublin's inner city to represent New York. One sequence required covering a Dublin park in artificial snow. Several months after filming was completed additional scenes had to shot in Dublin.

Before its release the film was screened at many international film festivals where it was critically acclaimed.

In extreme contrast to these productions is *Last Days in Dublin*, the feature directorial debut by young Dubliner Lance Daly. The film is inspired by Daly's work as a courier and was produced for the ridiculously low sum of €70,000. The money was spent on stock and processing and the 23 members of the cast and crew worked for nothing and borrowed equipment whenever necessary. When the film-makers were strapped for cash the Servants of Love, a Wicklow-based religious sect, supplied equipment and a camera. The production used locations throughout Dublin without getting permission in advance and had to make repeated quick exits. They even managed to shoot scenes in Cairo, New York and Paris with a single camera.

Twenty-year-old, Grattan Smith stars as Monster, a diminutive Dubliner who wants to leave his hometown to go travelling but his plans are thwarted by an array of oddball characters. Others in the cast include M. C. Wuzza, John Kavanagh and Jimmy Keogh with such well-known faces such as David Norris and Nell McCafferty making cameo appearances. The story in black and white is played out against a soundtrack of Dublin band Go Blimp Go. Daly shows a strong sense of originality from the opening credits on T-shirts.

Sarah Bolger, Paddy Considine, Samantha Morton and Emma Bolger in Jim Sheridan's *In America*.

# 37

# BROSNAN'S IRISH DREAMTIME

Despite his international success with James Bond, Pierce Brosnan remained loyal to his own production company, Irish Dreamtime. He had formed the company with Beau St Clair and produced the mediocre *The Nephew* in Ireland and the highly successful remake of *The Thomas Crown Affair* in the US. For their third production they chose *Evelyn* based on the true story of Evelyn Doyle. The story tells of a Dublin man, Desmond Doyle, whose four children are taken into care when his wife runs off and he loses his job. Doyle fights the Irish government and Catholic church to overturn an out dated custody law.

The film, set in 1953, was shot under Bruce Beresford's direction in inner city Dublin and Ardmore Studios where a large realistic set of the High Court was constructed on Stage D. Filming concluded only days before Christmas, allowing Brosnan to begin work on the twentieth Bond film, *Die Another Day*, in January 2002. A top line cast was assembled for *Evelyn* with Brosnan as Doyle and supported by Aidan Quinn, Julianna Margulies, Alan Bates, Stephen Rea and John Lynch. Sophie Vavasseur carries off the demanding central role of Evelyn with aplomb. Despite the strong human-interest element the story was told in an over-sentimental fashion. On its release a controversy broke out between members of the Doyle family over the authenticity of the facts portrayed in the film.

With so much media coverage of the abuse and the ill-treatment of young women in the Magdalene laundries it was obvious that a feature film would be produced on the subject. Actor/director Peter Mullan was so appalled by a documentary on the topic that he began researching and writing a screenplay, *The Magdalene Sisters*. He based his film in the 1960s when young girls were sent to these laundries by their parents to atone for their 'sins'. There they worked unpaid and often abused, in the harsh conditions of the institutions run by religious orders. Mullan's powerful, emotional drama focuses on four young women who are incarcerated in a Magdalene asylum. The four young actresses, Anne Marie Duff, Eileen Walsh, Dorothy Duffy and Nora Jane Noone give excellent performances. Geraldine McEwan plays the multi-faceted, Sr Bridget and Britta Smith is outstanding as a long serving inmate.

It was Mullan's intention to film in Ireland but the negative vibes from religious sources encouraged him to move the production to Dunfermline in Scotland.

The film was well received by critics and audiences alike. At the Venice Film Festival it won the Best Film Award and at the Toronto Film Festival the Discovery Award.

Two interesting Irish original screenplays went into production during the summer months of 2002. *The Actors*, written and directed by Conor McPherson, based on a short story by Neil Jordan, stars Michael Caine and Dylan Moran as two eccentric actors. Caine is Anthony O'Malley who dreams of playing Hamlet. He starts hanging out with criminals in one of the roughest pubs in Dublin and befriends the crime boss, Barreller. Caine and Moran don a series of disguises to swindle the gang out of a large sum of cash. Caine even appears in drag as their plan backfires. In one glaring error the same scene is repeated with the same audience walking out of two different performances of the play. In one amusing sequence Caine plays Richard III as a Gestapo officer.

Throughout the film Caine and Moran had fun ad-libbing many of the lines. Over the nine-week shoot the production filmed in Raheny, the SFX, the Olympia Theatre, St Anne's Park and Howth. Among the supporting players are Miranda Richardson, Michael Gambon, Lena Headley, and Deirdre O'Kane. Nine-year-old Abigail Iversen as Mary and Dylan Moran steal the acting honours.

The other film featuring minor Dublin criminals is *Intermission* termed as an Irish Short Cuts or Magnolia. The black comedy-drama set in contemporary suburban Dublin marks the first feature film for theatre director, John Crowley, from a screenplay by Mark O'Rowe. The film, produced by Neil Jordan, Stephen Woolley and Alan Moloney, interweaves the individual stories of a diverse bunch of individuals and their search for love. A misguided break-up between two young lovers initiates a series of events affecting everyone around them with cataclysmic results.

Niall Beagan, Sophie Vavasseur, Pierce Brosnan and Hugh MacDonagh in *Evelyn*.

Phyllis McMahon, Dorothy Duffy, Nora Jane Noone and Anne Marie Duff in *The Magdalen Sisters*.

Colin Farrell as the unsavoury Lehiff in *Intermission*.

Colin Farrell plays a small time crook, Lehiff, who is planning one last heist before going straight. Highlights of the film are a singles club, a double decker bus toppling over and a wheelchair race. Unglamorous locations for the film were shot in Finglas, Tallaght, Smithfield, the North Circular Road and Bray. Heading the cast is Colin Farrell, Colm Meaney, Cillian Murphy, Shirley Henderson, Kelly MacDonald, Ger Ryan, Deirdre O'Kane, Owen Roe and Brian F. O'Byrne. Despite Farrell's demand in Hollywood working with Tom Cruise, Bruce Willis and Al Pachino he honoured his commitment to this film which was delayed to accommodate his US schedule on *Daredevil*. *Intermission* was screened at the Cannes Film Festival to an enthusiastic audience. It grossed €2.8 million at the Irish box office.

# 38

# VERONICA GUERIN

The film version of *Song for a Raggy Boy*, based on the book by Patrick Galvin, was directed by Aisling Walsh in Ballyvourney, Co Cork. This was the first screenplay for the 76-year-old Cork born author. It took four years to get the package together and Subotica, the Dublin-based majority co-producers had to look abroad for much of the €3.7 million budget. Eventually Danish, Spanish and British investors were brought on board.

The film, set in 1939, is based on a true story and documents one man's courage to stand up against the tough regime at an Irish reform school for boys. Aidan Quinn plays Franklin who on returning from the Spanish Civil War, is appointed to St Jude's Reformatory School as the only lay teacher amongst the Christian Brothers. He attempts to build up a relationship based on trust with the boys, who are used to verbal, sexual and physical abuse from the brothers. However, the consequences of his actions prove disastrous and he is forced to decide whether to abandon the school and follow his idealistic principals or work within the system he despises. Others in the cast include Iain Glen, Marc Warren, Alan Devlin, Dudley Sutton and John Travers. Many locals from Ballyvourney were cast as extras in the production. The film received good notices and was chosen for competition at the Sundance Film Festival where it received a standing ovation.

Filming simultaneously in Dublin, Derry and Barcelona was *Mystics*, from a script by Wesley Burrowes. As with *The Actors*, the two central characters are old time performers who had earned their living as members of a theatrical company. Nowadays, to sustain themselves, they hold seances at their self-styled Temple of

Cate Blanchett and Don Wycherley in a scene from *Veronica Guerin*.

Anne Hathaway in the title role of *Ella Enchanted*. The film cost €35million to make.

Aidan Quinn in a poignant and tragic scene from *Song for a Raggy Boy*.

Truth (a room above a pub). They earn money with the harmless scam of pretending to communicate with the dead. Unexpectedly they find themselves in danger when a local criminal dies and his family want to communicate with him. The cast in this black comedy is headed by two veteran actors, David Kelly and Milo O'Shea, as the con-mystics. The film directed by David Blair also features Liam Cunningham, Don Baker and Maria Doyle Kennedy.

An extremely contrasting production is *The Roman Spring of Mrs Stone*. With exterior shooting completed in Rome this production transferred to Ardmore Studios and Dublin's City Hall for lavish interior scenes. The film is a remake of the controversial 1961 drama starring Vivien Leigh and Warren Beatty, which was banned in Ireland. The new production directed by Robert Allan Ackerman from a screenplay by Martin Sherman was adapted from the Tennesse Williams' novella and produced by the US Showtime Networks.

Helen Mirren stars as the frustrated, middle-aged, recently widowed American actress, Mrs Stone, who retreats to Rome. There she buys a fling at romance from a young Italian gigolo. Anne Bancroft plays her waspish friend and Olivier Martinez the gigolo. In a party scene in Dublin's City Hall the actor/director and husband of Bancroft, Mel Brooks, made a cameo appearance.

In the second film based on the life of the murdered Dublin journalist, Veronica Guerin, Australian actress Cate Blanchett was cast in the leading role. Behind the camera there was an impressive line-up of cinema talents with one of Hollywood's most powerful and successful figures, Jerry Bruckheimer, producing the film. Veteran film-maker Joel Schumacher directed from a screenplay by Carol Doyle and Mary Agnes Donoghue. Schumacher remains true to the story of the life and death of Guerin and uses real names and locations that featured in her dramatic life. With ongoing court cases of those accused of her murder aspects of the script had to be altered. Blanchett threw herself into the part and achieved a remarkably authentic Dublin accent and an uncanny likeness to the crusading journalist.

The film commences on 26 June 1996 as Guerin is driving back to Dublin following a court case in Naas and her assassin on a motorbike cold-bloodedly shoots her.

In an anti-drug march staged for the film in Dublin's Summerhill area following the death of Guerin, the situation became extremely realistic when real drug addicts from the area turned on actors and extras. The cast also features Brenda Fricker as Guerin's mother and Barry Barnes as her husband. The meatiest roles are those of the criminals with Gerard McSorley portraying a menacing John Gilligan, Ciaran Hinds as John Traynor, Paudge Behan as Brian

Meehan and Gerry O'Brien as Martin Cahill. Emmet Bergin, Des Cave and Joe Taylor played other leading roles. Colin Farrell, whom Schumacher launched on his Hollywood career by casting him in *Tigerland*, plays a cameo role in the Guerin film as a Manchester United supporter. Veronica Guerin proved a massive hit at the Irish box office where it clocked up over €4 million but failed to register in the US where it received mixed reviews.

The most expensive film shot in Ireland in 2002 was *Ella Enchanted*, based on the best selling children's book by Gail Carson Levine. Following the success of the Harry Potter films Miramax Films decided to shoot this $35 million film for younger audiences in Ireland. The cast is headed by the young star of *The Princess Diaries*, Anna Hathaway, as Ella and the English actor, Hugh Darcy, as the prince. Other well-known faces in the cast include Joanna Lumley, Minnie Driver, Patrick Bergin and Eric Idle. The film, directed by Tommy O'Haver, is set in a fictional medieval world and tells of a young woman, Ella of Frell, who is put under a spell of obedience by a fairy, making her follow all orders given. When Ella realises that the gift is actually a curse, she sets about trying to break the spell to avoid losing the love of her life, Prince Charmant. The film is a retelling of the Cinderella story in which Ella meets a fascinating range of characters. Over 200 extras and sixty dancers, dressed in medieval costumes were employed for the spectacular ball, coronation and wedding scenes on an elaborate castle interior constructed on Stage D in Ardmore Studios. Other scenes were filmed at Humewood House, Powerscourt House, Driminagh Castle, Luttrelstown and Lough Dan.

# 39

## COMEDY AND LOW BUDGETS

Glenarm, Co Antrim was chosen as the main location for the comedy-drama *The Boys and Girls from County Clare* (shot under the title *The Great Céilí War*). The story is set in the mid-1960s and centres on two fiddle-playing brothers. In the era of Beatlemania in Liverpool building contractor Jimmy MacMahon is still playing céilí music with his band at the Shamrock Club while his brother John Joe is leading another band in Co Clare. The brothers meet for the first time in 25 years as band-leaders and bitter rivals at the finals of the All-Ireland Traditional Music Championships. Further complications arise when John Joe's beautiful fiddle player falls for a player in Jimmy's band. Other locations for the film are Belfast and the Isle of Man doubling as Clare. John Irvine directs the whimsical screenplay by Nicholas Adams. The formidable and large cast includes Bernard Hill, Andrea Corr, Colm Meaney, Philip Barantini, James Nesbitt, Stephen Brennan, Catherine Byrne, Charlotte Bradley and David Kelly.

Northern locations also feature in *Puckoon*, based on Spike Milligan's profoundly funny tale. The story is set in 1924 when the boundary commission from Britain and Ireland is deciding on the new border between Northern Ireland and the Irish Republic. The border finds its way down the middle of Puckoon, dividing house from outhouse, man from wife, pub chairs from bar, church from cemetery. One morning Dan Madigan wakes to find beer cheaper on the wrong side of the pub and a border patrol demanding passports. Something has to be done. Writer/director Terence Ryan extracts every ounce of satire and humour from his top line cast headed by Sean Hughes, Elliott Gould,

Richard Attenborough, Daragh O'Malley, John Lynch and Griff Rhys Jones.

The filming of James Joyce's classic novel *Ulysses* by Irish director Sean Walsh was the end of a ten-year quest by the director. Walsh, who owns the Millbrook Studios in Dublin, began his project in 1993 when he wrote the screenplay. The producers found it difficult to encourage backers to invest in their effort to adapt this complex novel for the screen. The film set on one day (16 June 1904) in Dublin incurred additional costs for period costumes and props. With dogged determination Walsh finally got the finance in place and shooting of the low budget film was undertaken in Howth, Dublin Castle and other period settings in the Dublin area. The novel and film explores the consciousness of the three central characters: Leopold Bloom, Molly Bloom and Stephen Dedalus. The film begins with Molly reviewing the events in her life from her affair with Blazes Boylan, her marriage to Bloom and her childhood. Stephen Rea plays Bloom, Angeline Ball his wife Molly, Hugh O'Connor is Stephen and Patrick Bergin the Citizen. On completion of the film Walsh changed the title from *Ulysses* to *Bloom*.

*Spin the Bottle* is an irreverent comedy written by the team of Ian Fitzgibbon and Michael McElhatton, who created the successful RTÉ television series of *Paths of Freedom* and *Fergus' Wedding*. Fitzgibbon directs the strong cast headed by Michael McElhatton, Peter McDonald, Donal O'Kelly, Simon Delaney, Bronagh Gallagher and the last screen role of Pat Leavy as Rat's Ma.

The plot follows Rats on his release from prison and his bad start at readjusting. He discovers that the money he saved to send his aunt to Lourdes in search of a miracle cure for obesity has been stolen. He embarks on a series of schemes to replace the money before it is too late. Finally he decides that his only alternative is to reform his old band Spermdotcom with comical results.

The film was a remarkable achievement being made on a budget of less than €1 million and shot in 18 days on super 16mm film without lighting. McElhatton and his crew filmed in actual locations including Mountjoy Prison, corporation flats, streets, pubs and RTÉ.

Liz Gill is one of the few female director/screenwriters amongst the latest crop of film-makers. Her *Goldfish Memory* takes a light-hearted look at the dangers and delights of sexuality in contemporary Dublin. When Clara sees her boyfriend Tom kissing Isolde, it sets off a chain reaction of romances and heartbreaks, each trying to solve the pressing question of the perfect relationship. The film, the second feature for Gill, was shot with a small crew on digital video on a tight four-week schedule. Sean Campion, Flora Montgomery, Keith McErlean, Jean Butler, Fiona O'Shaughnessy and Stuart Graham head the cast, with Ritchie Buckley providing the haunting music score. The witty script, that portrays characters switching from straight to gay relationships at will, stretched credibility. Quinn and Gill's films were premiered at the Dublin International Film Festival but did not register too successfully at the box office.

On paper *The Honeymooners* seemed doomed to fail but it surprisingly succeeds. The production was filmed on a minuscule budget of £65,000 in 18 days by writer/director Karl Golden on location in Dublin and Portmagee, Co Antrim. By undertaking some of the shoot in Northern Ireland the film qualified for funding from their film board. Employing only natural light the film was shot entirely with hand-held DV cameras creating an authentic atmosphere. Following the wedding reception scene the cast and crew were informed that they could consume the props of rolls and sandwiches as their lunch. Alex Reid, Jonathan Byrne, Justine Mitchell, Gladys Sheehan and Conor Mullen star in this quirky comedy tale of a jilted groom and a waitress who make an unlikely alliance. Together they begin a hilarious and chaotic adventure that will change both their lives.

Over the past decade trends in Irish film production have been unpredictable. In 2001 twelve Irish films were released in cinemas with the comedies *About Adam* and *When Brendan Met Trudy* proving highly successful at the Irish box office but not abroad. In 2002 there was a decline of indigenous Irish films on release in cinemas, but the numbers in production remained at a healthy level. With the exception of *Veronica Guerin* and *Ella Enchanted* with budgets of $17 and $35 million respectively, Ireland failed to attract any major Hollywood productions in the *Braveheart, Saving Private Ryan* and *Reign of Fire* league. Ironically *Bloody Sunday* and *The Magdalene* Sisters, the two most successful Irish films of recent years, have been directed by an English and Scottish director, Paul Greengrass and Peter Mullan, respectively. It is therefore encouraging to see a number of talented Irish writer/directors emerging.

With the budget of December 2002 the Minister for Finance, Charlie McCreevy announced a tightening up of Section 481 tax incentives, with a ceiling of €10.48 million per production and the process ending in 2004. The abolition of the tax breaks would greatly curtail or end any further big budget productions being produced in Ireland. Prior to the budget there was speculation that the minister would abolish the Irish Film Board as a means of saving revenue but he rejected this suggestion. Despite their vulnerability the Film Board launched an enlightened project entitled Low Budget Feature Initiative in which they would finance up to fifteen feature films over a three-year period. Strict guidelines were applicable specifying that the budget of each production must be

*Left*: Jane Milligan and Sean Hughes in a scene from Terrence Ryan's *Puckoon*.

*Below*: Michael McElhatton as Rats in *Spin the Bottle*.

Sexual experimentation in *Goldfish Memory*.

under €1 million with the producer providing at least forty per cent and the board putting up the balance. The board received many submissions and the following were some of the first films qualifying under the scheme: *The Halo Effect, Head Rush, Bloom, Dead Bodies* and *Goldfish Memory.*

All these productions had much in common and with the exception of *Dead Bodies* had the same writer/director. To remain within their budgets each production also appealed for crew members and actors to work at reduced rates. Friends, neighbours and relatives dutifully filled in as lowly-paid extras. In some instances extras gave their services free.

For writer/director Lance Daly the experience on his second feature, *The Halo Effect* was considerably less stressful than on his shoestring *Last Days in Dublin*. For this production he had a budget of €1 million. *The Halo Effect* is set in a chip shop, run by Fatso, in Dublin's inner city during the last days of the Celtic Tiger boom. The chipper is where an assortment of characters is employed and hang out. Fatso employs hopelessly incompetent staff and generally manages to keep the entire community ticking over. His compulsive gambling is getting the better of him and he has to contend with an endless succession of loan sharks and debt collectors. In a poker game against a local crime boss he bets his chipper. Again the filming concentrates on a Dublin not featured in the tourist guides and the set designer constructed a replica chip shop in Dorset Street. Heading the strong cast is Stephen Rea as Fatso, Grattan Smith, Kerry Condon, Simon Delaney, John Kavanagh and Mick Lally.

Covering similar territory is *Head Rush*, the feature debut of Shimmy Marcus (son of the documentary film-maker Louis Marcus). This crime comedy features an assortment of Dublin characters against the background of the Celtic Tiger. It focuses on two disillusioned youths, Charlie and T-Bag, struggling through a haze of cannabis. When Charlie gets dumped by his girlfriend Vicky, and is knocked off the dole he becomes desperate to win her back. On hearing that a leading criminal is looking for new mules they devise an elaborate scam to smuggle a consignment of cocaine back from Amsterdam. Their plan backfires and in a series of amusing incidents they find themselves up to their necks in trouble. During location work one Saturday morning at the Bank of Ireland in Rathmines there was anxiety, as some locals believed that the bank was being robbed. *Head Rush* also required a short stint of location work in Amsterdam. Featuring in the film are Wuzza Conlon, Gavin Kelly, Laura Pyper, Tom Hickey and Maura O'Neill. Marcus pulled off a major coup in acquiring the services of the distinguished British actor, Steven Berkoff for a cameo role.

First time director, Robert Quinn (son of the veteran film-maker Bob Quinn), also chose a black comedy as the subject for *Dead Bodies*. With cinematographer Donal Gilligan he shot the film on High Definition Video in contemporary Dublin.

The plot revolves around Tommy, a young carefree supermarket assistant, who lives life to the full. Everything abruptly changes with the return of his high maintenance, anti-everything, ex-girlfriend, Jean. When she accidentally slips and dies he panics and fearful of the consequences, decides to bury the body in a local wood. As he digs a shallow grave he discovers another body and so begins an even greater dilemma.

The cast includes Andrew Scott, Kelly Reilly, Sean McGinley, Gerard McSorley and Des Nealon. This is an assured black thriller shot over a four-week stint in Dublin with post-production undertaken in Windmill Lane.

# 40

# KING ARTHUR

For the first six months of 2003 there was a pessimistic air amongst film-workers in Ireland with the threat of the abolition of Section 481, with only commercials and television series in production but no feature films. Then word filtered through that a major film was to be shot entirely in Ireland. The film, *King Arthur*, saw the return of the leading Hollywood producer, Jerry Bruckheimer, to Ireland. The previous year he had produced *Veronica Guerin* and for a number of factors had decided to film the $100 million epic of the Dark Ages in Ireland. Bruckheimer had been pleased with the professionalism of the Irish cast and crew, the diverse locations and the tax breaks under Section 481.

The location managers scoured the country for suitable locations for *King Arthur* before choosing many of the leading Co Wicklow beauty spots including Glenmalure, Wicklow Gap, Powerscourt, Hollywood, Turloughhill, Glendalough and Lugglaugh for sequences in the film. At Ballymore Eustace, Co Kildare, the largest set ever constructed in Ireland, featuring a village and a replica of Hadrian's Wall, was built by the construction team. Industry analysts estimated that the film would contribute €54 million to the Irish economy.

The epic *King Arthur*, is directed by Antoine Fuqua, who directed *Training Day* and *The Replacement Killers,* with the screenplay by David Franzoni and John Lee Hancock. The production is a demystified take on the tale of King Arthur and the Knights of the Round Table and a more realistic portrayal of Arthur than had previously been presented on screen. The film focuses on the history and the politics of the period during which Arthur ruled – when the Roman Empire collapsed and skirmishes over power broke out in outlying countries. The film attempts to place Arthur within his historical context, between the fall of the Roman Empire and the long road through the Dark Ages.

The film stars Clive Owen as Arthur, Stephen Dillane as Merlin, Keira Knightly as Guinevere, Ioan Gruffudd as Lancelot, Ray Winstone as Bors, Til Schweiger as Cynric and Stellan Skarsgard. Although no Irish names feature in prominent roles thousands of extras were recruited for the village and battle scenes. Before filming commenced there were large-scale photo shoots in counties Wicklow, Dublin and Kildare for extras to take the roles of knights, Saxons, Romans, Welsh and Scottish villagers. Over 5,000 people turned up for the casting sessions. Four hundred members of the FCA and other selected extras were taken to boot camp for special training to rehearse the bloody battle scenes. They were trained in marching, military manoeuvres, use of shields, long bows and swords. Filming was an arduous ordeal for all involved with the working day extending from sunrise to sunset, June to November.

In contrast to *King Arthur*, *Laws of Attraction* is a contemporary comedy set in New York and Ireland. In the film Pierce Brosnan portrays a divorce lawyer who falls in love with and marries another attorney, Julianne Moore, a top New York lawyer who handles high-profile divorce cases. Brosnan takes on the spouses of the people she is representing. After falling in love, the couple find that they are not immune to the same marital difficulties that bring their clients to court. Also in the cast are Parker Posey, David Wilmot and David Kelly.

The director, Peter Howitt, who also directed the box office hit *Johnny English*, began his career as an actor in the popular television series *Bread*. He proved to be a witty, friendly character who was still jovial after a twelve-hour working day.

*Laws of Attraction* was produced by Brosnan's own production company Irish Dreamtime. This was the fourth production for Brosnan and his business partner, Beau St Clair and their third production to be filmed in Ireland following *The Nephew* and *Evelyn*. Originally the story was set in Los Angeles but the producers were so keen to work in Ireland that the locations were transferred to New York and Ireland. Some New York scenes were shot in pubs and restaurants in the Temple Bar area of Dublin and a large American courtroom set was constructed in Ardmore Studios. Other Irish locations include Powerscourt, the Sugarloaf, Humewood House, Roundwood and Croke Park.

One extremely 'Oirish' segment of the film was shot over two days in the Bray Head Hotel that was transformed into a country pub for the Ballygra Annual Festival. During their visit Brosnan and Moore experience a céilí, a beer-drinking contest, a disco; they perform a karakoe duet and attend a mock

Keira Knightley and Clive Owen star in *King Arthur*.

wedding. The majority of Irish people present were not impressed by this stage Irish aspect in which Pierce is dragged onto the floor by a fat woman with a moustache and Joanne by a pig farmer. On winning the beer drinking competition Pierce is awarded a miniature leprechaun.

The producers had hoped to produce a classic comedy in the Spencer Tracey and Katherine Hepburn tradition.

The multi-billion dollar Indian film industry that produces over 1,000 films per year came to Ireland for location work on *Ayodhiya*. The title refers to the holy site in southern India which has been a place of conflict between the Muslim and Hindu communities. This was the first Bollywood film, co-produced with the Irish Pulcan Films to be shot in Ireland. The production centred their activities around eighteen-year-old Reena Rama and Eswar Rajamani and is directed and written by Eswar's brother Jayaprakash.

Many of the scenes were shot spontaneously when they director spotted a scenic location and set up his camera. On one occasion a guided tour around the monastic site of Glendalough unexpectedly walked into a scene with Reena Rama in a wedding dress. A troupe of Irish dancers called Celtic Rhythm dressed in Indian costumes and performed Indian dance steps. The production team utilised taped Indian music for the many dancing sequences. The love story centres around a Hindu man who exiles himself to Ireland and is followed there by his Muslim lover who attempts to bring him home. The story covers the conflict between the two lovers from different communities. Prior to their Irish visit the company had filmed in the southern Indian province of Tamil Hadu. The producers were so impressed with the Irish scenery and co-operation that they plan to return.

Patrick McGrath's novel of passion and obsession, *Asylum*, adapted for the screen by Patrick Marber is set in 1959 in a remote psychiatric hospital in Wales. The film began a four-week shoot in Leeds before moving for five weeks to the Hanney Studio and St Bricin's Hospital in Dublin and locations in Co Wicklow. The tragic drowning sequence of the boy was also filmed at the Upper Lake in Glendalough. David Mackenzie directed the distinguished cast headed by Natasha Richardson, Ian McKellen, Hugh Bonneville, Marton Csokas, Joss Ackland and Judy Parfitt. Richardson plays Stella, the wife of a doctor who has an affair with a patient who has been admitted to the asylum after murdering his wife. She has a dark past herself and when her young son drowns while in her care she descends into depression.

*The Blackwater Lightship*, based on the Booker nominated novel by Colm Toibin, was adapted for the screen by Shane Connaughton. The veteran

American actress, Angela Lansbury, who has a holiday home in Co Cork, returned to Ireland to take the central role. She stars as the matriarch of the Devereux family, three generations of women who are forced together when they discover that a male relative is dying of Aids. The novel is set in a bleak house on the Wexford coast but director John Erman filmed in the Co Wicklow locations of Greystones, Enniskerry, Brittas Bay and interiors in Ardmore Studios. The €5 million film for CBS TV also features Dianne Wiest, Keith McErlean, Gina McKee and Brian F. O'Byrne.

# 41

# FROM DOGS TO DEAD MEAT

Following a fallow period the summer of 2003 proved to be an exceptionally busy one on the film front as many productions went before the cameras. The American director, Kevin Reynolds, who directed *The Count of Monte Cristo* in Ireland returned to the Clifden area of Co Galway to shoot a new version of *Tristan and Isolde*. The film, under executive producer Ridley Scott, stars young American actor James Franco as Tristan and Sophie Myles as Isolde. Co-starring in the production are David O'Hara, Rufus Sewell, Bronagh Gallagher and Dexter Fletcher. Following the Irish shoot the production moved to Prague for completion.

Simultaneously on the east coast Paddy Breathnach was shooting his fourth feature film, *Man About Dog*, on location in Wicklow, Dublin, Kildare and Belfast. Shelbourne Park and many of the greyhound tracks throughout the country feature in the film. The screenplay for this black comedy is by Belfast writer Pearse Elliott and the producers are Robert Walpole and Simon Channing Williams. The raucous comedy is set in the world of greyhound racing in Ireland and centres around three young men from West Belfast who hatch a scheme to beat the bookies in the Republic. They are lumbered with a greyhound that only runs when it suits him. The cast features Sean McGinley, Pat Shortt, Alan Leech, Ciaran Nolan, Tom Jordan Murphy and Fionnula Flanagan.

Aiden Gillen and Renée Weldon star as young lovers in the modern love story, *Bite*, the second feature film from director Fintan Connolly. Connolly co-wrote the screenplay with Catríona McGowan. In supporting roles are Mannix

Flynn, Eamonn Morrissey, Susan Fitzgerald, Darragh Kelly and Declan Conlon. The story revolves around a chance encounter between a woman, Michelle, on the run from a messy relationship and a man, Conor, on the run from himself. Their relationship, against a Dublin background, develops into a strong sexual bond.

The award-winning Irish director, Damien O'Donnell, who had directed the critically acclaimed *East is East* and *Heartlands,* shot *Inside I'm Dancing*, his first Irish film in the Dublin area. While filming at the Markievicz Flats in Pearse Street the film-makers recruited locals as extras. The screenplay of the comedy drama by Jeffrey Caine is based on an original story by Christian O'Reilly. The life of twenty-four-year-old Michael, a long term resident of Carrigmore Residential Home for the Disabled is transformed when rebellious Rory moves in. Michael is astonished to discover that fast-talking Rory, who can only move his right hand, can understand his almost unintelligible speech. Soon Rory's dynamic nature sparks a flame in Michael, introducing him to a new life outside the institution. The cast for this humorous drama includes Romola Garai, James McAvoy, Steven Robertson, Brenda Fricker, Ruth McCabe and Tom Hickey.

A real life incident that occurred in 1999 was to become the subject of a feature film, *Sliding Dice*. The film is based on a major scam when 41 Romanians tricked the Irish authorities into believing they were a choir and received visas to participate in a music festival in Sligo. On their arrival at Dublin airport they disappeared. *Sliding Dice*, a fictionalised account of the scam that caused embarrassment in diplomatic circles is co-produced by Barry Mulligan, the Irish honorary consul in Bucharest. Mulligan, co-writer of the screenplay plays an Irish conman who helps to organise the scam and fool the Irish authorities. The film was shot in Romania over a six-week spell before moving to Dublin to conclude the shoot.

Galway is the setting for a supernatural thriller, *The Turlough*, for Maxim Pictures, an independent Irish/Australian film company. The storyline centres on John, who inherits some land following his father's death. John, who has not spoken to his father in fifteen years, has made it big in the Celtic Tiger and decides to develop the land. As a consequence a series of things go wrong as he has upset the spirits of the land.

Director Justin O'Brien was shooting the low budget production in Galway city, Craughwell and Oranmore.

*Dead Meat*, written, edited and directed by Conor McMahon is situated in the unusual setting of Co Leitrim. The topical storyline tells of the destroying of a group of infected cows. Unfortunately one slips through the net and begins an infection that quickly spreads throughout the countryside. People become cannibalistic and a young woman, Helen, seeks to find a safe escape across the treacherous landscape. Marian Araujo, David Muyllaert and Eoin Whelan feature in the cast.

*Adam and Paul* is a comedy drama set in Dublin and recalls a day in the life of two heroin addicts searching for a score. The camera follows the friends as all their efforts are devoted to scrounging and robbing money for drugs. The film marks a feature film debut for Lenny Abrahamson who shot from a screenplay by Mark O'Halloran who stars in the film with Tom Murphy.

Limerick-born director and screen-writer, David Gleeson made his feature film debut with *Cowboys and Angels*, a comedy drama set in present day Limerick. Gleeson's love for cinema can surely be attributed to his father who ran a small cinema in the village of Cappamore, Co Limerick. *Cowboys and Angels*, shot on a small budget and tight schedule avoided the image of the city as the crime capital of Ireland with gang feuds and stabbings. The story centres around two young men with nothing in common who share an apartment. Shane is a shy civil servant who has difficulty relating to girls while Vincent is an extrovert gay fashion design student. Shane finds his life transformed as he encounters a period of discovery in this new life style. Gleeson shot the film entirely on location in a variety of unglamorous locations. The mainly young cast includes Michael Legge as Shane, Allan Leech as Vincent, Amy Shiels, David Murray, Maeve McGrath and Frank Kelly as an old civil servant.

Surprisingly for a low budget Irish film it received a wide distribution in Ireland and favourable reviews.

*Omagh*, a film dealing with the Omagh car bombing of 15 August 1998, went into production in Dublin in December. The screenplay written by the screenwriter-director of the award-winning *Bloody Sunday*, Paul Greengrass, and Guy Hibbert is co-produced by Ed Guiney. The leading British director Pete Travis directs the cast headed by Gerard McSorley from Omagh as Michael Gallagher, whose 21-year-old son died in the blast. He spoke on behalf of the families and is the focal point of the film.

Others in the cast include Michelle Forbes, Pauline Hutton, Fiona Glascott, Des Cave, Brenda Fricker and Ian McIlhenney.

The film tells of the horrendous atrocity on a summer's day when 29 innocent people lost their lives in the Co Tyrone town. The film covers the rescue of victims from the rubble and the frantic search by relations through the blood stained hospital wards for missing loved ones. It also portrays the family's reactions and coming to terms with the grief and their dogged pursuit of justice.

Director of photography, Donal Gilligan and Ciaran Tanham on second unit

James McAvoy and Romola Garai in a scene from *Inside I'm Dancing*.

Michael Legge as the not-so-shy civil servant in *Cowboys and Angels*.

shot the film in semi-documentary style, with hand held cameras. This device had been employed to great success in Greengrass's award-winning *Bloody Sunday*.

Amputees were employed to add an extra degree of reality to the graphic reconstruction of the aftermath as the casualties were conveyed to hospital. In a dramatic sequence Brenda Fricker, playing Ombudsman, Nuala O'Loan, announced various short-comings in the investigation and that it is unlikely that anyone will be charged with the mass murder. The Co Meath town of Navan was chosen to represent Omagh. The town's Watergate Street bears a strong resemblance to Market Street in Omagh and was transformed into the set of the aftermath of the bomb.

Another film with a Northern Ireland setting is *Boxed* that tells of an idealistic priest who is mistakenly abducted by an IRA group and forced to hear the last confession from a suspected informer awaiting execution. When he refuses to comply there is a stand-off between the priest and his abductors. Writer/director Marion Comer filmed in Tipperary, Belfast and London. Tom Jordan Murphy, Darragh Kelly, Catherine Cusack, Jim Norton and Éanna MacLiam head the cast.

Eighty-year-old, actor/director Richard Attenborough came to Belfast for location work on his twelfth film as director, *Crossing the Line*. The $20 million production is set in North Carolina and Belfast and covers two periods, 1943 and 1993. The cast features Dennis Hopper, Shirley MacLaine, Colin Hanks and Mena Suvari.

Another film set against the strife in Northern Ireland is *Mickybo and Me*, based on the award-winning stage play by Owen McCafferty. The €3 million film tells the story of two boys who become friends in Belfast at the onset of sectarian strife in the early 1970s. They live in a fantasy world and share an obsession with *Butch Cassidy and the Sundance Kid*. The movie eventually inspires them to run away to Australia. This was the first feature film for writer-director Terry Loane whose credits include the Oscar-nominated short film, *Dance Lexie Dance*. Stephen Daldry is executive producer, for Working Title, producers of *Bridget Jones's Diary* and *Billy Elliot*. The nine-week shoot covers many locations across Northern Ireland including Banbridge and Portrush. The film stars Julie Walters, Ciaran Hinds, Adrian Dunbar, Gina McKee and in the leading roles two Belfast newcomers – Niall Wright as Jonjo and John Joe McNeill as Mickybo.

Belfast is also the setting for *Freeze Frame* by writer/director John Simpson. A paranoid murder suspect constantly videotapes himself to establish an alibi in case he is ever accused of another crime. His problems begin when the one tape that could prove his innocence of a new murder mysteriously disappears and he has to go on the run. Lee Evans, Sean McGinley, Ian McNeice, Colin Salmon and Rachael Stirling feature in the cast.

*You Looking at Me?,* a love story set in a similar locale, centres on a Chinese girl, Mei, who falls in love with a Protestant boy, Kenny. Life for the young couple is complicated as they try to adjust to their cultural differences and local politics in contemporary Belfast. The film directed and written by Margo Harkin features the young cast of Packy Lee, Kelly Flynn, Julie Lam and Kevin Breen.

Two diverse films featuring Irish characters, but not an Irish setting are *Blind Flight* and *Timbuktu*. *Blind Flight* reconstructs the four-and-a-half years that Belfast teacher Brian Keenan and journalist John McCarthy spent in capacity in the Lebanon in the late 1980s. The screenplay co-written by Keenan and director John Furse was based on Keenan's book *An Evil Cradling*. Ian Hart as Keenan and Linus Roache as McCarthy give outstanding performances as the captives with a common bond to survive. The film took thirteen years of planning and fund-raising to actually get into production. Shooting was undertaken in Belfast and Morocco on a tight schedule. The photography of Ian Wilson captures vividly the claustrophobia of the cell in which the two men are confined.

Morocco was also a location for *Timbuktu* directed by Alan Gilsenan from a screenplay by Paul Freaney. The multi-talented Gilsenan who moves at ease between film, television and theatre chose a dramatic road movie set in North Africia as his next project. Cinematographer P. J. Dillon again employed hand-held digital camera work for much of the frantic feel to the film. The story centres on a young woman Isobel, and her transvestite friend who search for her brother, a monk who has been kidnapped by Algerian rebels. Eva Birthistle, Karl Geary, George Jackos and Liam O'Maonlai head the cast.

# 42

# A BRIGHT FUTURE

W the looming threat that the Section 481 tax incentive scheme would be discontinued or greatly altered from the end of 2004. A number of productions were put on hold while others moved to locations such as Romania and the Isle of Man. In the main Section 481 applied to big budget films while low budget Irish films continued to be produced at an encouraging rate. Many proved highly successful at the Irish box office where Irish audiences flocked to see them in great numbers. In the past Irish productions would only enjoy a limited release for a week before disappearing and reappearing on video but as their subject matter became more contemporary and appealing to a younger audience attendances rose dramatically.

The year was to end on a positive note when the Minister for Finance, Charlie McCreevy, announced in his budget that not alone was Section 481 to be extended to 2008 but that the limit on qualifying productions was to be raised from €10.48 million to €15 million.

With the release of a diverse range of Irish-made films, 2003 proved to be one of the most successful years ever for the Irish film industry. In particular there was the overwhelming success of *Veronica Guerin* and *Intermission*. *Veronica Guerin* took the top place at the Irish box office, clocking up over €4.1 and *Intermission* in sixth place with a take of €2.8 million.

In the past decade more Irish films have been produced here than within the previous century and especially by indigenous directors. In 1918 Willie Power had begun the trend with his silent films to be followed by Tom Cooper who achieved astonishing results with *The Dawn* in the 1930s. Unfortunately their efforts were 'one-off' novelties with no follow-ups.

The majority of other major films were Hollywood versions of Irish rural life as with John Ford's *The Quiet Man* and *The Rising of the Moon* and David Lean's *Ryan's Daughter*. In many other productions Irish locations have doubled as a variety of diverse settings from Germany in *The Spy who Came in from the Cold* and *The Red Baron*, France in *The Blue Max* to China in *The Face of Fu Manchu*.

With the opening of Ardmore Studios in 1958 the majority of productions were by English film companies. There was also an over-reliance on successful Abbey plays as material for films. In the late 1950s and early '60s producers applied this lazy approach of filming stage plays rather than commissioning original screenplays. *Home is the Hero*, *The Big Birthday* and *This Other Eden* are prime examples of this method of production. In that era film production was more cumbersome with heavy arc lamps and cameras essential for interior scenes which were primarily shot on studio stages and exteriors on actual locations. In the main with more accessible equipment this method of operation has become obsolete and the tendency now is to film entirely on location.

With a list of award-winning films to their credit Neil Jordan and Jim Sheridan still maintain their international status. Sheridan and his daughters, Kirsten and Naomi have won many awards for their screenplay for *In America* including Best Writer at the Critics Choice Awards and the Stanley Kramer Award from the Producer's Guild.

The major achievement for *In America* was receiving three Oscar nominations for the 2004 Awards. The awards were for Samantha Morton in the Best Actress category, Djimon Hounson for Best Supporting Actor and Jim, Kirsten and Naomi for Best Original Screenplay. Unfortunately the film did not pick up any Oscars.

Equally encouraging is the emergence of a new wave of Irish directors including Gerry Stembridge, Conor McPherson, Robert Quinn, Paddy Breathnach, Kirsten Sheridan, Shimmy Marcus, John Crowley, Liz Gill and Michael McElhatton. Each has broken barriers and expressed their own individual style of film.

The Irish Film Board is to be congratulated for their support of low budget and micro-budget films allowing first time directors an opportunity to display their talents. Hopefully in coming years we can look forward to these new directors to produce international hits of the calibre of *My Left Foot* and *The Crying Game*.

With the uncertainty over Section 481 American film production companies were reluctant to make commitments without a gilt-edge assurance. In the first

Cillian Murphy (right) and Gavin Friday (left) in Neil Jordan's *Breakfast on Pluto*, adapted from Patrick McCabe's novel of the same name.

Aidan Gillen as Conor and Renée Weldon as Michelle, from *Trouble with Sex*.

six months of 2004 no indigenous or foreign companies went into production.

Many films were in various stages of development but nothing was certain until the budget was in place and the camera begins to roll. Fortunately in the latter part of the year a number of films went into production. Noel Pearson brought Maeve Binchy's novel *Tara Road* to the screen. Gillies MacKinnon returned to direct Andie McDowell, Olivia Williams and Sarah Bolger on location in Dublin, Wicklow and South Africa. For the big screen version of the hit television series *The Honeymooners,* New York settings were reconstructed in Ardmore and on Dublin locations. John Schulz directed Cedric the Entertainer in the leading role. Another popular television series the quirky *The League of Gentlemen* received the big screen treatment in *The League of Gentlemen's Apocalypse.* The familiar faces popped up in many Irish locations.

Indigenous film makers were lead by Neil Jordan. For his latest project he adapted another Pat McCabe novel, *Breakfast on Pluto,* for the screen. He assembled an outstanding cast headed by Liam Neeson, Cillian Murphy, Brendan Gleeson and Stephen Rea. Filming was undertaken in Dublin, Wicklow, Kilkenny and London.

Other Irish films to go before the camera in the latter months of the year were Billy O'Brien's *Isolation*, Stephen Bradley's horror film *Boy Eats Girl* and Fintan Connolly's *Trouble with Sex*. Commencing the new year Paul Mercier brought his highly successful stage play *Studs* to the screen with Brendan Gleeson again playing the leading role.

The Minister for the Arts, John O'Donoghue led a group of Irish film-makers to the major studios in the United States to promote Ireland as an ideal film location with tax and auxiliary benefits.

Hopes are high that with the minister's trip and the extension of Section 481 film production will increase dramatically. The reprieve could also see some other major Hollywood backed productions being filmed in Ireland, giving a boost to the industry and local economy. At present the film industry in Ireland employs 4,300 people directly and about 3,000 indirectly.

# FILMOGRAPHY

F The Lad from Old Ireland (1910)
D Sidney Olcott
C Gene Gauntier, Robert Vignola

F Rory O'Moore (1911)
D Sidney Olcott
C Gene Gauntier, Jack P. McGowan

F The Colleen Bawn (1912)
D Sidney Olcott
C Brian MacGowan, Sidney Olcott

F Arragh-na-Pogue (1912)
D Sidney Olcott
C Jack P. McGowan, Robert Vignola

F The O'Neill (1912)
D Sidney Olcott
C Pat O'Malley, Gene Gauntier

F The Shaughran (1912)
D Sidney Olcott
C Gene Gauntier, Jack Clarke

F You'll Remember Ellen (1912)
D Sidney Olcott
C Gene Gauntier, Jack Clarke

F Shane The Post (1913)
D Sidney Olcott
C Jack Clarke, Pat O'Malley

F The Kerry Gow (1913)
D Sidney Olcott
C Gene Gauntier, Jack P. McGowan

F Ireland the Oppressed (1913)
D Sidney Olcott
C Robert Vignola, Jack Clarke

F The Kerry Dancer (1913)
D Sidney Olcott
C Gene Gauntier, Jack Clarke

F A Girl of Glenbeigh (1914)
D Sidney Olcott
C Gene Gauntier, Jack Clarke

F The Fishermaid of Ballydavid (1914)
D Sidney Olcott
C Gene Gauntier, Robert Vignola

F The Gypsies of Old Ireland (1914)
D Sidney Olcott
C Annie O'Sullivan, Valentine Grant

F  Ireland a Nation (1914)
D  Walter MacNamara
C  Barry O'Brien

F  Robert Emmet (1914)
D  Sidney Olcott
C  Jack Melville, Pat O'Malley

F  Bunny Blarneyed (1914)
D  Larry Trimble
C  Larry Trimble

F  Fun at Finglas Fair (1915)
D  F. J. McCormick
C  F. J. McCormick

F  Puck Fair Romance (1916)
D  J. M. Kerrigan
C  J. M. Kerrigan, Kathleen Murphy

F  Molly Bawn (1916)
D  Cecil M. Hepworth
C  Alma Taylor, Stewart Rome

F  O'Neill of the Glen (1916)
D  J. M. Kerrigan
C  J. M. Kerrigan, Nora Clancy,
    Fred O'Donovan

F  The Miser's Gift (1916)
D  J. M. Kerrigan
C  J. M. Kerrigan, Kathleen Murphy,
    Fred O'Donovan

F  An Unfair Love Affair (1916)
D  J. M. Kerrigan
C  Nora Clancy, Fred O'Donovan

F  Widow Malone (1916)
D  J. M. Kerrigan
C  J. M. Kerrigan

F  Food of Love (1916)
D  J. M. Kerrigan
C  Kathleen Murphy, Fred O'Donovan

F  Woman's Wit (1916)
D  J. M. Kerrigan
C  Kathleen Murphy, Fred O'Donovan

F  The Eleventh Hour (1917)
D  Fred O'Donovan
C  Brian MacGowan, Kathleen Murphy

F  The Upstart (1917)
D  J. M. Kerrigan
C  Kathleen Murphy, Fred O'Donovan

F  Blarney (1917)
D  J. M. Kerrigan
C  Kathleen Murphy, J. M. Kerrigan

F  The Byeways of Fate (1917)
D  J. M. Kerrigan
C  Nora Clancy

F  The Irish Girl (1917)
D  J. M. Kerrigan
C  Kathleen Murphy

F  In the Days of Saint Patrick (1917)
D  Norman Whitton
C  Ira Allen, Alice Cardinall,
    George Gnffin

F  Knocknagow (1916)
D  John McDonagh
C  Brian McGowan, J. McCarra,
    Alice Keating

F  Rafferty's Rise (1918)
D  J. M. Kerrigan
C  Fred O'Donovan, Kathleen Murphy,
    Arthur Shields

F  When Love Came to Gavin Burke
    (1918)
D  Fred O'Donovan
C  Brian Moore, Kathleen Murphy

F Willie Scouts While Jessie Pouts
(1918)
D William Power
C William Power

F Rosaleen Dhu (1919)
D William Power
C William Power, Kitty Hart

F An Irish Vendetta (1920)
D William Power
C William Power, Kitty Hart

F Willie Reilly and the Colleen Bawn
(1919)
D John McDonagh
C Brian MacGowan, Kathleen Alexander

F The Life of Michael Dwyer (1919)
D John McDonagh
C F. J. McCormick

F The O'Casey Millions (1922)
D John McDonagh
C Jimmy O'Dea, Nan Fitzgerald,
Fred Jeffs

F Wicklow Gold (1922)
D John McDonagh
C Jimmy O'Dea

F Paying the Rent (1922)
D John McDonagh
C Jimmy O'Dea

F Land of her Fathers (1924)
D John Hurley
C Mícheál MacLiammóir,
Phyllis Wakeley

F Cruiskeen Lawn (1924)
D John McDonagh
C Tom Moran, Jimmy O'Dea,
Fay Sargent

F Irish Destiny (1925)
D I. J. Eppel
C Dennis O'Dea, Una Shields,
Daisy Campbell

F Ireland's Rough-Hewn Destiny (1929)
D Victor Haddick
C Gearóid O'Lochlinn

F Song of my Heart (1930)
D Frank Borzage
C John McCormack, Maureen O'Sullivan

F Some May Change (1933)
D Michael Farrell
C Sheila Fay

F Sweet Inniscarra (1934)
D Emmet Moore
C Sean Rogers, Mae Ryan

F Guests of the Nation (1934)
D Denis Johnson
C Barry Fitzgerald, Shelagh Richards
Hilton Edwards

F General John Regan (1934)
D Henry Edwards
C Henry Edwards, Chrissie White,
W. G. Fay

F Jimmy Boy (1934)
D John Baxter
C Jimmy O'Dea, Guy Middleton,
Vera Sherburne

F Irish Hearts (1934)
D Brian Desmond Hurst
C Lester Matthews, Nancy Burne,
Sara Allgood

F Riders to the Sea (1935)
D Brian Desmond Hurst
C Sara Allgood, Kevin Gutherie,
Ria Mooney

F  The Luck of the Irish (1935)
D  Donovan Pedelty
C  Richard Hayward, Kay Walsh,
   Niall McGinnis

F  Irish for Luck (1936)
D  Arthur Woods
C  Athene Seyler, Margaret Lockwood

F  The Voice of Ireland (1936)
D  Victor Haddick
C  Richard Hayward, Victor Haddick,
   Barney O'Hara

F  Wings of The Morning (1936)
D  Harold Schuster
C  Annnbella, Henry Fonda,
   John McCormack

F  Irish and Proud of It (1936)
D  Donovan Pedelty
C  Richard Hayward, Dinah Sheridan,
   Liam Gaffney

F  The Early Bird (1936)
D  Donovan Pedelty
C  Richard Hayward, Jimmy McGeean

F  Man of Aran (1936)
D  Robert Flaherty
C  Tiger King, Maggie Dirrane,
   Aran Islanders

F  The Dawn (1937)
D  Tom Cooper
C  Tom Cooper, Eileen Davis,
   Brian O'Sullivan

F  Uncle Nick (1938)
D  Tom Cooper
C  Val Vousden

F  Blarney (1938)
D  Harry O'Donovan
C  Jimmy O'Dea, Myrette Morven

F  West of Kerry (1938)
D  Dick Bird
C  Eileen Curran, Cecil Ford

F  The Islandman (1938)
D  Patrick Heale
C  Gabriel Fallon, Brian O'Sullivan

F  Devil's Rock (1938)
D  Germaine Burger
C  Richard Hayward, Geraldine Mitchell

F  Henry V (1943)
D  Laurence Olivier
C  Laurence Olivier; Robert Newton,
   Leslie Banks

F  Hungry Hill (1946)
D  Brian Desmond Hurst
C  Margaret Lockwood, Dennis Price,
   F. J. McCormick

F  Captain Boycott (1946)
D  Frank Launder
C  Stewart Granger, Cecil Parker,
   Kathleen Ryan

F  Crime on the Irish Border (1946)
D  Maurice J. Wilson
C  Kieron Moore, Barbara White

F  Odd Man Out (1946)
D  Carol Reed
C  James Mason, Kathleen Ryan,
   Robert Newton

F  Black Narcissus (1946)
D  Michael Powell, Emeric Pressburger
C  Deborah Kerr, Sabu, David Farrar

F  I See a Dark Stranger (1946)
D  Frank Launder
C  Deborah Kerr, Trevor Howard

F   The Courtneys of Curzon Street (1947)
D   Herbert Wilcock
C   Anna Neagle, Michael Wilding

F   Another Shore (1948)
D   Charles Crichton
C   Robert Beatty, Moira Lister, Stanley Holloway

F   My Hands are Clay (1948)
D   Patrick McCrossan
C   Shelagh Richards, Bernadette Leahy, Cecil Brook

F   The Greedy Boy (1948)
D   Richard Massingham
C   Joyce Sullivan, Jim Phelan

F   Transatlantic Flight (1948)
D   Joseph Ryle
C   Gene Kelly, Betsy Blair

F   At a Dublin Inn (1949)
D   Desmond Leslie
C   Valentine Dyall, Joseph O'Connor

F   No Resting Place (1950)
D   Paul Rotha
C   Michael Gough, Eithne Dunne, Noel Purcell

F   The Strangers Came (1950)
D   Alfred Travers
C   Seamus MacLocha, Gabriel Fallon

F   Jack of All Maids (1951)
D   Tomás MacAnna
C   Jack McGowran

F   The Promise of Barty O'Brien (1951)
D   George Freedland
C   Eric Doyle, Eileen Crowe, Harry Brogan

F   The Gentle Gunman (1952)
D   Basil Dearden
C   John Mills, Dirk Bogarde, Gilbert Harding

F   The Quiet Man (1952)
D   John Ford
C   John Wayne, Maureen O'Hara, Barry Fitzgerald

F   Knights of the Round Table (1953)
D   Richard Thorpe
C   Robert Taylor, Ava Gardner, Mel Ferrer

F   Captain Lightfoot (1954)
D   Douglas Sirk
C   Rock Hudson, Barbara Rush, Jeff Morrow

F   Jacqueline (1955)
D   Roy Baker
C   John Gregson, Kathleen Ryan, Jacqueline Ryan

F   Moby Dick (1955)
D   John Huston
C   Gregory Peck, Orson Welles, Richard Basehart

F   The March Hare (1956)
D   George More O'Farrell
C   Terence Morgan, Peggy Cummins, Cyril Cusack

F   Rising of the Moon (1956)
D   John Ford
C   Jimmy O'Dea, Noel Purcell, Cyril Cusack

F   Boyd's Shop (1957)
D   Henry Cass
C   Geoffrey Golden, Eileen Crowe

F  Professor Tim (1957)
D  Henry Cass
C  Ray McAnally, Márie O'Donnell

F  Rooney (1957)
D  George Pollock
C  John Gregson, Murial Pavlow,
    Barry Fitzgerald

F  Dublin Nightmare (1958)
D  John Pomeroy
C  William Sylvester, Marie Landi,
    Richard Leech

F  Home is the Hero (1958)
D  Fielder Cooke
C  Arthur Kennedy, Máire O'Donnell,
    Walter Macken

F  Sally's Irish Rogue (1958)
D  George Pollock
C  Julie Harris, Tim Sheehy,
    Harry Brogan

F  The Big Birthday (1958)
D  George Pollock
C  Barry Fitzgerald, Tony Wright,
    June Thorburn

F  She Didn't Say No! (1958)
D  Cyril Frankel
C  Eileen Herlie, Niall MacGinnis

F  Shake Hands with the Devil (1958)
D  Michael Anderson
C  James Cagney, Don Murray,
    Dana Wynter

F  This Other Eden (1959)
D  Murial Box
C  Leslie Phillips, Audrey Dalton,
    Norman Roadway

F  A Terrible Beauty (1960)
D  Tay Garnert
C  Robert Mitchum, Anne Heywood,
    Dan O'Herlihy

F  Gorgo (1960)
D  Eugene Lourie
C  Bill Travers, William Sylvester,
    Barry Keegan

F  Fr Brown (1960)
D  Helmut Ashley
C  Heinz Ruhmann

F  The Siege of Sidney Street (1960)
D  Roy Baker, Monty Berman
C  Donald Sinden, Nicole Berger,
    Kieron Moore

F  Ambush in Leopard Street (1960)
D  J. H. Piperno
C  James Kenny, Michael Brennan,
    Bruce Seton

F  Johnny Nobody (1960)
D  Nigel Patrick
C  Nigel Patrick, William Bendix,
    Aldo Ray

F  The Big Gamble (1960)
D  Richard Fleischer
C  Stephen Boyd, Juliette Greco,
    David Wayne

F  Sword of Sherwood Forest (1960)
D  Terence Fisher
C  Richard Greene, Peter Cushing,
    Nigel Greene

F  Middle of Nowhere (1960)
D  Don Chaffey
C  John Cassavetes, Elizabeth Sellars,
    David Farrar

F  Lies My Father Told Me (1960)
D  Don Chaffey
C  Betsy Blair, Harry Brogan

F  The Mark (1961)
D  Guy Greene
C  Stuart Whitman, Rod Steiger,
   Maria Schell

F  Murder in Eden (1961)
D  Max Varnell
C  Ray McAnally, Norman Rodway

F  A Question of Suspence (1961)
D  Max Varnell
C  Peter Reynolds

F  Enter Inspector Duval (1961)
D  Max Varnell
C  Anton Diffring

F  Freedom to Die (1961)
D  Frances Searle
C  James Maxwell, T. P. McKenna

F  Stork Talk (1961)
D  Michael Furlong
C  Tony Britton, Anne Heywood

F  Term of Trial (1961)
D  Peter Grenville
C  Laurence Olivier, Simone Signoret,
   Sarah Miles

F  The List of Adrian Messenger (1962)
D  John Huston
C  George C. Scott, Dana Wynter,
   Kirk Douglas

F  The Quare Fellow (1962)
D  Arthur Dreyfliss
C  Patrick McGoohan, Walter Macken,
   Sylvia Syms

F  The Very Edge (1962)
D  Cyril Frankel
C  Richard Todd, Anne Heywood,
   Jack Hedley

F  The Running Man (1962)
D  Carol Reed
C  Laurence Harvey, Lee Remick,
   Alan Bates

F  Dead Man's Evidence (1962)
D  Frances Searle
C  Conrad Phillips, Jane Griffith

F  A Guy Called Caesar (1962)
D  Frank Marshall
C  Conrad Phillips, George Moon

F  The Playboy of the Western World
   (1962)
D  Brian Desmond Hurst
C  Siobhan McKenna, Gary Raymond,
   Liam Redmond

F  The Devil's Agent (1963)
D  John Paddy Carstairs
C  McDonald Carey, Peter Van Eyck,
   Christopher Lee

F  Dementia 13 (1963)
D  Francis Ford Coppola
C  Patrick Magee, Eithne Dunne,
   William Campbell

F  Of Human Bondage (1963)
D  Ken Hughes, Henry Hathaway
C  Laurence Harvey, Kim Novak,
   Robert Morley

F  I Thank A Fool (1963)
D  Robert Stevens
C  Peter Finch, Susan Hayward,
   Diane Cilento

F Never Put It in Writing (1963)
D Andrew Stone
C Pat Boone, Milo O'Shea,
 Fidelma Murphy

F Girl with Green Eyes (1963)
D Desmond Davis
C Peter Finch, Rita Tushingham,
 Lynn Redgrave

F Ballad in Blue (1964)
D Paul Henreid
C Ray Charles, Mary Peach, Tom Bell

F The Spy Who Came in from the
 Cold (1964)
D Martin Rirt
C Richard Burton, Claire Bloom,
 Oscar Werner

F Finnegan's Wake (1964)
D Mary Ellen Bute
C Martin J. Kelly, Jane Reilly

F Sherlock Holmes and the Deadly
 Necklace (1964)
D Terence Fisher
C Christopher Lee, Senta Berger,
 Thorley Walters

F Ten Little Indians (1964)
D George Pollock
C Hugh O'Brian, Shirley Eaton,
 Stanley Holloway

F Face of Fu Manchu (1965)
D Don Sharp
C Christopher Lee, Tsai Chin,
 Nigel Green

F Young Cassidy (1965)
D Jack Cardiff
C Rod Taylor, Julie Christie,
 Maggie Smith

F The Blue Max (1965)
D John Guillermin
C George Peppard, James Mason,
 Ursula Andrews

F I Was Happy Here (1965)
D Desmond Davis
C Sarah Miles, Cyril Cusack,
 Julian Glover

F Rocket to the Moon (1966)
D Don Sharp
C Burl Ives, Troy Donoghue, Gert Frobe

F Robbery (1966)
D Peter Yates
C Stanley Baker, Joanne Pettet,
 James Booth

F The Viking Queen (1966)
D Don Chaffey
C Don Murray, Carita, Andrew Keir

F Casino Royale (1966)
D John Huston, Val Guest, Ken Hughes,
 Joseph McGrath
C David Nevin, Deborah Kerr,
 Peter Sellers

F Ulysses (1966)
D Joseph Strick
C Milo O'Shea, Barbara Jefford,
 T. P. McKenna

F Sinful Davey (1967)
D John Huston
C John Hurt, Pamela Franklin,
 Nigel Davenport

F 30 is a Dangerous Age, Cynthia
 (1967)
D Joseph McGrath
C Dudley Moore, Suzy Kendall,
 Patricia Routledge

F   The Lion in Winter (1968)
D   Anthony Harvey
C   Peter O'Toole, Katherine Hepburn,
    Jane Merrow

F   Lock Up Your Daughters (1968)
D   Peter Coe
C   Christopher Plummet, Glynis Johns,
    Susannah York,

F   Guns in the Heather (1968)
D   Robert Butler
C   Glenn Corbert, Kurt Russell,
    Alfred Burke

F   Darling Lili (1968)
D   Blake Edwards
C   Julie Andrews, Rock Hudson,
    Jeremy Kemp

F   The Prince and the Pauper (1968)
D   Elliott Geisinger
C   Tibi Lubin, Francis Herter

F   Where's Jack? (1968)
D   Jack Clavell
C   Stanley Baker, Tommy Steele,
    Fiona Lewis

F   The Italian Job (1968)
D   Peter Collinson
C   Michael Caine, Noel Coward

F   Alfred the Great (1968)
D   Clive Donner
C   David Hemmings, Michael York,
    Prunella Ransome

F   The Violent Enemy (1968)
D   Don Sharp
C   Tom Bell, Susan Hampshire,
    Ed Begley

F   Wedding Night (1969)
D   Piers Haggard
C   Dennis Waterman, Tessa Wyatt,
    Eddie Byrne

F   The Girl with the Paleface (1969)
D   Paul Gallico Jr
C   Fidelma Murphy, Donal McCann,
    Lee Dunne

F   McKenzie Break (1969)
D   Lamont Johnson
C   Brian Keith, Ian Hendry,
    Helmut Griern

F   Underground (1969)
D   Arthur Nadel
C   Robert Goulet, Daniele Gaubert

F   Paddy (1969)
D   Daniel Haller
C   Des Cave, Derbhla Molloy,
    Milo O'Shea

F   Country Dance (1969)
D   J. Lee Thompson
C   Peter O'Toole, Susannah York,
    Michael Craig

F   Ryan's Daughter (1969)
D   David Lean
C   Robert Mitchum, Sarah Miles,
    Trevor Howard

F   Quackser Fortune has a Cousin in the
    Bronx (1969)
D   Warris Hussein
C   Gene Wilder, Margot Kidder,
    Seamus Forde

F   Ace Eli and Rodgers of the Skies
    (1969)
D   Cliff Robertson
C   Cliff Robertson, Jack Watson

F Philadelphia Here I Come (1970)
D John Quested
C Donal McCann, Des Cave,
   Siobhan McKenna

F Flight of the Doves (1970)
D Ralph Nelson
C Ron Moody, Jack Wild,
   William Ruston

F Black Beauty (1970)
D James Hill
C Mark Lester, Walter Stezack,
   Patrick Mower

F The Red Baron (1970)
D Roger Corman
C John Phillip Law, Don Stroud,
   Tom Adams

F Zeppelin (1970)
D Etienne Perier
C Michael York, Elke Sommer,
   Anton Diffring

F Act Without Words (1971), unfinished
D Tom Blevins
C Rod Steiger

F Sitting Target (1971)
D Douglas Hickox
C Oliver Reed, Ian McShane,
   Jill St John

F Images (1971)
D Robert Altman
C Susannah York, Rene Auberjonois,
   Hugh Millais

F A Fistful of Dynamite (1971)
D Sergio Leone
C Rod Steiger, James Coburn

F The Hebrew Lesson (1972)
D Wolf Mankowitz
C Milo O'Shea, Patrick Dawson,
   Alun Owen

F And No One Could Save Her (1972)
D Kevin Billington
C Lee Remick, Milo O'Shea,
   Frank Grimes

F A War of Children (1972)
D George Schaffer
C Jenny Agutter, Vivien Merchant,
   Aideen O'Kelly

F Catholics (1973)
D Jack Gold
C Trevor Howard, Cyril Cusack

F The Mackintosh Man (1973)
D John Huston
C Paul Newman, James Mason,
   Dominque Sanda

F Zardoz (1973)
D John Boorman
C Sean Connery, Charlotte Rampling,
   John Alderton

F A Quiet Day in Belfast (1973)
D Milad Basada
C Barry Foster, Margot Kidder

F Horowitz of Dublin Castle (1974)
D William Kronick
C Harvey Lembeck, Cyril Cusack,
   Sinead Cusack

F Barry Lyndon (1974)
D Stanley Kubrick
C Ryan O'Neal, Marisa Berenson

F The Next Man (1975)
D Richard Sarafin
C Sean Connery, Cornelia Sharpe

F Victor Frankenstein (1975)
D Calvin Floyd
C Per Oscarsson, Leon Vitali,
Stacy Dorning

F Portrait of the Artist as a Young Man (1975)
D Joseph Strick
C Bosco Hogan, T. P. McKenna,
John Gielgud

F The Last Remake of Beau Geste (1976)
D Marty Feldman
C Marty Feldman, Ann Margaret,
Michael York

F The Purple Taxi (1976)
D Yves Boisset
C Peter Ustinov, Fred Astaire,
Charlotte Rampling

F The Inn of the Flying Dragon (1977)
D Calvin Floyd
C Curt Jurgens, Niall Toibin

F Down the Corner (1977)
D Joe Comerford
C Joe Keenan, Declan Cronin,
Kevin Doyle

F The First Great Train Robbery (1978)
D Michael Crichton
C Sean Connery, Lesley Anne Down,
Donald Sutherland

F The Outside (1978)
D Tony Luraschi
C Craig Wasson, Patricia Quinn,
Sterling Hayden

F Cry of the Innocent (1978)
D Michael O'Herlihy
C Rod Taylor, Cyril Cusack

F Exposure (1978)
D Kieran Hickey
C Catherine Schell, T. P. McKenna,
Bosco Hogan

F The Big Red One (1978)
D Samuel Fuller
C Lee Marvin, Mark Hamill

F Poitín (1978)
D Bob Quinn
C Cyril Cusack. Niall Toibin,
Donal McCann

F McVicar (1978)
D Tom Clegg
C Roger Daltry, Adam Faith

F North Sea Hijack (1979)
D Andrew V. McLaglen
C Roger Moore, James Mason,
Anthony Perkins

F The Flame is Love (1979)
D Michael O'Herlihy
C Linda Purl, Timothy Dalton

F Tristan and Isolde (1979)
D Tom Donovan
C Richard Burton, Kate Mulgrew,
Nicholas Clay

F The Hard Way (1979)
D Michael Dryhurst
C Patrick McGoohan, Lee Van Cleef,
Edna O'Brien

F Excalibur (1980)
D John Boorman
C Nicol Williamson, Nigel Terry,
Helen Mirren

F Inchon (1980)
D Terence Young
C Laurence Olivier, Jacqueline Bisset

F Light Years Away (1980)
D Alain Tanner
C Trevor Howard, Mick Ford

F It's Handy When People Don't Die
   (1980)
D Tom McArdle
C Garret Keogh, Bob Carisle,
   Brendan Cauldwell

F Wagner (1981)
D Tony Palmer
C Richard Burton, Vanessa Redgrave,
   Gemma Craven

F Fire and Sword (1981)
D Keith Von Fuerstenberg
C Peter Firth, Leigh Lawson

F Angel (1981)
D Neil Jordan
C Stephen Rea, Honor Heffernan,
   Ray McAnally

F Educating Rita (1982)
D Lewis Gilbert
C Michael Caine, Julie Walters

F The Outcasts (1982)
D Robert Wynn Simmons
C Cyril Cusack, Mary Ryan, Mick Lally

F Attracta (1982)
D Kieran Hickey
C Wendy Hiller, Kate Thompson

F State of Wonder (1983)
D Martin Donovan
C Anne Chaplin, Martin Donovan

F Pigs (1983)
D Cathal Black
C James Brennan, George Shane,
   Maurice O'Donoghue

F Anne Devlin (1983)
D Pat Murphy
C Bríd Brennan, Bosco Hogan

F The Country Girls (1983)
D Desmond Davis
C Sam Neill, Maeve Germaine,
   Niall Toibin

F Cal (1983)
D Pat O'Connor
C Helen Mirren, John Lynch,
   Ray McNally

F Eat the Peach (1985)
D Peter Ormrod
C Stephen Brennan, Eamonn Morrissey
   Catherine Byrne

F The Fantasist (1985)
D Robin Hardy
C Timothy Bottoms, Moira Harris,
   John Kavanagh

F Rawhead X (1986)
D George Pavlov
C David Dukes, Kelly Piper, Niall Toibin

F Budawanny (1986)
D Bob Quinn
C Donal McCann, Margaret Fegan

F The Dead (1987)
D John Huston
C Anjelica Huston, Donal McCann,
   Dan O'Herlihy

F The Courier (1987)
D Joe Lee, Frank Deasy
C Gabriel Byrne, Pádraig Ó Loingsigh,
   Cáit O'Riordain

F   Reefer and the Model (1987)
D   Joe Comerford
C   Ian McElhinney, Carole Scanlan,
    Ray McBride

F   The Lonely Passion of Judith Hearne
    (1987)
D   Jack Clayton
C   Bob Hoskins, Maggie Smith,
    Marie Kean

F   Taffin (1987)
D   Francis Megahy
C   Pierce Brosnan, Alison Doody,
    Ray McAnally

F   Da (1987)
D   Matt Clark
C   Martin Sheen, Barnard Hughes,
    Doreen Hepburn

F   The Dawning (1987)
D   Robert Knights
C   Anthony Hopkins, Jean Simmons,
    Trevor Howard

F   Now I Know (1987)
D   Robert Pappas
C   Matthew Modine, Maeve Germaine

F   High Spirits (1987)
D   Neil Jordan
C   Peter O'Toole, Daryl Hannah,
    Steve Guttenberg

F   Joyriders (1988)
D   Aisling Walsh
C   Andrew Connolly, Patricia Kerrigan,
    Billie Whitelaw

F   My Left Foot (1988)
D   Jim Sheridan
C   Daniel Day-Lewis, Brenda Fricker,
    Ray McAnally

F   Hidden Agenda (1989)
D   Ken Loach
C   Brad Dourif, Brian Cox,
    Frances McDormand

F   Fragments of Isabella (1989)
D   Ronan O'Leary
C   Gabrielle Reidy

F   Fools of Fortune (1989)
D   Pat O'Connor
C   Julie Christie, Ian Glen,
    Mary Elizabeth Mastrantonio

F   Hush-A-Bye-Baby (1989)
D   Margo Harkin
C   Emer McCourt, Sinéad O'Connor

F   December Bride (1989)
D   Thaddeus O'Sullivan
C   Donal McCann, Saskia Reeves,
    Ciaran Hinds

F   The Field (1989)
D   Jim Sheridan
C   Richard Harris, John Hurt,
    Tom Berenger

F   The Miracle (1990)
D   Neil Jordan
C   Beverly D'Angelo, Donal McCann,
    Niall Byrne

F   The Commitments (1990)
D   Alan Parker
C   Andrew Strong, Angeline Ball,
    Johnny Murphy

F   Hear My Song (1990)
D   Peter Chelsom
C   Ned Beatty, Shirley Anne Field,
    Adrian Dunbar

F  The Railway Station Man (1991)
D  Michael Whyte
C  Donald Sutherland, Julie Christie,
   John Lynch

F  Far and Away (1991)
D  Ron Howard
C  Tom Cruise, Nicole Kidman,
   Colm Meaney

F  Into the West (1991)
D  Mike Newell
C  Gabriel Byrne, Ellen Barkin,
   Ciarán Fitzgerald

F  The Playboys (1991)
D  Gillies MacKinnon
C  Albert Finney, Aidan Quinn,
   Robin Wright

F  The Crying Game (1992)
D  Neil Jordan
C  Stephen Rea, Adrian Dunbar,
   Jaye Davidson

F  High Boot Benny (1992)
D  Joe Comerford
C  Mark O'Shea, Frances Tomelty
   Alan Devlin

F  The Bishop's Story (1992)
D  Bob Quinn
C  Donal McCann, Margaret Fegan

F  The Snapper (1992)
D  Stephen Frears
C  Colm Meaney, Tina Kelleher,
   Ruth McCabe

F  In the Name of the Father (1993)
D  Jim Sheridan
C  Daniel Day-Lewis, Emma Thompson,
   Pete Postlethwaite

F  Broken Harvest (1993)
D  Maurice O'Callaghan
C  Colin Lane, Niall O'Brien,
   Marion Quinn

F  Widow's Peak (1993)
D  John Irvine
C  Mia Farrow, John Plowright,
   Natasha Richardson

F  All Things Bright and Beautiful
   (1993)
D  Barry Devlin
C  Gabriel Byrne, Tom Wilkinson,
   Ciaran Fitzgerald

F  War of the Buttons (1993)
D  John Roberts
C  Colm Meaney, Johnny Murphy,
   John Coffey

F  Moondance (1993)
D  Dagmar Hirtz
C  Ruaidhrí Conroy, Julia Brendler,
   Ian Shaw

F  The Secret of Roan Inish (1993)
D  John Sayle
C  Mick Lally, Eileen Colgan,
   Jeni Courtney

F  Aisla (1993)
D  Paddy Breathnach
C  Brendan Coyle, Andrea Irvine,
   Juliette Gruber

F  An Awfully Big Adventure (1994)
D  Mike Newell
C  Alan Rickman, Hugh Grant,
   Peter Firth

F  Braveheart (1994)
D  Mel Gibson
C  Mel Gibson, Sophie Marceau,
   Patrick McGoohan

F  Words Upon the Window Pane (1994)
D  Mary McGuckian
C  Geraldine Chaplin, Geraldine James, Donal Donnelly

F  Frankie Starlight (1994)
D  Michael Lindsay-Hogg
C  Ann Parillaud, Matt Dillon, Gabriel Byrne

F  A Man of No Importance (1994)
D  Suri Krishnama
C  Albert Finney, Brenda Fricker, Tara Fitzgerald

F  The Run of the Country (1994)
D  Peter Yates
C  Albert Finney, Matt Keeslar, Victoria Smurfit

F  Circle of Friends (1994)
D  Pat O'Connor
C  Chris O'Donnell, Minnie Driver, Geraldine O'Rawe

F  Korea (1994)
D  Cathal Black
C  Donal Donnelly, Andrew Scott, Fiona Molony

F  Undercurrent (1994)
D  Brian O'Flaherty
C  Owen Roe, Stanley Townsend, Tina Kelleher

F  Nothing Personal (1995)
D  Thaddeus O'Sullivan
C  Ian Hart, John Lynch, Michael Gambon

F  The Disappearance of Finbar (1995)
D  Sue Clayton
C  Jonathan Rhys-Myers, Luke Griffin, Fanny Risberg

F  Driftwood (1995)
D  Ronan O'Leary
C  James Spader, Anne Brochet, Barry McGovern

F  Guiltrip (1995)
D  Gerry Stembridge
C  Andrew Connolly, Jasmine Russell, Michelle Houlden

F  Moll Flanders (1995)
D  Pen Densham
C  Robin Wright, Morgan Freeman, Stockard Channing

F  Michael Collins (1995)
D  Neil Jordan
C  Liam Neeson, Julia Roberts, Alan Rickman

F  The Last of the High Kings (1995)
D  David Keating
C  Gabriel Byrne, Colm Meaney, Christine Ricci

F  This is the Sea (1995)
D  Mary McGuckian
C  Gabriel Byrne, Richard Harris, John Lynch

F  Joe My Friend (1995)
D  Chris Bould
C  John Cleere, Joel Grey, Schuyler Fox

F  The Boy from Mercury (1995)
D  Martin Duffy
C  Tom Courtenay, Rita Tushingham, James Hickey

F  The Van (1995)
D  Stephen Frears
C  Colm Meaney, Donal O'Kelly, Brendan O'Carroll

F   Space Truckers (1995)
D   Stuart Gordon
C   Dennis Hopper, Stephen Dorff,
    Debi Mazar

F   Some Mother's Son (1995)
D   Terry George
C   Helen Mirren, John Lynch,
    Fionnula Flanagan

F   The Sun, The Moon and The Stars
    (1995)
D   Geraldine Creed
C   Angie Dickinson, Jason Donovan,
    Elaine Cassidy

F   Spaghetti Slow (1995)
D   Valerie Jalango
C   Niamh O'Byrne, Guilio Di Marco,
    Brendan Gleeson

F   Trojan Eddie (1995)
D   Gillies MacKinnon
C   Stephen Rea, Richard Harris,
    Angeline Ball

F   A Further Gesture (1995)
D   Robert Dornhelm
C   Stephen Rea, Maria Doyle Kennedy,
    Brendan Gleeson

F   Bloodfist VIII – Trained for Action
    (1995)
D   Rick Jacobson
C   Don Wilson, J. P. White

F   The Devil's Own (1996)
D   Alan J. Pakula
C   Brad Pitt, Harrison Ford

F   The Fifth Province (1996)
D   Frank Stapleton
C   Brian F. O'Byrne, Lia Williams

F   The Last Bus Home (1996)
D   Johnny Gogan
C   Annie Ryan, Brian F. O'Byrne

F   Spagetti Slow (1996)
D   Valerio Jalongo
C   Brendan Gleeson, Giulio Di Mauro

F   Crushproof (1996)
D   Paul Tickell
C   Darren Healey, Jeff O'Toole

F   The Butcher Boy (1996)
D   Neil Jordan
C   Stephen Rea, Fiona Shaw

F   Matchmaker (1996)
D   Mark Joffey
C   Dennis Leary, Janeane Garofalo

F   I Went Down (1996)
D   Paddy Breathnach
C   Brendan Gleeson, Peter McDonald

F   Bogwoman (1996)
D   Tom Collins
C   Rachel Dowling, Peter Mullan

F   Seperation Anxiety (1996)
D   Mark Staunton
C   Susan Collins, Kevin Gildea

F   This is the Sea (1996)
D   Mary McGuckian
C   Richard Harris, Gabriel Byrne

F   Gold in the Streets (1996)
D   Liz Gill
C   Ian Hart, Jared Harris

F   November Afternoon (1996)
D   John Carney, Tom Hall
C   Michael McElhatton, Jayne Snow

F   The Nephew (1996)
D   Eugene Brady
C   Pierce Brosnan, Donal McCann

F   Night Train (1997)
D   John Lynch
C   John Hurt, Brenda Blethyn

F   Saving Private Ryan (1997)
D   Steven Spielberg
C   Tom Hanks, Mark Damon

F   Dancing at Lughnasa (1997)
D   Pat O'Connor
C   Merlyl Streep, Bríd Brennan

F   Sunset Heights (1997)
D   Colm Villa
C   Toby Stephens, Jim Norton

F   Lulu on the Bridge (1997)
D   Paul Anster
C   Harvey Keitel, Mira Sorvino

F   Cycle of Violence (1997)
D   Henry Herbert
C   Gerald Rooney, Mari Lennon

F   Serpent's Kiss (1997)
D   Philippe Rousselot
C   Ewan McGregor, Greta Scacchi

F   Divorcing Jack (1997)
D   David Caffrey
C   David Thewlis, Laura Frazer

F   The Boxer (1997)
D   Jim Sheridan
C   Daniel Day-Lewis, Emily Watson

F   Love and Rage (1997)
D   Cathal Black
C   Greta Scacchi, Daniel Craig

F   A Love Divided (1997)
D   Syd Macartney
C   Liam Cunningham, Orla Brady

F   Sweeney Barrett (1997)
D   Stephen Bradley
C   Brendan Gleeson, Liam Cunningham

F   Pete's Meteor (1997)
D   Joe O'Byrne
C   Mike Myers, Brenda Fricker

F   This is My Father (1997)
D   Paul Quinn
C   Aidan Quinn, James Cann

F   Angela's Ashes (1998)
D   Alan Parker
C   Robert Carlyle, Emily Watson

F   Resurrection Man (1997)
D   Marc Evan
C   Stuart Townsend, James Nesbitt

F   Agnes Browne (1998)
D   Anjelica Huston
C   Anjelica Huston, Marion O'Dwyer

F   Titanic City (1997)
D   Roger Mitchell
C   Julie Walters, Ciaran Hinds

F   Park (1998)
D   John Carney, Tom Hall
C   Claudia Terry, Des Nealon

F   The General (1997)
D   John Boorman
C   Brendan Gleeson, Jon Voight

F   The Last September (1998)
D   Deborah Warner
C   Fiona Shaw, Lambert Wilson

F  Animal Farm (1998)
D  John Stephenson
C  Pete Postlewaite, Joe Taylor

F  Nora (1998)
D  Pat Murphy
C  Ewan McGregor, Susan Lynch

F  Felicia's Journey (1998)
D  Atom Egoyan
C  Bob Hoskins, Elaine Cassidy

F  Accelerator (1998)
D  Vinny Murphy
C  Stuart Sinclair Blyth, Aisling O'Neill

F  Angela Mooney Dies Again (1998)
D  Tommy McArdle
C  Mia Farrow, Patrick Bergin

F  Ordinary Decent Criminal (1998)
D  Thaddeus O'Sullivan
C  Kevin Spacey, Peter Mullan

F  When the Sky Falls (1998)
D  John MacKenzie
C  Joan Allan, Patrick Bergin

F  Saltwater (1998)
D  Conor McPherson
C  Brian Cox, Brendan Gleeson

F  Flick (1998)
D  Fintan Connolly
C  David Murray, David Wilmot

F  About Adam (1999)
D  Gerry Stembridge
C  Stuart Townsend, Kate Hudson

F  When Brendan Met Trudy (1999)
D  Kieron J. Walsh
C  Peter McDonald, Flora Montgomery

F  An Everlasting Piece (1999)
D  Barry Levinson
C  Barry McEvoy, Brian F. O'Byrne

F  Chaos (1999)
D  Geraldine Creed
C  Jason Barry, Peter Lohmeyer

F  Borstal Boy (1999)
D  Peter Sheridan
C  Shawn Hatosy, Michael York

F  On the Nose (1999)
D  David Caffrey
C  Dan Aykroyd, Robbie Coltrane

F  On The Edge (1999)
D  John Carney
C  Cillian Murphy, Stephen Rea

F  The Most Fertile Man in Ireland (1999)
D  Dudi Appleton
C  Kris Marshall, James Nesbitt.

F  Disco Pigs (1999)
D  Kristen Sheridan
C  Cillian Murphy, Elaine Cassidy

F  The Tailor of Panama (1999)
D  John Boorman
C  Pierce Brosnan, Geoffrey Rush.

F  Country (1999)
D  Kevin Liddy
C  Dean Pritchard, Des Cave

F  Rat (1999)
D  Steve Barron
C  Pete Postlewaite, Frank Kelly

F  Mad About Mambo (1999)
D  John Forte
C  William Ash, Keri Russell

F   Puckoon (2000)
D   Terence Ryan
C   Richard Attenborough, John Lynch

F   Mapmaker (2000)
D   Johnny Grogan
C   Brian F. O'Byrne, Susan Lynch

F   The Abduction Club (2000)
D   Stefan Schwartz
C   Daniel Lapine, Mathew Rhys

F   Silent Grace (2000)
D   Maeve Murphy
C   Orla Brady, Cara Seymour

F   Not Afraid, Not Afraid (2000)
D   Annette Carducci
C   Diana Weist, Jack Davonport

F   Last Days in Dublin (2000)
D   Lance Daly
C   Grattan Smith, John Kavanagh

F   Peaches (2000)
D   Nick Grosso
C   Matthew Rhys, Kelly Reilly

F   How Harry Became a Tree (2000)
D   Goran Paskaljevic
C   Colm Meaney, Cillian Murphy

F   H3 (2000)
D   Les Blair
C   Brendan Mackey, Aidan Campbell

F   Count of Monte Cristo (2000)
D   Kevin Reynolds
C   Jim Cazaviel, Guy Pearse

F   Evelyn (2001)
D   Bruce Beresford
C   Pierce Brosnan, Aidan Quinn

F   Medallion (2001)
D   Alfred Chung
C   Jackie Chan, Lee Evans

F   Reign of Fire (2001)
D   Rob Bowman
C   Mathew McConnughey,
    Christian Bale

F   The Crooked Miles (2001)
D   Stephen Kane
C   Dayna McKiernan, Alan Smyth

F   In America (2001)
D   Jim Sheridan
C   Paddy Considine, Samantha Morton

F   Bloody Sunday (2001)
D   Paul Greengrass
C   James Nesbitt, Kathy Kiera Clarke

F   The Magdalene Sisters (2001)
D   Peter Mullan
C   Geraldine McEwan, Anne Marie Duff

F   The Escapist (2001)
D   Gilles MacKinnon
C   Johnny Lee Miller, Jodhi May

F   Ella Enchanted (2002)
D   Tommy O'Havers
C   Anne Hathaway, Patrick Bergin

F   Head Rush (2002)
D   Shimmy Marcus
C   Wuzza Conlon, Gavin Kelty

F   Dead Bodies (2002)
D   Robert Quinn
C   Andrew Scott, Kelly Reilly

F   Goldfish Memory (2002)
D   Liz Gill
C   Flora Montgomery, Sean Campion

F  Mystics (2002)
D  David Blair
C  David Kelly, Milo O'Shea

F  Veronica Guerin (2002)
D  Joel Schumacher
C  Cate Blanchette, Gerard McSorley

F  The Honeymooners (2002)
D  Karl Golden
C  Jonathan Byrne, Alex Reid

F  The Halo Effect (2002)
D  Lance Daly
C  Stephen Rea, Grattan Smith

F  The Actors (2002)
D  Conor McPherson
C  Michael Caine, Dylan Moran

F  Bloom (2002)
D  Sean Walsh
C  Stephen Rea, Angeline Ball

F  Intermission (2002)
D  John Crowley
C  Colin Farrell, Colm Meaney

F  Song for a Raggy Boy (2002)
D  Aisling Walsh
C  Aidan Quinn, John Travers

F  The Roman Spring of Mrs Stone
   (2002)
D  Robert Allan Ackerman
C  Helen Mirren, Anne Bancroft

F  The Boys and Girls from County
   Clare (2002)
D  John Irvine
C  Bernard Hill, Andrea Corr

F  Blind Flight (2003)
D  John Furse
C  Ian Hart, Linus Roache

F  Cowboys and Angels (2003)
D  David Gleeson
C  Michael Legge, Allen Leech

F  King Arthur (2003)
D  Antoine Fuqua
C  Clive Owen, Keira Knightly

F  Mad About Dog (2003)
D  Paddy Breathnach
C  Allen Leech, Tom Jordan Murphy

F  Inside I'm Dancing (2003)
D  Damien O'Donnell
C  Steven Robertson, James McAvoy

F  Asylum (2003)
D  David Mackenzie
C  Natasha Richardson, Ian McKellen

F  Spin the Bottle (2003)
D  Ian FitzGibbon
C  Michael McElhatton,
   Peter MacDonald

F  Laws of Attraction (2003)
D  Peter Howitt
C  Pierce Brosnan, Julianne Moore

F  Omagh (2003)
D  Pete Travis
C  Gerard McSorley, Michelle Forbes

F  Adam and Paul (2003)
D  Lenny Abrahamsom
C  Mark O'Halloran, Tom Murphy

F  Bite (2003)
D  Fintan Connolly
C  Aidan Gillen, Renee Weldon

F  Boxed (2003)
D  Marion Comer
C  Tom Jordan Murphy, Darragh Kelly

F  Dead Meat (2003)
D  Conor McMahon
C  Marian Araujo, David Muyllaert

F  Freeze Frame  (2003)
D  John Simpson
C  Lee Evans, Sean McGinley

F  Mickybo and Me (2003)
D  Terry Loane
C  Niall Wright, John Jo O'Neill

F  Starfish (2003)
D  Stephen Kane
C  Ailish Symons, Mark Huberman

F  Timbuktu (2003)
D  Alan Gilsenan
C  Eva Birthistle, Karl Geary

F  You Looking at Me? (2003)
D  Margo Harkin
C  Packy Lee, Kelly Flynn

F  Breakfast on Pluto (2004)
D  Neil Jordan
C  Cillian Murphy, Liam Neeson

F  Tara Road (2004)
D  Gillies MacKinnon
C  Andie McDowell, Olivia Williams
   Sarah Bolger

F  The Honeymooners (2004)
D  John Schulz
C  Cedric the Entertainer, Mike Epps

F  The League of Gentlemen's
   Apocalypse (2004)
D  Steve Bendelack
C  Jeremy Dyson, Mark Gatiss,
   Steve Pemberton

F  Isolation (2004)
D  Billy O'Brien
C  John Lynch, Ruth Negga

F  Boy Eats Girl (2004)
D  Stephen Bradley
C  Samantha Mumba, David Leon

F  Trouble with Sex (2004)
D  Fintan Connolly
C  Aidan Gillen, Renée Weldon

F  Mighty Celt (2004)
D  Pearse Elliott
C  Robert Carlyle, Gillian Anderson

F  Studs (2005)
D  Paul Mercier
C  Brendan Gleeson, Phelim Drew

*Note:*

The year indicates when the film was made, rather than when it was released.

F: Film;  D: Director;  C: Cast

# GLOSSARY OF FILM TERMS

| | |
|---|---|
| *Action* | Term used by director to start filming. |
| *Adaptation* | A film based on, or adapted from, a work in another medium. |
| *Art Department* | The people working under the production designer including illustrators, set painters and model makers. |
| *Assistant Director* | Usually performs more mundane tasks for director. |
| *Background Artist* | Or an extra who has no lines and is used in background or crowd scenes. |
| *Back Lot* | Area of studio grounds where large exterior sets are erected. |
| *Back Projection* | A technique where a film is shown on a giant screen and actors perform in front of it. The entire scene is then refilmed and appears as one. |
| *Best Boy* | The assistant to the chief electrician. |

| | |
|---|---|
| *Blue-Screen Process* | Technique used to create travelling mattes, where models or actors are filmed against a blue screen, and is added into another sequence by use of an optical printer. |
| *Boom* | Microphone on long pole used for recording sound. |
| *Cameo* | A brief unbilled screen appearance by a famous actor or director. |
| *Cut* | Term used by director to finish scene. |
| *Clapper Board* | A small board on which the number of each scene is recorded. The clap is used by the editor in synchronising sound with vision. |
| *Continuity* | Person who follows script closely to ensure continuity of story and costume are maintained. |
| *Credits* | Titles listing the people who make the film and their contribution. |
| *Crew* | The group of people involved in making a film. |
| *Dailies* | Rough prints of a day's shooting. |
| *Director* | Person responsible for instructing actors and the creative side of filming. |
| *Director of Photography* | Person responsible for lighting set and supervising camera crew. |
| *Dolly* | Truck on which the camera is fixed for moving shots. |
| *Double* | A double resembles the actor and stands in for dangerous scenes. |
| *Dresser* | A person who assists actors into their costumes. |

| | |
|---|---|
| *Dubbing* | Aligning the film with the sound. Also refers to a system whereby the sound track is replaced by one in another language. |
| *Editor* | The person who assembles the completed sections of film into proper sequences. |
| *Extra* | Person employed on a daily basis for crowd scenes. |
| *Feature* | Principal film in cinema programme. |
| *Flashback* | A scene depicting events that occurred prior to main narrative. |
| *Focus Puller* | Assistant cameraman. |
| *Grips* | A person who moves scenery and props and lays down tracks. |
| *Indie* | An independent film company. |
| *Lot* | The lot covers the area of the studio including inside and outside. |
| *Location* | Actual places and buildings away from studio where scenes are shot. |
| *Make-up* | Department where actors are made-up before going in front of camera. |
| *Mixer* | A person in post-production who blends several sound tracks into one master track for a film. |
| *Mcguffin* | Term used by Alfred Hitchcock for an object about which the main characters are interested in. |
| *Premiere* | First official viewing of a film usually a gala night. |

| | |
|---|---|
| *Preview* | An unofficial showing of a film to judge reaction. |
| *Producer* | Overall boss who controls the financial and business aspects of the film. |
| *Production Manager* | Their duty is to ensure the smooth running of the production. |
| *Property Master* | A person who supervises purchase and construction of props. |
| *Rushes* | The rough prints of the day's filming. |
| *Screenplay* | Also known as the script and is divided into scenes, dialogue and action. |
| *Score* | Musical soundtrack on film. |
| *Script Doctor* | Writer hired to rewrite a script or improve it. |
| *Second Unit* | A group of personnel, headed by second-unit director, that films separately from the main unit, handling action and crowd scenes. |
| *Set* | An artificial construction where the action of a scene takes place. |
| *Sound Track* | The combination of sounds, including dialogue, noise and music that accompanies the film. |
| *Special Effects* | Department where trick photography and miniatures are used to give a realistic effect. |
| *Stage* | The studio building. |
| *Stand-in* | People resembling main actors used in setting up scenes. |

| | |
|---|---|
| *Storyboard* | A series of sketches or photographs outlining plot of film. |
| *Stills* | Still photographs taken of scenes from the film. |
| *Stunts* | A specialist who deputises for main actors in dangerous scenes. |
| *Sub-titles* | A translation printed on the bottom of the screen. |
| *Take* | Term used for the filming of a single shot. A scene may had to be repeated several times. |
| *Technical Advisor* | A person from outside the film industry hired to advise the makers of a film about a particular area of expertise. |
| *Trailor* | A short preview of a forthcoming film. |
| *Treatment* | The storyline of the plot told in 20 or more pages. |
| *Visual Effects* | Special effects or trick photography added to the film. |
| *Wardrobe* | Department that looks after the costumes for a film. |

# INDEX

*All book, film and song titles are highlighted in italics.*

# PICTURE CREDITS

Acorn Pictures: p.154; Amblin/Universal/The Kobal Collection: colour section p.4 (*An American Tail*); AVCO Embassy/The Kobal Collection: p.109 (*The Lion in Winter*); BAC Films: p.159 (Kieran Hickey); BBC/The Kobal Collection: p.180 and front cover (*The Snapper*); BBC/Irish Films/The Kobal Collection: p.204 (*I Went Down*); Beacon Communications/20th Century Fox/The Kobal Collection: p.180 (*The Commitments*); BFI/The Kobal Collection: p.148; Bord Scannan/The Kobal Collection/Pat Redmond: p.226 (*About Adam*); British Film Institute: p.32; Canal +/Paradox Pictures/Cattleya/The Kobal Collection:p.230 (*How Harry Became a Tree*); Castle Rock/The Kobal Collection: p.191 (*The Run of the Country*); Clár Productions: p.141 (*Tristan and Isolde*); Clarence Pictures: p.195 (*Nothing Personal*); Collins Ave/Deadly Films 2/The Kobal Collection: p.226 (*When Brendan Met Trudy*); Columbia/The Kobal Collection/Ken Regan: p.210 (*The Devil's Own*); Columbia/Famous Artists/The Kobal Collection: p.90 (*Casino Royale*); Columbia Tristar/The Kobal Collection: colour section p.7 (Neil Jordan); Dreamworks LLC/The Kobal Collection: p.213 (*Song for a Raggy Boy*); Fantastic Films Ltd/LolaFilms SA/The Kobal Collection: p.244 (*Song for a Raggy Boy*); Ferndale Films/Jonathan Hession: p.176 (*The Field*); Ferndale/Capitol/Sony/Channel 4/The Kobal Collection: p.204 (*Dancing at Lughnasa*); Film 4/First City/The Kobal Collection: p.195 (*The Disappearance of Finbar*); Film Council/Momentum Pictures/.The Kobal Collection: p.241 (*The Magdalen Sisters*); Filmline/The Kobal Collection/Jonathan Hession: colour section: p.6 (*This is My Father*); Fubar: p.266 (*Trouble with Sex*); Geffen/Warner Bros/The Kobal Collection: p.199 and front cover (*Michael Collins*); Geffen Pictures/The Kobal Collection/Pat Redmond: p.204 (*The Butcher Boy*); Goldfish Films/The Kobal Collection: p.250 (*Goldfish Memory*); Granada/Miramax/The Kobal Collection: p.171 and back cover (Brenda Fricker); Granada TV/Portman Entertainment/The Kobal Collection/Bernard Walsh: p.235 (*Bloody Sunday*); Granada/Sovereign/The Kobal Collection: colour section p.6 (*The Field*); Grand Pictures: p.250 (*Spin the Bottle*); Handmade Films/The Kobal Collection: p.168 (*The Lonely Passion of Judith Hearne*); Tony Hanna: colour section p.8 and front cover (Colin Farrell); Icon/Ladd Co/Paramount/The Kobal Collection: p.191 (*Braveheart*); Icon Ent Int/The Kobal Collection: p.222 (*Ordinary Decent Criminal*); Insight Ventures/Y2K Productions/The Kobal Collection: p.250 (*Puckoon*); Jules Verne Films/The Kobal Collection: p.102 (*Rocket to the Moon*); The Kobal Collection: colour section p.7 (John Boorman); Lions Gate/Hemdale/The Kobal Collection: p.123 (*Images*); Majestic/BBC/Little Bird/The Kobal Collection: p.191 (*A Man of No Importance*); Majestic/Miramax/Film 4 Int/BR Screen/The Kobal Collection: colour section p.6 and spine (*Into the West*); MGM: colour section p.2 (*Ryan's Daughter*); MGM/The Kobal Collection: p.85 (*Of Human Bondage*), p.102 (*Young Cassidy*), p.109 (*Alfred the Great*), p.115, colour section p.7 (John Huston); MGM/United Artists/The Kobal Collection/Jonathan Hession: p.241 (*Evelyn*); Miramax Films: p.244 (*Ella Enchanted*); George Morrison: p.22 (*In the Days of Saint Patrick* still); p.50 (*I See a Dark Stranger*); National Film Studios of Ireland: p.137 (*Purple Taxi*); Nattore/Merlin Films/The Kobal Collection: p.222 and back cover (*The General*); October Films/The Kobal Collection/Jonathan Hession: p.218 (*Agnes Browne*); Orion/Warner Bros/The Kobal Collection: p.144, colour section p.4 and back cover (*Excalibur*); Palace/NFFC/ITC/The Kobal Collection: colour section p.4 (*Company of Wolves*); Palace/The Kobal Collection/Tom Hilton: colour section p.5; Parallel Films/The Kobal Collection: p.195 (*The Last of the High Kings*) p.241 (*Intermission*); Paramount/The Kobal Collection: p.109 (*Darling Lili*); Paramount Pictures: p.85 (*The Spy Who Came in from the Cold*), p.141 (*The Outsider*); Paramount/Universal/The Kobal Collection/Bill Kaye: p.218 (*Angela's Ashes*); Pathé Distribution Ltd: p.266 (*Breakfast on Pluto* © Pathé Productions Ltd 2005, all rights reserved); Polygram/The Kobal Collection/Marcus Robinson: p.210 (*Resurrection Man*); Portman/BBC/Wolfhound/The Kobal Collection: p.185 (*An Awfully Big Adventure*); Rafran/San Marco/The Kobal Collection: p.123 (*A Fistful of Dynamite*); Rank Film Distributors: p.60 (*Boyd's Shop*); Regal Films: p.72 (*The Siege of Sidney Street*); Republic/The Kobal Collection: p.54, colour section p.1 and front cover (*The Quiet Man*); RKO/The Kobal Collection: p.40 (*The Informer*); Romulus/Warner Bros/The Kobal Collection: p.80 (*Term of Trial*); Stoneridge Ent/The Kobal Collection: p.230 (*Peaches*); Strongbow: p.164 (*Eat the Peach*); 20th Century Fox: colour section p.3 (*Zardoz*); 20th Century Fox/The Kobal Collection: p.132, p.180 (*The Van*); 20th Century Fox/The Kobal Collection/Bernard Walsh: p.238, colour section p.7 (Jim Sheridan) and front cover (*In America*); Temple Film and TV Productions/The Kobal Collection: p.226 (*Disco Pigs*); Touchstone/The Kobal Collection/Jonathan Hession: p.235 (*Reign of Fire*) p.244 (*Veronica Guerin*); Touchstone/Spyglass/The Kobal Collection/Albert Watson: p.230 (*The Count of Monte Cristo*); Touchstone Pictures/Jerry Bruckheimer Films/The Kobal Collection/Jonathan Hession: p.255; United Artists/The Kobal Collection: p.137 (*The First Great Train Robbery*); United Artists Corporation: p.66 (*Shake Hands with the Devil*), p.80 (*Girl with Green Eyes*), p.118 (*The Red Baron*); United British Artists/MGM/The Kobal Collection: p.168 (*Taffin*); Universal/The Kobal Collection: p.176 (*Far and Away*), p.210 (*The Boxer*); Universal/The Kobal Collection/Jonathan Hession: p.185 and back cover (*In the Name of the Father*); VCI Entertainment: p.72 (*The Mark*); Walt Disney Productions: colour section p.3 (*Guns in the Heather*); Warner Bros: p.129 (bottom); Warner/Goldcrest/Enigma/The Kobal Collection: p.164 (*Cal*); Warner Bros/The Kobal Collection: p.129 (top) colour section p.2 (*Moby Dick*); Warner-Pathé: p.102 (*Ten Little Indians*); Wide Eye Films/Buena Vista International: p.261 and back cover (*Cowboys and Angels*); and WT2 Productions/The Kobal Collection: p.261 (*Inside I'm Dancing*).